ALTERNATIVE MARKET RESEARCH METHODS

Traditional research methods in marketing can be illuminating when used well, but all too often their data-driven results fail to provide the depth of understanding that organisations need to anticipate market needs. *Alternative Market Research Methods: Market sensing* is a new approach that enables researchers to get greater depth and meaning from their research and organisations to make smarter strategic decisions.

This book, the first text dedicated to the topic, explains market sensing simply and practically and demonstrates how it can benefit researchers. It teaches non-mainstream and alternative research methods which facilitate innovative research design, and achieves deep insights into the mindsets of consumers. The methods explored in this book include:

- emotional scaling;
- discourse analysis;
- consumer ethnography;
- social media networks;
- narrative and storytelling;
- gamification.

With a wealth of case studies and pedagogy to aid student learning, as well as online teaching aids including PowerPoint presentations and video content, this ground-breaking textbook is an essential resource for anyone who wants to expand their repertoire of marketing research methods to create a research project that will be original and insightful.

David Longbottom is a Reader in Marketing at the University of Derby, UK.

Alison Lawson is a Senior Lecturer in Marketing at the University of Derby, UK.

ALTERNATIVE MARKET RESEARCH METHODS

Market sensing

*Edited by David Longbottom
and Alison Lawson*

Routledge
Taylor & Francis Group

LONDON AND NEW YORK

Please visit the companion website for this title at: www.
routledge.com/cw/longbottom

First published 2017
by Routledge
2 Park Square, Milton Park, Abingdon, Oxon OX14 4RN

and by Routledge
711 Third Avenue, New York, NY 10017

Routledge is an imprint of the Taylor & Francis Group, an informa business

British Library Cataloguing in Publication Data
A catalogue record for this book is available from the British Library

Library of Congress Cataloging in Publication Data
A catalog record for this book has been requested

ISBN: 978-1-138-84371-4 (hbk)
ISBN: 978-1-138-84372-1 (pbk)
ISBN: 978-1-315-73090-5 (ebk)

Typeset in Bembo Std
by Swales & Willis Ltd, Exeter, Devon, UK

MIX
Paper from
responsible sources
FSC   FSC® C013056
www.fsc.org

Printed and bound in Great Britain by
TJ International Ltd, Padstow, Cornwall

CONTENTS

FIGURES

TABLES

CASE STUDIES

CONTRIBUTORS

Kuldeep Banwait is a senior lecturer in marketing at the University of Derby. His teaching interests are in marketing strategy, brand engagement and experiential marketing. His teaching philosophy is based upon integrating research, practice and creativity to help produce holistic marketers who can add value and make a commercial impact. His doctoral research looks at policy shift in English higher education: it evaluates the notion of the 'student as a customer' and considers the implications for future strategy making in universities. His commercial work focuses on helping brands engage and connect with their customers' hearts and minds. It challenges conventional wisdom, suggesting brands must collect deeper market intelligence to establish customers' needs and wants.

Polina Baranova is a senior lecturer in strategic management and programme leader for the fulltime MBA at the Derby Business School, University of Derby. She is a Member of the Chartered Management Institute (CMI) and a Fellow of the Higher Education Academy (FHED). She is in the final stages of her doctoral studies at the Nottingham University Business School, University of Nottingham. Her research interests include strategy and organisational strategising, capability building in the low-carbon economy and service design capabilities.

Lesley Crane is a consultant and author specialising in organisational change through effective learning and knowledge sharing. She is passionate about designing and implementing solutions which allow and motivate people to achieve their real potential through effective learning and knowledge sharing. Since completing her doctorial studies she has worked in a wide range of industries and sectors, both public and private, giving her a broad spectrum of insights, and her work has appeared in various organisational science journals and management publications. Her first book, *Knowledge and Discourse Matters*, was published in late 2015. She also serves as an official reviewer for a leading journal in knowledge management and contributes to international conferences as a speaker on the topics of learning, knowledge management and change.

Ian Churm is a senior lecturer and programme leader in marketing at the University of Derby. His specialist subject areas are in marketing communications and public relations. Prior to his career at university, Ian worked for several years in the aircraft industry with Rolls Royce.

Simon Dupernex is a senior lecturer in operations and strategy at the University of Derby. His teaching interests are in business improvement, modelling and postgraduate research methods. His research interests are also in business improvement and modelling. He is the editor of the journal *Critical Perspectives on Business Management*.

Charles Hancock specialises in the use of images and deep emotions to study consumer value in marketing contexts. He has just completed his doctoral studies which applied images and emotional scaling techniques to the UK higher education sector, examining the perceptions from the student perspective. He is a senior lecturer at the University of Derby and has had a strong commercial career.

Annmarie Hanlon is a trainer, consultant and adviser in digital marketing strategy and social media. Starting in 1999, when she worked in 'internet marketing', she has worked on digital marketing consultancy projects in various sectors including legal and financial services, software and IT, communications, advertising, media, health and leisure. Annmarie is a senior lecturer in digital marketing at the University of Derby where she is also studying for a PhD in the strategic business use of social media networks. She is a Fellow of the Chartered Institute of Marketing, a Member of the Marketing Institute Ireland and a Liveryman of the Worshipful Company of Marketors.

Alison Lawson is a senior lecturer in marketing at the University of Derby, teaching copywriting, marketing communications and research methods for independent study. Before going into academia she worked for twenty years in the book publishing industry and her passion for books and clear communication has not waned. Her research interests are in consumers' emotional response to products, especially books and other print products. Alison specialises in qualitative research and the use of interviewing, case study and appreciative inquiry approaches in particular.

David Longbottom has published more than fifty academic papers. His research has largely focused on internal marketing and services marketing within the financial services sector. He is a reader in marketing at the University of Derby. He also works as a consultant in financial services. He is an associate editor for the *International Journal of Quality and Service Sciences* and a reviewer for several academic journals.

Maria Potempski is a public relations practitioner who has held a number of senior positions in both advertising and PR agencies. She has worked as an account director, on both consumer and business-to-business brands, producing multi-media campaigns for a number of household names including M&S, Charnos, Lepel and Church's Shoes. Her particular areas of interest are the creative industries, fashion and retail sectors where she was engaged in forecasting, design and trends development for new product ranges. She is a senior lecturer in marketing and PR within the University of Derby.

INTRODUCTION AND RATIONALE FOR THIS BOOK

Editors: David Longbottom and Alison Lawson

This is a book about market sensing. For our purposes we define market sensing as:

> A selection of research methods, each of which has the aim of achieving deep insights into the mindsets of consumers.

We believe that market sensing lies at the very heart of marketing. It is about gathering intelligence at a deeper level – searching for the gemstones that will make your marketing different. We are passionate about it. We enjoy doing it. We want you to enjoy doing it. It is a great shame that so many marketing research texts and courses we see are much of a muchness, and frankly are dull. We want market sensing to be different, creative, enjoyable and, most importantly, distinguish your marketing work from the crowd.

Throughout the text we will present many examples of modern-day organisations that have used market sensing methods to achieve successful and enduring marketing campaigns: these are everyday organisations and brands that you will be familiar with. We will reveal some of the methods they have used to become market leaders in their fields.

We have been involved in marketing and marketing research for over twenty years, both in teaching the subject and in practical applications. In deciding to write this book we came to the view that although there are very many excellent texts on marketing research, they tend to focus on similar methods; what we will term 'traditional research methods'. These methods include surveys, focus groups, in-depth interviews and case studies. These are all fine basic skills for marketing research, but in our view traditional methods may not go deep enough into the complex mindsets of consumers, and only skim the surface of what determines consumer behaviour and consumer decision making. Market sensing aims to go deeper. In today's world of complex, well-informed, savvy consumers, this deeper level of understanding is essential for marketing managers looking for differentiation in strategy, brand building, advertising and promotion, and in internal marketing.

This, we believe, presents the marketing student or marketing practitioner with an alternative set of research methods which can help to differentiate a research project and produce results at a higher level.

Guide to using this book

We want you to enjoy this book and 'buy in' to some of the 'special' elements which we believe are present in market sensing and which make market sensing projects exciting and rewarding to be involved with. So in coming to this book we would advise you to go straight to the chapters in Part II and take a look at what methods are involved in market sensing. Check out anything that catches your eye and that you think you might like to get involved with. Get a basic understanding, and think about how you might apply it. Market sensing applied properly will give you fantastic results, and importantly you should enjoy the process.

When you have identified a method that really interests you, then go on to consider in more depth the associated issues of theory and process.

Guide to the structure of the book and its content

This book is arranged in three parts. Part I covers the underpinning theory of research based on market sensing methods in three chapters. Part II presents a selection of market sensing methods. Part III considers issues of presentation of your work and research ethics.

Part I: Theoretical underpinnings for market sensing

These are the three theory chapters which support all of the market sensing methods we describe in Part II. We recommend that you first choose a market sensing method that interests you and fits in well with your project objectives before getting too much embroiled in research theory. Research theory can, in parts, be heavy and difficult to comprehend, so use these theory chapters just as a point of reference to help you to explain the underpinning theory (for example, when writing up the final presentation of your work).

For students undertaking a research-based assignment (for example, an independent study/dissertation) it is normally required that a research methodology chapter be written to support the project and demonstrate academic underpinning. For practitioners it may be essential to demonstrate the credibility of a project by having a sound understanding of the underlying theoretical principles. This is all covered in Part I.

Chapter 1 presents market sensing as a qualitative methodology. This means that the focus is primarily on the analysis of words and meaning (for example, in talk or written text), on observation and on pictures and images. Some numerical content may also be included if this helps to build the analysis. Data is normally captured in a social setting. This means research usually takes place at the point where the activity being studied takes place (a natural environment rather than a scientific laboratory).

Chapter 2 takes you through the process of conducting qualitative research. It covers issues of deciding a research strategy, planning your research project and activities, and data collection methods.

Chapter 3 continues the research process by looking at methods for data analysis, and finally at issues involved in presenting your data and findings.

Part II: Marketing research methods for market sensing

In Part II you will find the following:

- *Theory Box*: Throughout the chapters in Part II you will find at the start of each chapter a Theory Box. Each will set out the structure and the basic principles needed to underpin a theoretical explanation of the method you are reading about. It is in essence a short summary of the theoretical underpinnings. If you are a student writing a methodology chapter for your independent study you can use this, for example, to structure your research methodology chapter. It will help you to make the main points of theory in a concise and clear way. You can then expand on the main points with more discussion (which you will find by referring back to the main body of Chapters 1, 2 and 3).
- *Mini-case studies*: We will use many examples to illustrate current practices. These are drawn from our own research and practice or contemporary sources. We have used a lot of pictures and images which we feel help to bring the subject matter to life. Pictures and images are a vital part of market sensing.
- *Process*: For each market sensing method we will take you through the process. This will look at what you need to do at each stage in the process, from planning, through to conducting the research, analysing the data and presenting the data.
- *Study exercises and seminar activities*: These will be included within the text, and at the end of each chapter.

In Chapter 4 Charles Hancock and David Longbottom present market sensing using images and emotional scaling. The authors present that understanding deep emotions is the key to understanding and predicting consumer decision making and behaviour. But uncovering deep emotions is no easy task, and traditional research methods may miss important indicators. Studies have shown that our thoughts and deep emotions are often stored in our minds not as well-structured words and expressions but rather as sets of un-coordinated pictures and images. In this scenario it is difficult for a research participant to describe exactly how they feel even if they really want to. You may be dealing with issues that are below the level of the conscious mind. In this method, pictures and images are used to structure discussions with participants and elicit deep thought processes and emotions.

In Chapter 5 Lesley Crane examines discourse analysis, a method for analysing talk and text. Discourse analysis seeks to study the language that people use in everyday conversation, to understand what is being said (explicit) and also to seek out hidden meaning (tacit). Lesley uses a detailed example to demonstrate the process; taking a political speech she interprets the data for explicit and tacit statements which are deeply revealing. In a growing age of social media use, really hearing and understanding what people are saying about us is vitally important for marketers.

In Chapter 6 Ian Churm investigates consumer ethnography: literally the study of folk in their own environments. Some fascinating early ethnographic studies of people and their environments show us the historical foundations of the method, with researchers moving into unchartered communities to explore undiscovered lifestyles (from one study of South Sea Islanders to another of the Chicago underclass). Ethnographers follow the principle of immersion in the environments they study, and this can take many months or, in some cases, years of study. In consumer ethnography timescales have to be considerably shorter (for commercial and practical reasons) and this chapter shows us ways of doing this without compromising on depth and immersion principles.

In Chapter 7 Annmarie Hanlon presents market sensing using social media networks. In an age of growing use of social media, Annmarie shows how savvy marketers can engage successfully with consumers to gain very valuable feedback on a range of issues, from service satisfaction to new product ideas. Techniques for mining data and selection of appropriate social media networks are considered.

In Chapter 8 Alison Lawson analyses market sensing in the context of narrative and storytelling. Narrative inquiry has its roots in sociology, with published studies dating back to the 1920s. Alison poses the questions: Who are you? What makes up your thought processes and opinions? How do you express yourself? Through use of examples and examination of question techniques, Alison explains the process and how stories can unfold which give us greater understanding of why things happen.

In Chapter 9 David Longbottom and Kuldeep Banwait explore gamification, investigating how game technology and game playing can create an environment for engaging with consumers. Game technology is defined in a broader sense than just playing games, and goes beyond simple marketing campaigns based on points and prizes. In using game technologies for research purposes, the designer is trying to stimulate those sensory attributes that make people want to spend valuable quality time engaging in activities, but in a business and marketing context.

In Chapter 10 Polina Baranova looks at service design methodology: this is rooted in understanding services marketing and related processes. It considers the use of flowcharting and blueprinting to map out customer processes and understand service landscapes. These methods are used to capture the journey from the customer perspective, mapping experiences and activities at each stage. Whilst such methods have been well used in operations and supply chain management, relatively few studies appear in marketing contexts. The ability to see the customer experience through this detailed analysis of their whole journey (including pre- and post-purchase) is very valuable.

Part III: Presenting your research and research ethics

In Chapter 11 Alison Lawson and Maria Potempski look at how you communicate your work. They explain how qualitative work can best be presented. The discussion covers preparation and planning for writing up, drafting a literature review, use of language to get your points across and, importantly in academic work, how to include critical analysis. The chapter concludes with an examination of writing in different contexts and for different media.

In Chapter 12 Simon Dupernex takes us through research ethics. He explains the main points that have to be taken into consideration, and provides an example. Whilst all institutions will vary in the process, the principles will remain the same.

Additional study materials

The book is supported by a number of short videos – 'talking heads' – and a set of PowerPoint slides for each chapter on the accompanying website. The videos give an insight into the market sensing methods outlined in the book in the authors' own words and the slides summarise the chapters' content with live links to related resources.

Additionally we have provided examples of student dissertations (which received high grades from their examiners).

We hope you find the book and other resources useful and wish you success with your research projects. We are happy to receive comments, feedback and stories about your own experiences of research and about your research projects. Research should not be a lonely endeavour – share your experiences and learn from each other, as we will learn from you.

David Longbottom
d.longbottom@derby.ac.uk

Alison Lawson
a.lawson@derby.ac.uk

PART I

Theoretical underpinnings for market sensing

1

MARKET SENSING AND QUALITATIVE RESEARCH

Context, philosophy, approach and strategy

David Longbottom

Purpose and context

The market sensing methods presented in this book follow a qualitative framework to research. This chapter considers qualitative research as a methodology for studies at undergraduate, postgraduate and PhD levels. It will discuss and critically examine those issues of context, philosophy, approach and strategy necessary for evaluating and justifying a methodology for a research-based study (including writing a research methodology chapter to support an independent study thesis) and in preparing to undertake research of a high academic standard. This chapter largely focuses on understanding the theoretical concepts and foundations on which qualitative methodology is based, whilst discussions of the practical implications of process are contained in subsequent chapters. Chapter 2 will examine issues of planning and data collection, and Chapter 3 those of qualitative data analysis and presentation.

Learning outcome

At the end of this chapter you will be able to design and critically evaluate the theoretical underpinnings for a qualitative research methodology for a research study at undergraduate and postgraduate levels, specifically to deal with issues of context, philosophy, approach and strategy.

THEORY BOX

A Theory Box will appear at the start of each chapter in Part II of this book. The purpose of the Theory Box is to present an overview of relevant theory

(continued)

(continued)

(in context and summary format) so that you can easily locate the particular research method that is being presented in Part II and see where it fits within a qualitative research framework. (This is an essential skill required when presenting an academic research study.) You can use the Theory Box to easily locate your chosen methodology within the theoretical framework provided. This is handy, for example, when setting out the structure and justification for your methodology if, perhaps, you are a student setting out to write the methodology sections for your independent study.

For the purposes of this book we will be following the theoretical framework:

- philosophy;
- approach;
- strategy;
- design;
- analysis;
- presentation.

Qualitative research: context

There has been a major growth in qualitative inquiry within social sciences over the past two decades. Miles and Huberman (2013) suggest a growth of qualitative-based research papers being accepted for academic journal publication and find evidence of significant growth in academic textbooks. The reasons for this may be, as Cassell and Symon (1995: 2) point out, that research in social sciences is mostly concerned with people, organisations and social interactions, and is not well disposed to positivist/scientific philosophy (for example, which are based on quantitative survey or experiment). This is also apparent in marketing research where increasingly marketers are striving to achieve a depth of understanding of consumers for important decisions in marketing strategy, brand development, internal marketing and marketing communications. In summary, the characteristics of qualitative research are:

- social context: people, behaviour, organisations and the environment;
- depth, meaning, in social settings;
- not conducive to experiments within controlled environments;
- not conducive to testing of predetermined hypotheses and survey-based methods.

From our own studies and observations we find a significant growth of qualitative-based studies within the marketing subject area. The objective of market sensing is to seek out qualitative methods that achieve depth and meaning from research, and this may not be achieved using some traditional methods of research (often described in mainstream research texts) such as surveys, focus groups and surface-level cases and interviews. In market sensing we are seeking out alternative research methods which have the objective of going deeper, to explore areas which may be more difficult to uncover, but which provide marketers with very rich insights into consumers and markets.

A word of caution on qualitative research methods

The market sensing methods we present in this book are based on qualitative methods which include words, images, emotions and observations collected and analysed in social settings. We will present and argue the strong case, importance and relevance of qualitative research and that, if conducted in a rigorous and robust way, the outcomes can make a meaningful contribution to knowledge in the field of social science studies. We should acknowledge at the outset, however, that there are some risks and challenges facing the researcher adopting this methodological approach. Some academics may challenge the credibility of the methodology, for example on grounds of the validity of the approach and consequently the reliability of the findings. There are, for example, arguments that the methods are non-scientific, open to personal opinions, biases and subjective interpretations. These are all challenges that the qualitative researcher will have to face (and we will examine the implications within this chapter, suggesting ways to add rigour and robustness into design which will significantly counter such issues).

FIGURE 1.1   Not everything that counts can be counted; not everything that can be counted counts (Albert Einstein, 1879–1955)

Source: Photo © 360b. Image courtesy of Shutterstock

Qualitative research: philosophy

Research philosophy is about examining beliefs (our own and those of others) on how knowledge is developed (for example, what is valid in adding knowledge in the marketing/social sciences field of study). How do we know what we know, and what will be regarded as adding acceptable knowledge within a particular field of study? A discussion on research philosophy usually commences with a consideration of two opposite research perspectives (sometimes referred to as paradigms): positivist and interpretive. Qualitative research falls within the interpretive philosophy. Interpretive philosophy may also be described by some authors as phenomenology.

There are good chapters on this in Bryman and Bell (2012) and in Saunders et al. (2012). Bryman and Bell describe the two philosophies as contrasting extremes, visualised as a sort of Likert-type scale with positivist at one extreme and interpretive at the other. Saunders et al. (2012) illustrate these concepts in the form of a 'Research Onion Model', where choosing a research philosophy represents the first important stage in constructing a research design (before peeling back further layers of the onion to construct a design). The model clearly implies that although there are two extreme philosophies, there may also be positions in between (or that have elements of each philosophy) and it may be that individuals have a research perspective somewhere within the scale (rather than at the extremes). It is, for example, quite common for researchers these days to use a combination of research methods; a mixed methods approach.

For the purposes of this text we take the position which we will define as the professional researcher. In the role of professional researcher the researcher takes no predetermined philosophical approach or subsequent research pathway based on the requirements of philosophical position (as implied by some models). Rather, the researcher determines the particular study and the defined research objectives. In this textbook we are starting from a common position that our research objectives require depth and meaning in social contexts; and therefore a predominantly interpretive philosophy is taken. The market sensing methods we have chosen will seek to describe how this depth and meaning might be achieved.

A good discussion and comparison of positivist and interpretive philosophies can be found in Chapter 1 of Cassell and Symon (1995); note these authors have also produced an edited series of textbooks covering a variety of methods in this field. *Positivism* as they describe it is based on the assumption that there is an objective truth (a reality) existing in the world which can be revealed through scientific methods where the focus is on measuring relationships between variables systematically and statistically. That quantification lies at the heart of scientific methods. The key concerns are that measurement is reliable, valid and generalisable. Studies frequently involve the determining of a research hypothesis which may be subsequently tested for validity. Methods follow strict scientific and statistical protocols.

Whilst such approaches may be predominant in scientific fields (where laboratory conditions may be applied to control variables and the environment), we will argue that such conditions may not be applied meaningfully in social sciences (such as marketing) where participants and the environment are naturally occurring and interacting in a social setting.

In contrast the *interpretive* philosophy is largely concerned with words and meaning arising in social contexts. There is an assumption that there is no single objective truth or reality, rather that relationships are socially constructed and rely on the subjective interpretations of the actors. Or as Fryer (1991: 3) presents it:

> Qualitative researchers are characteristically concerned in their research with attempting to accurately describe, decode and interpret the precise meanings to persons of phenomena occurring in their normal social contexts and are typically preoccupied with complexity, authenticity, contextualisation, shared subjectivity of researcher and researched and minimisation of illusion.

The market sensing methods we have chosen to present in this book align with the interpretive perspective. Aligned with decisions on where research fits and its philosophical perspective are issues of epistemology and ontology which are discussed below.

Epistemology

Bryman and Bell (2012: 13) define epistemology as a theory of knowledge, used to describe a philosophical stance. Within each stance lie underpinning principles and values, and associated procedures for capturing what may be considered acceptable or new knowledge.

So far, for example, we have identified two extreme and opposing research philosophies: positivist and interpretive. Table 1.1 illustrates the contrasting epistemological principles on which these are based.

TABLE 1.1 Comparing research philosophies: positivist and interpretive

Research philosophy	Positivist	Interpretive
Epistemological principles	Scientifically tested	Socially constructed
	For example: Results can be measured and compared, for example using quantitative analysis and statistical techniques.	For example: Results are interpreted from words, images and observations, in a social setting.
	Deductive	Inductive
	For example: A hypothesis is developed (from literature and secondary data) and is tested using scientific principles.	For example: There is no predetermined hypothesis; results are interpreted from emerging themes.
	Objective	Subjective
	For example: Results can be reported scientifically, free from bias, and may be capable of generalisation (from a sample to a wider population).	For example: Results are subject to interpretation and may not be generalised but rather are particular to the study.

TABLE 1.2 Comparing research philosophies: positivist and interpretive (epistemology and ontology)

Research philosophy	Positivist	Interpretive
Epistemological principles	Scientifically tested Deductive Objective	Socially constructed Inductive Subjective
Ontological assumptions	There is a single reality or truth which may be tested and proven	There is no single reality or truth; rather, understanding and meaning is subject to the interpretation of actors in in different social contexts

Ontology

Ontology is concerned with the nature of social entities and questions about what constitutes reality. For example, within the interpretive research philosophy the epistemological principle on which it is based is that knowledge is socially constructed, inductive and subjective. From this perspective an ontological interpretation would suggest a belief that there is no single reality or truth, but that reality is subjective and bound by the interpretations of the social actors (for example, the researcher and the participants). Table 1.2 continues the development contrasting the two philosophical extremes.

We can see from these two tables that designing a qualitative methodology will present some issues and challenges for the researcher. With quantitative techniques there are clear rules and statistical protocols and procedures which can be followed to produce objective and generalisable findings. Qualitative research, however, has to tackle issues of 'interpretation', 'subjectivity' and 'social construction', which are concepts far more difficult to pin down with simple rules and procedures. As Miles and Huberman (2013) write:

> The most serious and central difficulty in the use of qualitative data is that methods of analysis are not well formulated. For quantitative data there are clear conventions the researcher can use. But the analyst faced with a bank of qualitative data has very few guidelines for protection against self-delusion, let alone the presentation of unreliable or invalid conclusions to scientific or policy-making audiences. How can we be sure that our findings are not in fact wrong?'

These issues lead us to the important areas that a qualitative research design must tackle; namely, validity, reliability and bias, which we discuss in Table 1.3.

So questions with which the qualitative researcher must be concerned are:

- Validity: How do we make and demonstrate that the results are credible and valid (to what extent do our findings present a true picture of the situation)?

TABLE 1.3 Validity, reliability and bias

Validity
Definitions
• Validity is concerned with the integrity of the data gathered and the conclusions developed from it (Bryman and Bell, 2012).   • It is the extent to which data collection methods accurately record and measure what was intended (Saunders et al., 2012).
Reliability
Definitions
• Reliability is concerned with the question of whether the results of a study are repeatable (Bryman and Bell, 2012).   • It is the degree to which data collection methods and analysis will yield consistent findings, similar observations would be made and conclusions reached by other researchers repeating the process (Saunders et al., 2012).
Bias
Definition
• Bias refers to the extent to which the researcher or researched may seek to influence the process of data collection, analysis and findings.

- Reliability: How can we be sure that if the same research were carried out independently by different researchers, similar results would be achieved?
- Bias: How do we identify and eliminate our own and others' personal agendas, preferences and biases, to find the truth?

According to Miles and Huberman (2013), the task for the qualitative researcher is to build in robustness (will the design stand up in different and difficult situations?) and rigour (will the design demonstrate comprehensive attention to detail?) in the research design. This will involve careful attention to process, planning, data collection, data analysis and data presentation. These issues will be considered within Chapters 2 and 3 when we go on to look at the process and procedures involved in planning, data collection, analysis and presentation.

In quantitative-based studies a key objective is often to design the study to precise statistical rules so that results from samples can be generalised to a wider population. In qualitative research generalisation cannot be claimed. Results are subject to interpretation. The real value of qualitative research lies not in generalisation but in particularisation. In other words the richness and knowledge derives from understanding a particular situation or case study, in greater depth.

Research approach

So far we have presented that qualitative research is aligned with an interpretive philosophy, that it follows epistemological principles such as social construction,

TABLE 1.4 Approaches to research: inductive and deductive

Stage	Positivist: deductive process (theory then research)	Interpretive: inductive process (research then theory)
1	Theory: Develop theory from literature and secondary data	Theory: Develop understanding of critical factors from literature and secondary data
2	Hypothesis Develop a hypothesis (single or multiple) which may be tested using statistical protocols	Themes and factors Identify critical factors which may be used as a semi-structure to frame the research themes and research questions
3	Data collection Quantitative data is collected, for example using surveys, questionnaires	Data collection Qualitative data is collected, for example using interview and/or observational techniques
4	Findings Findings are presented using numbers following statistical analysis and protocols	Analysis and findings Findings are presented by interpreting and summarising words from interview transcripts, images, observations, recordings
5	Accept or reject hypothesis Hypothesis may be accepted or rejected following statistical protocols (to a level of statistical significance)	Conclusions Conclusions may be developed, for example identifying existing, new or emerging critical factors and themes
6	Generalise findings/theory Provided statistical protocols are followed, results may be generalised (from sample to wider population) to a level of statistical significance	Develop theory/not generalisable Theory may be developed from interpretation of results Results are not generalisable but are particular to the study

inductivism and subjectivism. It is based on the ontological assumption that there is no single truth or reality. The implications for the research process are now examined with a look at the processes for inductive and deductive approaches to research.

Table 1.4 illustrates the two contrasting approaches of deductive (sometimes described as 'theory then research') and inductive ('research then theory').

Both processes normally begin with a review of current theory. In the context of developing a thesis for an undergraduate or postgraduate independent study (dissertation) this is the review of literature and other data, with a view to determining current theory and identifying trends and, importantly, any gaps in knowledge.

Within the *deductive* approach this assumes that research will flow from developing a hypothesis (single or multiple) concerning the association or relationship between different variables (for example, does increased spend on advertising associate with higher customer spend?). Often such studies will seek to establish cause and effect relationships between data variables. Statistical tests or controlled experiments follow, with a view to confirming or rejecting the hypothesis. Following statistical protocols enables the researcher to present conclusions which claim to be predictive, or generalisable to a wider population (from the results of the sample).

Within the *inductive* approach the process assumes that the outcomes from the theory review will present a focus not on statistical relationships between data but more on the nature and understanding of the subject. Themes and factors (often referred to as critical factors) may emerge that are identified as important and these form the basis for the research. The emphasis is on depth and understanding in social contexts, not statistical measurement of relationships.

Data collection often proceeds in the form of interview and observation techniques (structured or semi-structured around emerging themes and critical factors). The strategies associated with data collection are considered in the final section of this chapter.

Research strategy

Research strategy is about choice, to determine appropriate methods to answer the emerging research questions and to form these into a research design and develop research instruments. We have presented that in qualitative research the research objectives and research questions emerge from a detailed review of literature and secondary data, in the form of themes and critical factors, and an awareness of gaps in knowledge. Research questions in qualitative studies will be concerned with depth, meaning and understanding in social contexts and will follow an inductive approach, within an interpretive philosophy.

Saunders et al. (2012) provide us with a useful list of possible strategies and methods, and a brief explanation of each. Commonly used qualitative strategies they identify are:

- case study;
- grounded theory;
- ethnography;
- action research.

Within the context of an inductive approach they also raise the possibility of utilising mixed methods, employing one or more qualitative techniques, or including some quantitative methods, for example surveys or experiments. Bryman and Bell (2012) suggest that in this way triangulation of results may be achieved, where findings from one source or method may be cross-checked and contrasted with those from another. Some authors have suggested that utilising a mixed method strategy can add to the robustness of the research design, with strengths and weaknesses being better balanced and complemented.

Cassell and Symon (1995 onwards) present a very useful series of 'Reader' textbooks (where a collection of highly regarded specialists contribute chapters on their specific area of expertise) with a good range of qualitative strategies and more detailed explanation covering issues of data collection, analysis and presentation. They cover, for example:

- case studies in organisational contexts;
- discourse analysis;
- repertory grid;
- action research;
- qualitative interviewing;
- 20 statements test;
- participant observation;
- tracer studies;
- intervention techniques.

Some of these methods are considered further in Chapter 2, which deals with planning, data collection and analysis.

Summary

This chapter has presented the main underpinning theory for composing a research methodology based on qualitative methods, in particular dealing with issues of context, philosophy, approach and strategy. We have argued that qualitative research is relevant and important and growing within social sciences, which are largely concerned with people and institutions in social contexts. We have presented that qualitative research aligns with a philosophy of the interpretive; epistemologically it is interpretive in nature, socially constructed, inductive and subjective, and ontologically it implies that there is no single truth or reality. This presents the qualitative researcher with challenges in dealing with issues of reliability, validity and bias within the research design. We discuss the inductive approach associated with qualitative research and finish with some suggested research strategies. Chapters 2 and 3 will go on to consider practical application of qualitative research designs, looking further at strategy before moving on to planning, data collection, analysis and presentation.

Bibliography

Bogdan, R. and Taylor, S. J. (1975). *Introduction to Qualitative Research Methods*. New York: Wiley.

Bryman, A. (1988). *Quantity and Quality in Social Research*. London: Unwin Hyman.

Bryman, A. and Bell, E. (2012 or later edition). *Business Research Methods*. Oxford: Oxford University Press.

Cassell, C. and Symon, G. (eds) (1995 or later edition). *Qualitative Methods in Organizational Research*. London: Sage.

Denzin, N. K. (1971). 'The Logic of Naturalistic Enquiry'. *Social Forces Journal* 50, pp. 166–82.

Denzin, N. K., and Lincoln, Y. (2012). *The Sage Handbook of Qualitative Research*. London: Sage.

Fryer, D. (1991). 'Qualitative Methods in Occupational Psychology: Reflections on Why they are so Useful but so Little Used'. *The Occupational Psychologist* 14, pp. 3–6.

Glaser, B. and Strauss, A. L. (1967). *The Discovery of Grounded Theory: Strategies for Qualitative Research*. Chicago: Aldine.

Holden, M. T. and Lynch, P. (2004). 'Choosing the Appropriate Methodology: Understanding Research Philosophy'. *The Marketing Review* 4, pp. 397–409.

Lincoln, Y. S. and Guba, E. G. (2012). *Naturalistic Enquiry*. London: Sage.

Marshall, C. and Rossman, G. B. (2012). *Designing Qualitative Research*. London: Sage.

Miles, B. M. and Huberman, A. M. (2013 or later edition). *Qualitative Data Analysis*. London: Sage.

Patton, M. Q. (1980). *Qualitative Evaluation Methods*. Beverley Hills, CA: Sage.

Patton, M. Q. (1988). 'Paradigms and Pragmatism', in D. Fetterman (ed.), *Qualitative Approaches to Evaluation in Education*. New York: Praeger.

Saunders, M., Lewis, P. and Thornhill, A. (2012 or later edition). *Research Methods for Business Students*. London: FT Prentice Hall.

Silverman, D. (2012 or later edition). *Doing Qualitative Research: A Practical Handbook*. London: Sage.

2

THE QUALITATIVE RESEARCH PROCESS PART 1

Strategy, planning and data collection

David Longbottom

Purpose and context

This chapter considers the practical steps and implications for implementing a qualitative research methodology and will examine issues of strategy, planning and data collection. These are the initial stages in the qualitative research process dealing with preparation and beginning the research. Chapter 3 will go on to consider the later stages of data analysis and data presentation.

Learning outcome

At the end of this chapter you will be able to describe and critically evaluate different qualitative research strategies, determine appropriate strategies for your own study, and begin the process of planning and data collection.

Further reading

This chapter introduces several different strategies which can help guide your choice for an appropriate strategy for your research. For the purposes of this chapter these are briefly identified and discussed, and we identify further readings that can be consulted to develop a deeper understanding. In Part II of this textbook we will explain in greater detail some of the strategies we have particularly selected as appropriate and contemporary for market sensing.

Introduction

We start this chapter with an overview of the qualitative research process and the stages and process are illustrated in Table 2.1. We have compiled the table from a number of sources, so it is the generic outline you will find in most research methods textbooks.

TABLE 2.1 The qualitative research process

Stage	Process
1. Strategy	Choice of method
2. Planning	Sample selection
	Background data gathering
	Gaining access
3. Data collection	Design of research instruments
	Conducting research: interview and observation methods
4. Data analysis	Methods and tools for analysis
	Data reduction; recording, transcription, coding, and analysis
5. Presentation	Methods and examples

Stage 1: strategies for qualitative research

At the end of Chapter 1 we identified some potential research strategies for qualitative research. This chapter begins with a brief overview of some of the most commonly employed for studies in marketing and organisation contexts, with a brief consideration of characteristics and suggested further readings. In Part II of this book we will present in greater detail some selected methods for market sensing. Table 2.2 identifies some research strategies for qualitative research.

TABLE 2.2 Research strategies for qualitative research

Case studies

Definition

A research strategy that takes as its subject a single case or a few selected examples of a social entity (Marshall, 1995: 56). A case might be an individual person, or a single organisation.

Key features

The focus is on selection of one or a few organisations, groups or individuals identified as having particular relevance and importance to the area of study.

Advantages

Intensive examination of single or small group of cases with particular relevance to the study. Can incorporate history and background for context.

Disadvantages

Internal validity; bias can be difficult to overcome.
External validity; to what extent results can be utilised outside of the specific case context.
Access to particular organisations and individuals might be difficult.
Identity of case might need to be restricted for reasons of confidentiality (and this may result in some loss of impact).

Reading

Hartley, in Cassell and Symon (1995), provides a good overview and example in one concise chapter. Major authors include Yin (2013), Silverman (2012), Glaser and Strauss (1967) and Eisenhardt (1989).

(continued)

TABLE 2.2 *(continued)*

Grounded theory

Definition

An approach to the analysis of qualitative data that aims to generate new theory from the data. The method is often associated with case study research. The method is very prescriptive and systematic, requiring the researcher to carefully observe and follow a series of steps to gather, analyse and present the data.

Key features

Sets out a series of steps that can be followed to add rigour and robustness into the research process. It is regarded as a landmark theory in the field of qualitative research.

Advantages

Logical sequence of steps to be followed, constantly checking and cross-checking data with theory.

Disadvantages

Can be seen as a very prescriptive process. Has become subject to abuse and modification, with researchers claiming grounded theory but often not following closely the protocols and procedures.

Reading

Glaser and Strauss (1967). For a more general brief overview see Bryman and Bell (2012).

Ethnography

Definition

The term ethnography refers to folk (ethno-) description (-graphy). The ethnographer's method is to live among the people in the study and record their way of life (frequently using modern media such as digital audio/visual recording).

Key features

Immersion into the lives of the subjects. Frequently designs are unstructured. Use of observation, field notes and modern media to record events.

Advantages

Rich insights into life and unfolding events as they occur. Data is recorded for later analysis.

Disadvantages

Immersion (over an extended period) can be difficult to achieve in practice. Time-consuming.
Difficult to prejudge whether anything of merit will emerge.

Reading

Hammersley and Atkinson (2007). Ethnography is used extensively within marketing; further theory and example studies can be found within marketing and marketing research texts.

Action research

Definition

Action research occurs where researcher and participants collaborate to solve problems and implement solutions. Examples might arise in organisational contexts in consultancy or in change programmes.

Key features

The researcher collaborates with participants and so gains practical insights into the process and procedures and problem-solving activities.

Advantages

Hands-on experience of working within the environment and tackling real problems that arise.

Disadvantages

Can be time-consuming. Can be difficult to gain access/sponsorship. Conflicts of interest might arise between researcher and sponsor/participants.

Reading

McNiff and Whitehead (2005).

Discourse analysis

Definition

Discourse analysis focuses attention on language in social settings, both verbal and written (Marshall, 1995: 91).

Key features

Focus shifts away from individuals and cases as the unit of analysis, to language and context. Language is seen as a variable means of communication and expression of feelings, and not a standardised transparent medium.

Advantages

Allows the researcher to pick up on informal messages and feelings within communications. Enables an understanding of how language (use and interpretation) influences behaviours in a variety of settings. Promotes a better understanding of emerging and developing cultures.
The method may be particularly relevant to analysing talk and text in modern environments using digital and social media.

Disadvantages

Involves collection and study of large amounts of data/transcripts. Analysis of large amounts of data is time-consuming and ambiguities may arise which require clarification. Presentation of findings is difficult to keep concise (whole extracts are often needed, plus narrative, to understand the context).

Reading

Marshall (1995), presents a good concise chapter and example. See also Potter and Wetherell (1987), Paltridge (2012), Jones (2012) and Bryman (2012).

Benchmarking

Definition

Seeks to establish emerging critical factors and best practices using a process-based approach.

Key features

Focuses on understanding how systems and processes work in organisational contexts. Compares and contrasts methods to identify and develop critical factors and emerging best practices.
Uses flow charts to illustrate and analyse processes, activities and procedures.
Used largely in organisational studies but can be adapted for use in consumer studies.

(continued)

TABLE 2.2 *(continued)*

Advantages

Semi-structured method built around process. Uses interview, observation and some quantitative data (measures of performance, for example). Can involve collaboration with participants in problem solving and creative elements.

Disadvantages

Issues concern access (particularly where data is competitive or sensitive). Time-consuming process.

Reading

Zairi (1999).

There are, of course, many different strategies and methods that have been developed by researchers and those above are just a snapshot of common strategies. Often methods or constructs have particular relevance in specific subject areas, and will emerge as common strategies from the review of subject literature. Some other strategies are listed very briefly below.

TABLE 2.3 Further research strategies for qualitative research

Strategies	Used in	Characteristics
Repertory grid	Psychology, organisation behaviour, marketing	Attempts to identify personal constructs and arrange into a grid/matrix for analysis
20 statements test	Psychology, organisation behaviour, HR, marketing	Based on 20 areas commonly used by individuals to assess the self and values
Participant observation	Psychology, organisation behaviour, HR, marketing	Similar to ethnography, involving immersion in the field of study, and involvement in the process
Tracer studies	Organisation behaviour, decision making, operations	Critical events or tags are used to trace events in processes
Intervention techniques	Psychology, organisation behaviour, marketing	Similar to action research in that researcher is involved with the process and problem solving
SERVQUAL	Services marketing	Survey-based instrument for assessing performance in service organisations
Mystery shopper	Services marketing	Fly-on-the-wall method, placing the researcher in the role of the customer
Personal diary	Psychology, organisation behaviour, HR, marketing	Recording of events as they are experienced over a prolonged period
Critical incident	Marketing, HR	Questioning technique based on selecting a specific event or issue for close examination

Means–end chain	Marketing, psychology, organisation behaviour	Questioning technique based on tracing terminal values from observed behaviours
Focus group	Marketing, multi-disciplines	Technique involving group interview and observation where interaction important, often to generate or explore new ideas
Projective techniques	Marketing, multi-disciplines	Technique involving extrapolation or creation of new ideas

Stage 2: planning

Sample selection

In quantitative research there are very clear and specific methods, rules and protocols which can be followed. These present the researcher conducting a quantitative-based study with a set of rules and protocols which can be followed and provide a good basis to support and defend the accuracy and reliability of the findings. However, as we have argued previously, such methods may not produce the depth and meaning that we are seeking in market sensing, and so we have to look at alternative qualitative-based methods either used separately or as part of a combined (or mixed methods) design. In qualitative research, careful consideration and justification is necessary for each individual study, to build a position which may later be defended if challenged on the accuracy of the findings on issues of reliability, validity and bias. Qualitative researchers are not concerned with rules for probability and non-probability, association and statistical significance, and the outcomes in qualitative research will not be generalisable (predictive of a population). In qualitative research the results will be as Thomas (2004: 131) describes them – 'particularisable' – in other words, the results are specific to the context, case study or individual. Application to other contexts may be inferred by the researcher (where similar characteristics are evident) but this is subject to interpretation (the researcher makes inferences, or others interested in the research outcomes interpret relevance and meaning to their own situations).

Sampling in qualitative research is therefore normally based on selection (not randomised) and this brings into discussion the merits of the selection, the selection process and the judgement of the researcher. In short the researcher will need to justify the sample selection (who is included and why) and sample size (how many are included and why). This task is further complicated by the fact that we must be aware that in qualitative research emphasis is on depth and meaning, and this can mean that interventions are necessarily time-consuming and relatively costly. It is, for example, unlikely we can achieve sample sizes of similar proportions to that which may be achieved by survey. It also brings into consideration issues of timing; that is, are we able to collect our data using cross-sectional interventions (a single sample at a single point in time)? Or does the study require longitudinal interventions (multiple or repeated samples spread over a long time period)?

Bryman and Bell (2012) present that in seeking to justify the sample selection researchers need to refer to the relevance and context of the study (for example, close attention to the objectives of the study). The outcomes from the literature review may be a good source for justification (for example in case selection), for reported examples in the literature, and for frequently identified examples of good (or bad) practice. Another source may be through expert interview (the considered opinions of those considered to be expert or close to the field of study).

In terms of sample size an often-used principle is that of 'saturation'. Here the researcher proceeds with a set of semi-structured themes or research questions, and conducts interviews and observations until a point is reached where it may be argued that 'no new information is being revealed, and similar findings are being repeated or confirmed'. A paper by Guest et al. (2006) considers this further, posing the question 'How many interviews are enough?' The authors examine a number of qualitative studies and draw some general guidelines; for example, samples of 5 to 25 are normally adequate for interpretive studies, 20 to 30 for grounded theory studies.

From our own experiences we would say as a general rule of thumb Table 2.4 might be used as a guide.

However, these must be viewed as general guidelines only, and it will be for the researcher to present and justify sample selection and size in the context of the specific study.

A major concern for the researcher is to be aware of the risk of bias in the selection process, and to take steps to ensure that the sample can be justified as representative in the study context. Before entering the field it is vital that the researcher is confident of achieving a defendable and representative sample. Sample selection is often a 'hot topic' in presenting qualitative studies.

TABLE 2.4 How many in-depth interviews are enough?

Undergraduate independent study: 4–6 in-depth interviews

Studies at this level are designed so that the student can demonstrate competence in applying appropriate research methods. Some interesting findings may emerge but these are not likely (or expected) to be conclusive (the main purpose is to demonstrate competence in carrying out the research process).

Postgraduate independent study: 6–12 in-depth interviews

Studies are designed principally so that the student can demonstrate competence in applying appropriate research methods. Some interesting findings may emerge and further themes may be identified which would be suitable for further study at PhD or commercial levels.

PhD: 20–30 in-depth interviews, following the principles of saturation

Studies are designed to develop new theory in a defined and focused area (i.e. new knowledge emerges in a defined field of study which will inform academics and practitioners).

Some students may wish to include some elements of quantitative data or measures to support key areas (thus taking a 'mixed methods' approach). This also achieves 'triangulation' of findings; that is, results from qualitative and quantitative analysis may be compared and contrasted (for similarities or differences).

Commercial studies: 50 + in-depth interviews

This, of course, is very much a rule of thumb and depends on the size of organisation, scope of the project, and available funding and resources. Large organisations will often require a sizeable database to be gathered and stored (for example, using software packages such as NVivo). The advantage of this data store may be in 'holding stock' for future studies and references.

Note: These are rule of thumb guidelines only based on our own collective experiences in this area. Researchers must check the requirements of their own institution to ensure that they are consistent and meet the standards expected.

Gathering background data

It is good practice, and a vital part of preparation before entering the field, to trace the history, background and context to the case, individual or unit to be researched. This saves unnecessary time in the field being taken up seeking information which is already published or generally available. The researcher should exhaust all sources before entering the field, for example:

- literature review;
- secondary data;
- company documentation (for example, published accounts, website, etc.);
- expert interviews;
- recent conferences, events, exhibitions, trade fairs;
- industry and professional bodies.

Good preparation is vital for:

- saving time in the field on unnecessary activity;
- giving greater credibility and professionalism to the research;
- understanding the wider context of the study;
- assessing the importance of including enough within the final thesis to give the reader an overall context for the study.

Gaining access

This can be difficult and needs to be discussed very early within the context of the study and study objectives. Qualitative research is very time-demanding, and there are clearly major issues in engaging participants.

Aligned with availability and access, the researcher also needs to consider, for example, how ethical arrangements might impact the study. Within the NHS (and UK public sectors), for example, there are very precise guidelines that must be followed, and increasingly large corporations in the public and private sectors have well-developed procedures that must be followed. The process for getting approval for access may be long and difficult, and so must be identified early. Students at university or similar institutions will find detailed guidance which needs to be followed. Clarity on ethical processes, such as confidentiality and the right to withdraw, can be very important credentials which the researcher in the field can assert. This has the advantage of giving the participants in the study confidence and trust in the professional nature of the researcher and the study.

Saunders et al. (2012) make some suggestions for negotiating appropriate access:

- make early contact;
- make initial contacts short and easy;
- build up networks;
- have contingency plans;
- use attendance at conferences, events, exhibitions, etc.;
- use other research groups and experts active in the field;
- use professional and trade bodies;
- arrange presentations, disseminations of your work.

From our own experiences we have found attendance at conferences and exhibitions to be particularly useful in building more personalised networks.

Stage 3: data collection

Interviewing

A good chapter entitled 'The Qualitative Research Interview' written by Nigel King can be found in Cassell and Symon (1995). According to King, the qualitative interview will generally have the following characteristics:

- a low degree of structure imposed by the researcher;
- a preponderance of open-style questions;
- a focus on situations and actions in the world of the interviewee.

These characteristics give weight to the interview taking place within the interviewee's natural environment, thus affording the researcher the additional benefits of understanding context and of observing behaviours and the environment, thus facilitating the use of examples and evidence gathering. King argues that even natural interruptions that occur within the field can be useful for the researcher to better understand the environment and context.

King's view of a low degree of structure is supported by Thomas (2004:162–70). He discusses the issues involved in preparing an interview plan or schedule.

He suggests that it should not be in the form of a checklist of questions (more relevant to survey work) but designed to facilitate a conversation with purpose. He advocates the use of key themes (emerging as the critical factors for the research from the literature review), supported by prompts and probes (to guide and assist the researcher). Similar ideas for developing frameworks can be found in Miles and Huberman (1994: 16–38). In Table 2.5 we present an example of an interview plan and interview questioning techniques which we have developed from our own collective experiences of interviewing over many years. The work also draws on interviewing methods described by Cooper and Branthwaite (1997), which Hancock and Longbottom develop further in Chapter 4 of this book.

In this particular example case study we were engaged with representatives from Hewlett Packard and our research was investigating critical factors in building knowledge management systems. Hewlett Packard had been referenced many times within the literature review we had conducted and was considered by many authors to be at the forefront of knowledge management (KM)

TABLE 2.5 Example interview plan

	Interview Plan: Study of Knowledge Management (KM) Hewlett Packard Consulting (HPC) Photo © Ken Wolter. Image courtesy of Shutterstock
	Name: AB Position: Senior Consultant, HP Consulting Photo © drserg. Image courtesy of Shutterstock Background: Joined HP in last three years from MBA Cranfield, age 45, specialises in KM, IT for KM. Previous experience with PriceWaterhouse on KM IT development. Has a team of four consultants. Looking to generate own HP specialist section. Client base covers mostly UK (60%), France (20%) and Germany (20%).

(continued)

TABLE 2.5 *(continued)*

Purpose: Establish the status of KM within HPC, to include critical factors, implementation process, key performance measures and future directions.

Date: 24 April 2010 (Easter Geneva site visit)

Time: 11am–5pm (including lunch and site visit, IT facility, HP museum)

Place/location: HPC HQ, Geneva

Photo © GlobalVision 360. Image courtesy of Shutterstock

Present: Interviewers Dave Longbottom, Pieris Chourides, Rick Edgemann
Interviewed: AB

Transcript: Formal tape recording two hours for full transcription, plus notes as supplementary evidence. Various policy documents and internal training materials gathered reference appendices 1–5.

Themes 1 and 2 of 34

Theme 1: Discuss the status of KM within HPC
Definition (1)
Start date (1)
Time (1)
Resources (2)
Responsibility (2)
Effectiveness (3)
Competencies (3/4)
Theme 2: Discuss approach to implementation and methods used

Describe the approach (2)
Evaluate the approach (3)
Describe methods (2)
Lessons learned (3)
Key performance measures and impact (3/4)

Note: Numbers in brackets for each theme denote 'difficulty levels' which we discuss in the next section. For each difficulty level we try to anticipate potential issues which may arise, for example:

systems (a justification for including them within the primary data collection phase).

- trust and confidentiality;
- expressions of personal opinion or evaluation;
- sensitive information;
- possibility of bias;
- evidence.

We then consider what questioning strategies might be most useful in overcoming any issues that might arise and that we need to secure the depth of understanding that is the purpose of our study. Questioning strategies are considered in the following sections.

We might also identify sub-themes or probes (probing questions) to help if responses seem incomplete or unclear.

We also will normally indicate on the plan projected timings to help keep the interview within the timescale agreed (though researchers have to be alert to emerging issues which may extend times in certain areas or which introduce new themes not anticipated; such is the nature of this inductive learning process).

The important issue with the plan is to use it as a guide to process, to help anticipate events and to ensure some measure of consistency across a range of participants. Taking detailed notes during the interview is not recommended. Rather we prefer to use audio or video to record events. This allows the researcher to concentrate fully on the conversation and to take important readings of body language and emotion (which may be cues for further questions and probes).

Questioning strategies

Aligned with the interview plan we suggest that some attention to preparation of question strategies is important. Here we are trying to anticipate difficulty levels and choose appropriate questioning strategies to elicit meaningful responses. An example is illustrated in Table 2.6.

Table 2.7 illustrates the relationship between time and trust in gaining interview data. Developing trust over extended time periods may simply be impractical in many research situations which are time-constrained, so the researcher has to consider strategies to capture the information needed within the limitations of the interview. It suggests that the researcher can prepare a questioning and interpretation strategy based on four levels, each incremental level becoming progressively more difficult.

TABLE 2.6 Interview difficulty levels

Awareness	*Response*
Level 1	Level 1
Aware, communicable, public	Spontaneous, reasoned, self-explanatory
Level 2	Level 2
Aware, communicable, private or personal, not public	Protective, reserved, may need clarification
Level 3	Level 3
Aware, difficult to communicate, private, personal or confidential	Sensitive, difficult, may be partial or slow release, or withheld
Level 4	Level 4
Not aware, unable to communicate	Confused, incoherent, withdrawn, open to misrepresentation

Source: adapted from the work of Cooper and Branthwaite (1977)

TABLE 2.7 Levels of questioning: trust and time relationships

TRUST

High				Level 4
^^^			Level 3	
^^^		Level 2		
Low	Level 1			
	Short	>>>	>>>	Long TIME

Table 2.8 suggests some interviewing strategies that may help, presenting that questioning style, degree of probing, and interviewer/interviewee speaking ratios may change depending on the question level. For example, at level 3 you would expect much greater use of prompts and probes and the interviewer might seek to employ particular questioning techniques (for example, critical incident or means–end chain). Prolonged use of silence may also increase as levels rise, a useful technique for the interviewer to attempt to engage the interviewee further by being suggestive that more information is desired (whist allowing thinking and reflective time). Silences should be noted within the interview transcripts to help the reader understand the context and tone of the conversation.

TABLE 2.8 Levels of questioning: style implications

Level	Dominant question style	Probing	Interviewee: interviewer ratio
Level 1	Open	Low level, clarification seeking	80:20
Level 2	Open and closed	Moderate level, clarification seeking and explanation building	50:50
Level 3	Open, closed and cross-examining	High level, clarification seeking, explanation building, evidence gathering	20:80
Level 4	Open, closed, cross-examining and observation	High level, clarification seeking, explanation building, evidence gathering, moving to cross-checking and observation methods	Moving to observation

Table 2.9 suggests some questioning strategies that might be used. In particular, these may be helpful in eliciting responses at the more difficult levels (levels 3/4).

Skill and practice

Whilst we have shown techniques for interview planning and developing appropriate questioning strategies we must stress that interviewing is a very difficult skill

TABLE 2.9 Questioning strategies

Questioning strategies	Characteristics
Critical incident	Questions focus on a specific event or incident to gain rich insights into an actual example
Means–end chain	Questions move from understanding actual behaviour through to terminal values (Why fundamentally do you behave that way?)
Prisoner's dilemma	Introduces other evidence or opinion which may contradict what the respondent is saying
Devil's advocate	Interviewer is well rehearsed on opposing point of view and takes on this role
Chief executive diary	Seeks to check out interview answers by observation of actual behaviour
Process	Seeks to gain depth by asking the respondent to talk through the process stage by stage
Storytelling	Similar to process where respondent is asked to talk through an example, real or simulated
Silence	Use of prolonged and deliberate silences during an interview to tease out more comment
Perspective	Asks the respondent to look at the situation from another angle or point of view
Projective	Asks the respondent to engage in creative thought or exploration of trends
Group (focus)	Introduces group opinion and dynamics into discussion
Empathy	Interviewer plays on building relationship with respondent and sympathising with situation or events
Rank/rate scales	Useful for positioning opinion when answers not clear-cut
Metaphorical analysis	Based on theory that suggests 'deep emotions' are revealed in metaphorical expressions

to master. In our experience it requires considerable practice and evaluation. We would always recommend a rehearsal, with self- and peer review of performance.

Summary

This chapter has considered the research process for qualitative research. Unlike quantitative research, the process is less prescriptive and influenced by the particular field of study. The qualitative researcher must therefore draw on some general rules of practice, but also from best practice emerging from their field of study. Drawn from a number of sources we identify a generic process, the principal stages in the process and main activities within the stages. This chapter deals specifically with qualitative strategies, planning and data collection. Within the strategies section we have presented examples of commonly employed strategies and some further examples which are related to the field of study. Within the planning section we have considered and made some suggestions for preparation, background data gathering, gaining access and dealing with ethical issues. Within the data collection section we presented examples of preparing an interview plan and developing an interview design and questioning strategy. Chapter 3 will consider the remaining stages in the qualitative research process: data analysis and data presentation.

Bibliography

Atkinson, P. and Hammersley, M. (1994). 'Ethnography and Participant Observation', in N.K. Denzin and Y. S. Lincoln (eds), *Handbook of Qualitative Research*. London: Sage.

Bogdan, R. and Taylor, S. J. (1975). *Introduction to Qualitative Research Methods*. New York: Wiley.

Bryman, A. (2012). *Social Research Methods*. Oxford: Oxford University Press.

Bryman, A. and Bell, E. (2012 or later edn). *Business Research Methods*. Oxford: Oxford University Press.

Cassell, C. and Symon, G. (eds) (1995). *Qualitative Methods in Organizational Research*. London: Sage.

Cooper, P. and Branthwaite, A. (1997). 'Qualitative Technology; New Perspectives on Measurement and Meaning through Qualitative Research'. *Proceedings of the Market Research Society Conference 1997*.

Denzin, N. K. (1971). 'The Logic of Naturalistic Enquiry'. *Social Forces Journal* 50, pp. 166–82.

Denzin, N. K. and Lincoln, Y. S. (eds) (1994). *Handbook of Qualitative Research*. Thousand Oaks, CA: Sage.

Denzin, N. K. and Lincoln, Y. S. (2005). *The Sage Handbook of Qualitative Research*. Thousand Oaks, CA: Sage.

Eisenhardt, K. M (1989). 'Building Theories from Case Study Research'. *Academy of Management Review* 14, pp. 532–50.

Fryer, D. (1991). 'Qualitative Methods in Occupational Psychology: Reflections on Why they are so Useful but so Little Used'. *The Occupational Psychologist* 14, pp. 3–6.

Glaser, B. and Strauss, A. L. (1967). *The Discovery of Grounded Theory: Strategies for Qualitative Research*. Chicago: Aldine.

Guest, G., Bunce, A. and Johnson, L. (2006). 'How Many Interviews are Enough? An Experiment with Data Saturation and Variability'. *Field Methods* 18, no. 1, pp. 59–82.

Hammersley, M. and Atkinson, P. (2007). *Ethnography: Principles in Practice*. London: Sage.

Hartley, J. (1995). 'Case Studies in Organisational Research', in C. Cassell and G. Symon (eds), *Qualitative Methods in Organizational Research*. London: Sage.

Holden, M. T. and Lynch, P. (2004). 'Choosing the Appropriate Methodology: Understanding Research Philosophy'. *The Marketing Review* 4, pp. 397–409.

Jones, R. H. (2012). *Discourse Analysis: A Resource Book for Students*. London: Routledge.

King, N. (1995). 'The Qualitative Research Interview', in C. Cassell and G. Symon (eds), *Qualitative Methods in Organizational Research*. London: Sage.

Lincoln, Y. S. and Guba, E. G. (1985). *Naturalistic Enquiry*. Beverley Hills, CA: Sage.

Marshall, H. (1995). 'Discourse Analysis in Occupational Context', in C. Cassell and G. Symon (eds), *Qualitative Methods in Organizational Research*. London: Sage.

Marshall, C. and Rossman, G. B. (1989). *Designing Qualitative Research*. Newbury Park, CA: Sage.

McNiff, J. and Whitehead, J. (2005). *All You Need to Know about Action Research*. London: Sage.

Miles, B. M., and Huberman, A. M. (1994). *Qualitative Data Analysis*. London: Sage.

Paltridge, B. (2012). *Discourse Analysis: An Introduction*. London: Bloomsbury.

Patton, M. Q. (1980). *Qualitative Evaluation Methods*. Beverley Hills, CA: Sage.

Patton, M. Q. (1988). 'Paradigms and Pragmatism', in D. Fetterman (ed.), *Qualitative Approaches to Evaluation in Education*. New York: Praeger.

Potter, J. and Wetherell, M. (1987). *Discourse and Social Psychology*. London: Sage.

Saunders, M., Lewis, P. and Thornhill, A. (2012). *Research Methods for Business Students*. London: FT Prentice Hall.

Silverman, D. (2012). *Doing Qualitative Research: A Practical Handbook*. London: Sage.

Thomas, A. B. (2004). *Research Skills for Management Studies*. London: Routledge.

Yin, R. K. (2013). *Case Study Research: Design and Methods*. Beverley Hills, CA: Sage.

Zairi, M. (1999). *Benchmarking for Best Practice*. London: Butterworth Heinemann.

3

THE QUALITATIVE RESEARCH PROCESS PART 2

Data analysis and data presentation

David Longbottom

Purpose and context

This chapter considers the final stages in the research process; data analysis and data presentation. It will consider issues of recording and transcribing, summarising data, analysis of data, drawing conclusions, constructing solutions, testing and further research.

Learning outcome

At the end of this chapter you will be able to describe and critically evaluate the different qualitative research methods for data analysis and data presentation necessary to complete and evaluate primary research to a high professional standard.

Introduction to data analysis and presentation

In quantitative scientific enquiry the researcher has statistical rules and protocols which should be followed in order to produce results which can be presented as accurate and meaningful. In qualitative research the procedures that should be followed are not so clear and are subject to interpretation and application by the researcher, who will have to justify the design and process. This places more emphasis on the researcher to demonstrate robustness and rigour in the process chosen.

The process of analysis for qualitative data requires what is often termed data reduction. Here the researcher is moving from a lengthy interview transcript to a more concise summary and analysis of key points. The challenge is to do this in a robust and rigorous way so that readers can see the raw data and how interpretations have been made. The raw data (often in the form of transcripts or images) represents the researcher's evidence base. It is necessary therefore that the researcher takes care to make transcripts and images fully available to the reader, and introduces some form of referencing system so that extracts can be easily located (in transcripts or in collages of images).

We would identify the following key stages in the data reduction process:

1. recording and transcribing;
2. summarising data;
3. analysis and evaluation of data;
4. drawing conclusions, constructing solutions, and further research.

Figure 3.1 illustrates the main stages in the data reduction process.

Recording and transcribing

There are considerable advantages in using audio or video recording for interviews:

- saves time;
- removes the need for note taking;
- allows the researcher to focus on the participant for important signals: language and discourse, body language, facial expression, emotions;
- provides a permanent record if stored in a database;
- audio or video may add value to presentations.

Disadvantages relate mostly to the risk that it may inhibit the interviewee. On balance we favour recording in most situations and through the use of unobtrusive modern technology and skilful interviewing the drawbacks may be largely overcome. Sometimes a mixture of formal recording and informal conversation may be employed if it is judged that there are concerns or sensitivities.

Typically a 1-hour interview will equate to around 6,000/8,000 words of transcribed data. It can be seen therefore that the issue of recording and transcription is

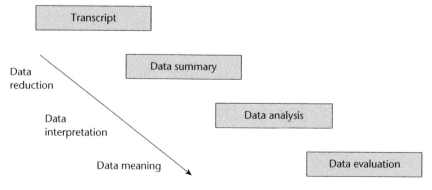

FIGURE 3.1 Data reduction process

a difficult and time-consuming task, and presents the researcher with considerable issues when deciding on presentation (which we discuss in later sections). There are many good voice recognition software packages that are available commercially which can drastically reduce the time needed to type up a full transcript. At the time of writing the market leader within the UK is Dragon software, and we have found that with careful practice in dictation an accuracy level of around 80% is possible (leaving only final grammar, spelling checks and proofreading to complete the transcript). At the time of writing we have not been successful in using any voice recognition satisfactorily for live recordings in the field (voice recognition between researcher and participants is just too different and complex for the software to handle). So at the moment our practice is to dictate the audio file using speaker/earphone headsets. Transcripts are then annotated to show expressions of emotion, body language, etc., but can never replace the feel of the live recording. Future advances in technology which could accommodate multiple voice recognition would be a major breakthrough for qualitative researchers.

There is no prescriptive or one best way of transcribing that we can advise the researcher to follow. Some useful hints and tips can be found in Bryman and Bell (2012) on interviewing in qualitative research. In Table 3.1 we present an example interview transcript illustrating some of the main issues. This is a continuation of

TABLE 3.1 Example interview transcript

Theme	Question/response	Ref.
Theme 1: Status of KM		
DL (interviewer)	Alan, in this first part I would like to spend a little time trying to understand what KM [knowledge management] is within your organisation. I have a number of questions, but perhaps we could start by you telling me a little bit about it, for instance, when did your project start, who is involved and so on.	T1.1
AB (participant)	*Well . . . I suppose our first concerns started to come out after we separated from HP Corporate and became HP Consulting . . .* AB hands me the 'New Direction' document April 1992 and we have a brief interlude on this (see appendix 12.4).	1.1
	This was a big move for us but entirely consistent with our routes. I suppose you must know of our mission to keep the values of a small business within a major global organisation . . .	1.1.1
DL	Yes, please continue	
AB	*Well, the problem as we saw it was splitting up the business gave us lots of opportunities; independence, competitive spirit, greater flexibility and so on . . . all vital I might add and we had been wanting a long time . . . but we saw some risks too. There were some areas where we might be exposed and we wanted to be able to bring in expertise from the wider group and did not want to lose access to this. We wanted to still retain elements of shared expertise, knowledge if you like. The way it worked was like this . . .*	1.1.2

the case study of Hewlett Packard Consulting (HPC) and knowledge management (KM) introduced in Chapter 2.

Comments on the transcript

At this point in the interview AB went into the project in some detail for over 20 minutes, describing the background and how events unfolded. The information was useful to us in the context of our study and as we had good time available we did not interrupt. Having a detailed interview plan (and using audio tape recording to capture the conversation) enabled the interviewee to 'tick off' issues that were being addressed (naturally in conversation) by AB (wholly or partially) and without the need to be distracted from listening and observation (which can be the case if involved with extensive note taking). For example, looking back at the interview plan we were able to tick that we had received in the initial exchange several items: a definition (and explanation and documents to support it), start date, time, resources, responsibilities. We had some responses on process (but needed to go back on this for much more detail) but no comment yet on effectiveness. Some elements were beginning to emerge as important: for example, issues concerning competitiveness, relationships between units, and individual roles, which we noted as later themes that we would need to explore further and address within our plan.

This introductory question and conversation is at level 1; most of the information AB is aware of and familiar with, able to describe and explain, and his response is spontaneous (not reserved) and easy to interpret. Some of it confirms data that we already knew from background preparation, such as documents within the public domain (so the interviewer faces the decision of whether to interrupt the flow and move on, which may be important if there are time pressures). Allowing the interviewee to provide a full, if somewhat lengthy introduction can, however, be important for setting the tone for the meeting, also for judging overall attitude to the subject and the building of trust. It might also lead to the identification of important issues emerging that may be off-plan: for example, AB revealed early on that there were tensions between some departments (which we noted down as an issue for further investigation at a later stage in the research).

Note that in the 'Ref.' column we have started a theme and paragraph numbering system. This will enable us to reference the transcript within the main text of our final report (and thesis). This will be important in data reduction when we summarise and draw extracts from transcripts (still allowing the reader to locate the extract from the transcript if further context is required). Similarly we will edit the audio tape recording so that themed sections can be referenced in our final report and located by a reader wanting to hear an extended version.

General points arising from the transcript

Within the transcript we identify the themes structuring the discussion as main headings, with prompts and questions as they occur. We provide a numbering system (right-hand column) so that when writing up summaries in the main thesis references can be used (transcripts and tape recordings are then normally included in appendices, increasingly in digital computer format). In this example, numbering is by paragraph, but some researchers use line-by-line (particularly if itemised or content analysis is used).

This structure tends to assume that interviews flow logically and according to plan, which often is not the case. For this we also suggest that commentaries are added: for example to illustrate where the conversation has referred back to previous issues, or has raised new issues, or simply to note context (interruptions, observations, change in mood or behaviour, prolonged silences, etc.).

There is a further issue of the coding of data which the researcher may wish to introduce. This can help to shorten the transcription process, aid recall and analysis, or highlight key themes and features that are emerging. It may be particularly useful if the researcher is planning to use formal content analysis procedures to analyse and present data. Content analysis can take extreme forms such as searching out and counting the number of times an issue is raised. Some qualitative researchers, however, would feel uncomfortable that such extreme approaches may be too simplistic and really just a means of imposing quantitative analysis not appropriate to an essentially qualitative study.

The issue of coding, however, will also be important if computer-aided qualitative data analysis (CAQDAS) is being employed. Within the UK the market leader is NVivo, formerly NUD*IST (Non-numerical Unstructured Data Indexing Searching and Theorising). The software enables the researcher to design and construct a language-based database which is useful for data storage, retrieval and analysis. This can be particularly useful for storage of large volumes, and where the researcher wishes to create an archive (allowing for repeated analysis over long time periods). The drawback is that it can take some time to design and set up, and some researchers feel that it can lead to some detachment of the researcher from the data. There is a useful website available for NVivo which includes sample software, an online tutorial, and a short presentation of the main product features.

In the example provided we have presented transcripts with reference codes by paragraph. Some researchers prefer to present transcripts in line-by-line format; in that case each line is numbered, allowing the researcher to reference very specific areas and keywords from the transcript (and this allows the reader to look up the points from the transcript if additional context is wanted).

Summarising data from a transcript to be presented in the main text

Presenting qualitative data is difficult. Unlike quantitative research, there are no rules and conventions about using numbers and statistics that may be followed. So the qualitative researcher has to follow general guidance on good practice from a variety of sources, and keep in mind the study objectives, the research philosophy and strategy underpinning the study, plus the need in all qualitative research to demonstrate rigour and robustness. As we have stated already, a good general discussion of presentation issues can be found in Bryman and Bell (2012) and Miles and Huberman (2012). For specific research strategies you can also refer to specialist texts which cover the particular research strategy you have selected.

Case or thematic analysis

A key decision to be taken is whether to present the analysis on a case-by-case basis, or by theme. In case-by-case analysis the responses from each individual participant is summarised and presented with illustrative extracts from the case transcript. This may be the preferred option if the researcher feels that it is important to build individual case-by-case profiles. The alternative is to adopt a thematic approach where the analysis is presented by emerging key themes. In thematic analysis the researcher summarises the key aspects of the theme, then draws on extracts from transcripts across the full range of participants to illustrate the views being expressed.

An example of presenting a summary from the main transcript is presented below. In this example we have chosen a thematic approach. Our justification for the thematic approach rested on the principle that our main objective was to gain an understanding of the knowledge management process (and that this might best be achieved by assessing views and themes across a range of diverse participants). Continuing with our example of HPC, themes were presented following our semi-structured format but also noting emergent (inductive) themes. Here, for example, we discovered that an emerging theme concerned inter-departmental attitudes and arguments which were seen as important and a cause of problems in implementation of the knowledge management programmes. A short extract from our summary report is given in Table 3.2 to illustrate an example of a summary derived from transcript.

Comments on the summary

The summary presentation is structured by key themes, then issues and questions arising within themes. Note that some researchers will prefer to adopt a less structured approach and attempt to build the presentation from word repositories (abandoning the semi-structured themes in favour of emerging groups and characteristics). It can also be useful in adding rigour to the process to cross-check interpretations, either by involving others in the process or going back to respondents to clarify meaning. The researcher might also seek out documents or other evidence to confirm an interpretation.

Illustrative quotes are selected and used and the author references the full transcript (allowing the reader to locate the extract within the full transcript or recording if further reading or context is wanted). A commentary is provided, which at this stage seeks to stress similarities and differences but avoids being over-analytical, preferring to take the reader into the situation.

TABLE 3.2 Example summary derived from transcript

Theme: IT lead/dominance

When we began discussing the roles of the main departments, issues began to emerge. It became apparent from a number of sources that the driving force for the new system was the IT department. Some managers were of the view that IT had become a dominant player at corporate level and was able to secure substantial investment denied to others. There were concerns expressed about a dominant attitude from IT analysts, a lack of consultation on key implementation issues, and an indifference to people and resource issues.

'We were being told that we must transfer all our client data onto the central system. All our personal job records, diaries, and CVs too. There was no real discussion, ... just, like, do it . . . by next week. Well, a lot of us were uneasy. We talked among ourselves. I guess if I'm honest we sort of decided to play a game. Most of us put data on . . . to be seen to be engaging . . . but in reality most of the stuff was old, outdated, and not much good. Most of the real stuff we kept back.'

MT, Senior Consultant

Ref: MT T5.2.2, p. 101

'There was no real thought about planning or disruption. The timings were just unrealistic. We can't just stop everything whilst a new system is going in. We have jobs to get done. There was a lot of resistance . . . and frankly many thought it was a waste of time anyway. I'm not sure they knew what they were doing anyway.'

SKH, Head of Operations

Ref: SKH T5.2.5, p. 133

'There was clearly a clash between DS [head of HRM] and JOD [head of IT]. It got so bad that I don't think they were speaking to each other. DS had a point, I feel. It was all going ahead too quickly and we could see trouble. Fact is DS just withdrew his support, but it didn't seem to matter. I don't think he has a big say on the Board any more . . . I think they just ignored him.'

RH, Supervisor HRM

Ref: RH T1.4.2, p. 24

The problem of data reduction and summarisation is particularly difficult for qualitative researchers presenting academic papers for conference or journal publication, where often editors will limit word counts and this places a difficult discipline on qualitative researchers. Use of audio and video attachments is becoming more common, also the insertion of text extracts (and sometimes images and illustrations) within an appendix to the main report.

Whilst data reduction through summarising is perhaps the most commonly applied presentation method for qualitative research, Miles and Huberman (2012) suggest that there are many different ways to present data and they give examples of use of metrics, diagrams, structures and pattern matching (which can be used as alternatives or in conjunction with summarising methods). This introduces the opportunity for some element of creativity, which could be important in the context of the study and communicating the findings.

Analysis and evaluation of data

For some researchers the presenting of summaries with reference to transcripts may be the limit of the analysis, leaving the reader to make their own further interpretations and judge the relevance for their own contexts. In some disciplines, however, it is becoming more normal to carry out further analysis and evaluation (business and marketing disciplines, for example). In these scenarios the researcher will carry out further analysis and interpretation of data, leading to evaluation of data and in some instances development of new theory (or suggesting practical business solutions).

There are good examples of different methods for further reducing and analysing and presenting data to be found in Miles and Huberman (2012). Again, you will find particular examples within specialist texts dealing with the various particular research strategies (for example, in case study, grounded theory, discourse analysis, etc.), and you may find these useful reference points. Table 3.3 illustrates a matrix type of analysis based on cross-tabulation of results. This works well in case or thematic analysis, multi-interview situations, and also for focus groups. (Table 3.3 is again extracted from our Hewlett Packard example).

Table 3.3 illustrates a snapshot of responses to key themes from respondents (in practice for this study there were many more respondents and themes that are not shown here), enabling the data to be reduced down to single pages. Further analysis can take the form of cross-tabulation analysis (horizontal and vertical).

Horizontal analysis enables patterns to be identified for each theme. For example, in this study, under the theme of 'IT role' there is an emerging consensus that the project is 'IT-dominated'. We also find that 'Marketing' are 'not engaged'. Within the theme 'Resources' there are differences between departments, some being 'under-resourced' while others are 'well-resourced'. Table 3.4 shows an example of horizontal/thematic analysis.

TABLE 3.3 Example of further summary analysis using cross-tabular method

Themes	Respondents			
	AB	DH	SKH	MT
KM status	High	High	Low	High
Approach	Participative	Project structured	Top-down IT-driven	Involving but IT focus
Resources	Good	Good	Under-resourced	Moderate/ reviewing
Performance	Financial improvements	Too early to say	No evidence	Some improvements
Future	Important	Will continue	May drop	Needs longer
Competencies	Need more time	Will be longterm	Very weak	Weak
Strategic role	Some input	Part of plan	Lip service	Needs more effort
IT role	High involvement	Main driver	IT focus	IT focus
Marketing role	Need to engage	Don't see benefits	Against the idea	Not involved
HRM role	Getting more involved	Need more input	Ineffective	Minor role

TABLE 3.4 Example of horizontal/thematic analysis

Themes	*Respondents*				KEY OUTCOME BY THEME
	AB	DH	SKH	MT	
KM status	High	High	Low	High	
Approach	Participative	Project structured	Top-down IT- driven	Involving but IT focus	
Resources	Good	Good	Under-resourced	Moderate/reviewing	
Performance	Financial improvements	Too early to say	No evidence	Some improvements	
Future	Important	Will continue	May drop	Needs longer	
Competencies	Need more time	Will be longterm	Very weak	Weak	
Strategic role	Some input	Part of plan	Lip service	Needs more effort	
IT role ↑	High involvement ↑	Main driver ↑	IT focus ↑	IT focus ↑	IT FOCUS
Marketing role ↑	Need to engage ↑	Don't see benefits ↑	Against the idea ↑	Not involved ↑	MARKETING NOT ENGAGED
HRM role	Getting more involved	Need more input	Ineffective	Minor role	

TABLE 3.5 Example of vertical/case analysis

Themes	Respondents			
Key outcome by participant	'Positive supporter'		'Negative sceptic'	
	AB	DH	SKH	MT
KM status	High ↑	High	Low ↑	High
Approach	Participative ↑	Project structured	Top-down IT driven ↑	Involving but IT focus
Resources	Good ↑	Good	Under-resourced ↑	Moderate/ reviewing
Performance	Financial improvements ↑	Too early to say	No evidence ↑	Some improvements
Future	Important ↑	Will continue	May drop ↑	Needs longer
Competencies	Need more time ↑	Will be long-term	Very weak ↑	Weak
Strategic role	Some input ↑	Part of plan	↑	Needs more effort
IT role	High involvement ↑	Main driver	IT focus ↑	IT focus
Marketing role	Need to engage ↑	Don't see benefits	Against the idea ↑	Not involved
HRM role	Getting more involved	Need more input	Ineffective	Minor role

Vertical analysis in this study may be important in identifying individual perspectives by case. For example, respondent AB displays responses that are generally 'positive and supportive' and he is 'optimistic' about the future of the project. In contrast, SKH is much more 'negative' and 'pessimistic'. Table 3.5 shows an example of vertical/case analysis.

Drawing conclusions, constructing solutions, and further research

Practice in qualitative research is again variable and there are no strict rules that must be followed. Within business disciplines it is normal practice to expect the researcher to develop the analysis further and suggest a summary of the main conclusions: what was discovered, what the immediate implications are for the study sample, and possible wider implications for others (subject to interpretation). Some researchers may wish to further engage with respondents and other experts (before final writing up) to review and check the findings (within a focus group, presentation or discussion). This can add rigour to the overall process.

In drawing conclusions, the researcher must be careful not to imply that the results are generalisable, but rather that the strength lies in the results being particularisable to the case and respondents in the study. Many students go on to suggest or create new models which address some of the issues identified and provide a basis for further discussion and a focus for future research. It is generally considered good practice at the end of a thesis to reflect on the outcomes and discuss further research areas.

In Part II of this textbook we present a variety of different market sensing methods. For each method the authors will present a practical example which takes you through all of the theoretical processes we have described in Part I. In some of the examples the authors have developed frameworks or business solutions and these provide interesting and relevant practice outcomes.

Summary

This chapter has examined the final stages in the research process; those of data analysis and data presentation. It has discussed issues of recording and transcribing, summarising data, analysis of data, drawing conclusions, constructing solutions, testing and further research. Particular examples have been presented drawing from published studies in marketing and business disciplines. Presentation of data may vary across the disciplines and researchers may need to be adaptive to practices that are closely aligned with their chosen research strategy and accepted within their particular field of study.

In Part II of this book a variety of different market sensing methods are discussed in detail.

Bibliography

Atkinson, P. and Hammersley, M. (1994). 'Ethnography and Participant Observation', in N.K. Denzin and Y.S. Lincoln (eds), *Handbook of Qualitative Research*. Thousand Oaks, CA: Sage.

Bogdan, R. and Taylor, S. J. (1975). *Introduction to Qualitative Research Methods*. New York: Wiley.

Bryman, A. and Bell, E. (2012 or later edn). *Business Research Methods*. Oxford: Oxford University Press.

Cassell, C. and Symon, G. (eds) (1995). *Qualitative Methods in Organizational Research*. London: Sage.

Cooper, P. and Branthwaite, A (1977). 'Qualitative Technology; New Perspectives on Measurement and Meaning through Qualitative Research.' *Proceedings of the Market Research Society Conference 1997*.

Denzin, N. K. (1971). 'The Logic of Naturalistic Enquiry'. *Social Forces Journal* 50, pp. 166–82.

Denzin, N. K. and Lincoln, Y. S. (eds) (1994). *Handbook of Qualitative Research*. Thousand Oaks, CA: Sage.

Denzin, N. K. and Lincoln, Y. S. (2005 or later edn). *The Sage Handbook of Qualitative Research*. London: Sage.

Eisenhardt, K. M (1989). 'Building Theories from Case Study Research'. *Academy of Management Review* 14, pp. 532–50.

Fryer, D. (1991). 'Qualitative Methods in Occupational Psychology: Reflections on Why they are so Useful but so Little Used'. *The Occupational Psychologist* 14, pp. 3–6.

Glaser, B. and Strauss, A. L. (1967). *The Discovery of Grounded Theory: Strategies for Qualitative Research*. Chicago: Aldine.

Guest, G., Bunce, A. and Johnson, L. (2006). 'How Many Interviews are Enough? An Experiment with Data Saturation and Variability'. *Field Methods* 18, no.1, pp. 59–82.

Hammersley, M. and Atkinson, P. (2007). *Ethnography: Principles in Practice*. London: Sage.

Hartley, J. (1995). 'Case Studies in Organisational Research', in C. Cassell and G. Symon (eds), *Qualitative Methods in Organizational Research* (or later edn). London: Sage.

Holden, M. T. and Lynch, P. (2004). 'Choosing the Appropriate Methodology: Understanding Research Philosophy'. *The Marketing Review* 4, pp. 397–409.

King, N. (1995). 'The Qualitative Research Interview', in C. Cassell and G. Symon (eds), *Qualitative Methods in Organizational Research*. London: Sage.

Lincoln, Y. S. and Guba, E. G. (1985). *Naturalistic Enquiry*. Beverley Hills, CA: Sage.

Marshall, C. and Rossman, G. B. (1989). *Designing Qualitative Research*. Thousand Oaks, CA: Sage.

Marshall, H. (1995). 'Discourse Analysis in Occupational Context', in C. Cassell and G. Symon (eds), *Qualitative Methods in Organizational Research*. London: Sage.

McNiff, J., and Whitehead, J. (2005). *All You Need to Know about Action Research*. London: Sage.

Miles, B. M., and Huberman, A. M. (1994 or later edn). *Qualitative Data Analysis*. London: Sage.

Patton, M. Q. (1980). *Qualitative Evaluation Methods*. Beverley Hills, CA: Sage.

Patton, M. Q. (1988). 'Paradigms and Pragmatism', in D. Fetterman (ed.), *Qualitative Approaches to Evaluation in Education*. New York: Praeger.

Potter, J. and Wetherell, M. (1987). *Discourse and Social Psychology*. London: Sage.

Saunders, M., Lewis, P. and Thornhill, A. (2012 or later edn). *Research Methods for Business Students*. London: FT Prentice Hall.

Silverman, D. (2012 or later edn). *Doing Qualitative Research: A Practical Handbook*. London: Sage.

Thomas, A. B. (2004). *Research Skills for Management Studies*. London: Routledge.

Yin, R. K. (2013). *Case Study Research: Design and Methods*. Beverley Hills, CA: Sage.

Zairi, M. (1999). *Benchmarking for Best Practice*. London: Butterworth Heinemann.

PART II

Market research methods for market sensing

4

MARKET SENSING USING IMAGES AND EMOTIONAL SCALING

Charles Hancock and David Longbottom

Purpose

This chapter explores how the use of images can reveal deep insights into understanding the minds of consumers, and help to explain or predict their behaviours. Images are closely related to expression of feelings and emotions, and we will include a discussion of emotional scaling techniques.

Context

Understanding consumer mindsets is vitally important for modern marketing; for example, in order to inform marketing strategy, brand development, promotion and advertising. Traditional research methods such as surveys and focus groups simply do not go deep enough to understand consumers' minds and behaviours. As a consequence, organisations may miss vital signals which may have serious consequences for their future.

Learning outcomes

At the end of this chapter you will be able to confidently design, plan, conduct and present a research project based around the use of images and emotional scales to gain deeper insights into the mindsets of consumer participants.

THEORY BOX

Philosophy: interpretive

- ontology: no single reality, results are subject to interpretation;
- epistemology: knowledge and meaning derived from the study of social interactions in social and organisational settings.

(continued)

(continued)

Approach: inductive

There is no pre-determined hypothesis; theory development emerges from the research.

Strategy: depth interview using images and emotional scales for planning, analysis, evaluation and presentation of research.

Design: creation of images around an emerging research theme.

An in-depth interview plan based around semi-structure (research theme and indicative research questions) making use of images to frame the discussion. Use of images in planning, analysis, evaluation, and presentation stages.

Analysis:

- by case: images and transcripts; data reduction is by case by case summaries and cross-tab analysis of cases and emerging themes;
- by theme: images and transcripts; data reduction is by theme by theme summaries and cross-tab analysis of themes and cases.

Presentation:

- by case: images and annotations by case; discussion and key findings, implications for strategy, branding and promotional activity;
- by theme: images and annotations by theme; discussion and key findings, implications for strategy, branding and promotional activity.

Introduction, background and context

In this chapter we will be considering the following questions:

- How can images be used in marketing research?
- How can emotional scales be used in marketing research?

A recurring theme of this textbook is the issue of adding depth and meaning into marketing research projects. Traditional methods such as focus groups, interviews and surveys may just not go deep enough into understanding the mindsets of modern-day consumers.

Research work from the disciplines of psychology and the neurosciences tells us that people most often think in abstracts and images (such as may occur in dreams and imagination) rather than in structured words and sentences. In seeking to discover deep insights into thoughts, feelings and behaviour, this presents challenges for the researcher. It may be that when only conventional interview methods are used, participants are just simply not able to express in structured words and sentences what their inner thoughts and feelings are.

In this context the use of images to inform research in depth interview situations may be a useful approach, allowing the participant to select images related to the research topic (which can then be used by the researcher to explore deeper meaning). The use of images may provide us with a framework for research (for example, to start, conduct and analyse a depth interview) and may therefore have potential advantages in providing opportunities to explore the consumer mindset and elicit thoughts and feelings which may otherwise remain hidden.

In mini–case 4.1 we present an indicative example from a study we conducted at the University of Derby.

Mini-case 4.1

Exploring consumer attitudes towards the Apple brand

In this example we engaged a small group of consumers who had identified themselves as 'loyal owners of Apple products'. Typically, they had owned multiple Apple products such as iPhone, iPod, desktops, lap tops or tablets.

Prior to interview we asked each participant to select six to eight images which reflected their 'attitude and relationship with the Apple brand'. We gave each participant seven days to think about, select and prepare their images.

In conducting the interview, some of the images were relatively easy for the participants to describe and explain; for example, recognising the company logo, recognising the range of products and particular design features. In choosing and discussing these images the participants were generally comfortable and conscious of the reasons for selection, and they could easily articulate their thoughts. This is typical of what we find in interviews of this nature and we will later go on to describe these as level 1 responses.

Photo © Zeynep Demir. Image courtesy of Shutterstock

(continued)

(continued)

Photo © 1000 Words. Image courtesy of Shutterstock

Photo © Dmitro2009. Image courtesy of Shutterstock

Some of the images selected, however, were not so easy to explain. For example, one participant, Ben, a 21-year-old American student studying in the UK, selected amongst his collection an image of US President Barak Obama, with a background caption which read; 'Re-evaluating the role of America'.

There are some additional images of what look like war scenes with damaged and destroyed buildings. In asking Ben to describe and explain these images he had initially only vague thoughts as to why he had selected them: 'Something to do with Apple and . . . you know . . . innovators and those people who are meant to think differently . . . outside the box.'

Ben reflected on issues of 'American values' and revealed he had developed concerns over 'the American role in world influence' and 'loss of status and credibility in the light of financial scandals and in the behaviours of prominent

Photo © Fotokon. Image courtesy of Shutterstock

Photo © David Peterlin / Shutterstock.com

Photo © oneinchpunch. Image courtesy of Shutterstock

businesses and celebrities'. The image of Apple to Ben of being 'the cool brand of his youth', of 'deep' and 'different thinkers', might be starting to be 'eroded'.

Other participants raised issues touching on concerns about ethics and long-running disputes with Samsung.

The use of images in mainstream marketing research literature

Whilst the use of images and visual stimulation can be traced back over many years within research disciplines, we have found relatively little has been presented within the mainstream marketing texts and marketing research texts. As a consequence we feel the methods may often be overlooked by researchers and practitioners and good opportunities for valid research missed. This is particularly strange given the advances in audio and visual technologies and the widespread availability of and access to images.

The best work we can find covering the use of images in research is in *Visual Methodologies* by Gillian Rose (2014). The text provides several very good examples in organisational studies and in marketing. The author presents that the methods allow probing into deep and hidden areas and suggests that this can add richness; it 'also builds on the pleasure, thrills, fascination, wonder, fear, revulsion, of the person looking at the images' and proposes you should 'use your methodology to discipline your passion not to deaden it' (Rose, 2014: preface). The author believes that images are useful alongside traditional interview methods to elicit responses, increase the level of participation and engagement, and tap into the creative dimensions of the participants by providing a means for expression. There are several good examples included in the book from a range of invited authors including:

- TV and film promotion;
- computer gaming;
- advertising and promotion;
- consumer behaviour.

The work of Gerald Zaltman, Harvard Business School Emeritus Professor of Business Administration, describes a methodological approach in consumer marketing based around the use of images and metaphorical expression (Zaltman and Zaltman, 2008). The authors cover a range of examples and include links to a companion YouTube broadcast by Harvard Business School on the Zaltman Metaphorical Elicitation Technique (ZMET) (2012); several examples, including Coca Cola and Michelin Tyres, are presented.

In *Market-Led Strategic Change*, Nigel Piercy (2008) sets out a very strong case for a different approach to identifying value from the consumer perspective, suggesting that researchers need to go beyond traditional methods in order to develop new ways of thinking.

To place the methodological approach in the context of qualitative research methodologies we would recommend Symon and Cassell (2012), a text which sets out the rationale for qualitative research. This is the latest edition in a series of books where top academics in the field of qualitative methodologies present their perspectives. Within the 2012 edition Vince and Warren present a very good chapter covering 'Participatory Visual Methods' (pp. 275–95). The authors trace examples back many years in organisation studies, psychology, anthropology and sociology.

In mini-cases 4.2 and 4.3 below we show how images have played an important role in contemporary marketing strategy and in advertising and promotion.

Mini-case 4.2

Use of images in strategy formulation at Apple Inc.

A classic case often recited in marketing strategy texts is the case of the rise of Apple Inc. under the leadership of iconic leader Steve Jobs.

In the 1980s Apple had fallen on hard times and was struggling to keep pace with major competitors in the computer technology markets.

In a re-appraisal of Apple's strategy, Jobs presented that a return to their core values was needed, and in a recorded speech to senior employees (see Steve Jobs, 'An oldie but goodie', available on YouTube) he outlines his feelings on Apple strategy: 'Apple is not about making boxes for people to do their work (although we do that rather well) . . . it is about being creative, innovative, and thinking differently.'

Photo © Bangkokhappiness. Image courtesy of Shutterstock

Photo © Leonard Zhukovsky. Image courtesy of Shutterstock

(continued)

(continued)

In presenting the strategy to the organisation and later communicating the brand to consumers, Jobs and his marketing team made good use of images to illustrate the powerful new strapline for Apple 'Think different'.

As Jobs commented in the same speech: 'If they owned a computer you just know it would have been a Mac'.

Photo © dimitris_k. Image courtesy of Shutterstock

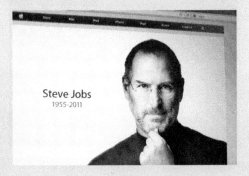

Photo © Annette Shaff. Image courtesy of Shutterstock

The powerful strategy message helped turn around the fortunes of Apple and has endured for many years with the creation of many market-leading and iconic products.

Mini-case 4.3

Use of images for promotional activity at John Lewis

John Lewis in the UK has become famous for the production of emotive Christmas advertising campaigns, to such an extent that they are anticipated by consumers and feature widely in the news and media reviews.

In 2013 the campaign, said to have cost in the region of £7–10 million, attracted record audiences and was rated as the highest recalled advert over the Christmas period by *Marketing Week*.

Photo © Nando Machado. Image courtesy of Shutterstock

The television advert features no products or service details but presents a story based on two animation characters, the 'Bear and the Hare'.

The images evoked emotional responses from consumers of 'nostalgia', 'family', 'friends', 'Christmas', 'celebration', 'holidays' and 'togetherness', and appealed to 'both children and adults'.

Promotional campaigns for leading brands rarely focus on the product or its functional or service dimensions, but rather give emphasis to emotional values and abstract thoughts and feelings which represent the brand in the mind of the consumer. In the 2015 Christmas campaign JL has again focused on deep emotional content with a 'lonely man on the moon'.

Study exercise

- Make a study of current advertisements.
- Consider what product or service is being offered.
- Consider what images are being used to tap into emotional rather than functional dimensions.
- Consider how the use of images fits with the strategy message.

Given the prominent use of images in marketing strategy, branding and promotional activity, it is therefore very surprising that little academic attention to methods and practice appears in mainstream marketing texts. We believe that using market sensing methods such as we describe in this chapter (using images and emotional scales) can contribute to building a skills-based approach into creative processes.

We also find that images used in marketing research projects tend to be applied in a very limited way (usually to introduce a research project or in order to provide a framework for subsequent interview). In this scenario, typically the pre-selection of images is used by the researcher only to provide the basic framework and structure for the interview process. In the process that we will describe we will also show how images can be used in later stages and in fact contribute throughout the entire process (for example, in planning, starting, conducting, analysing, evaluating and presenting).

We will also show how images may be subsequently used in developing marketing practice (for example, in formulating and communicating marketing strategy, in developing the brand, and in promotional activity).

We can summarise this as follows:

The use of images in the research process:

- interview planning: images form the framework (and semi-structure) for interview planning and questioning strategies;
- analysis: images are analysed for content and interpretation;
- evaluation: images are used to develop findings and conclusions;
- presentation: images are used to present the results.

The use of images to inform marketing practice:

- in formulating and communicating marketing strategy;
- in developing the brand;
- in promotional activity.

In using images within the research process, as we have illustrated, feelings and values may be revealed (which perhaps otherwise would remain hidden). The method is therefore very closely linked with understanding emotion and examining emotional responses for meaning and context. In the next section we will explore the issue of emotions and consider how emotional scales might be helpful to the researcher in analysing and evaluating research where images and depth interviews are involved.

ETHICS BOX

It is important to stress that the researcher must be aware of ethical considerations when conducting research. In using images and exploring emotional content this is particularly relevant.

The participant must be well briefed and in particular the researcher and participant must be mindful of the right to withdraw at any time.

Emotional scaling methods

Aligned with the use of images are emotions. Using images in research may, as we have demonstrated, help to uncover deeper thoughts and feelings. These may be initially below the level of consciousness and reveal themselves only fully during the depth interview where the skilled researcher delves and probes into key issues for meaning and relevance.

There are vast literatures on the role of emotion in framing our thoughts and behaviour patterns. This is beyond the scope of this text, and we present here just a brief overview of some of the key works that have informed our methods.

A deeper understanding of customer needs may be required and emerges from the literature as a recurring theme; for example, in understanding value from the customer's perspective (Piercy, 2008; Anderson et al., 2007; Palmer and Koenig-Lewis, 2009); developing system and internal marketing solutions (Seddon, 2008; Jackson, 2003; Womack et al., 1990; Longbottom and Hilton, 2011); and in understanding the minds of customers (Zaltman, 2003; Zaltman and Zaltman, 2008).

Zaltman (2003), for example, suggests that many traditional approaches to consumer research may be shallow and misleading, and he proposes a more serious approach based on qualitative interview (using images). Based on a method of metaphorical analysis (defined for his purpose very broadly as 'analogy, simile and other non-literal descriptions'), he advocates 'deep dives' into understanding customer feelings and emotions. Methods involve using images and metaphorical expression.

Early works often cited in the development of emotional scales for marketing purposes include Baggozzi et al. (1999), who define emotion as

> a mental state of readiness that arises from cognitive appraisals of events or thoughts; has a phenomenological tone; is accompanied by physiological processes; is often expressed physically (e.g. in gestures, posture, facial features); and may result in specific actions to affirm or cope with the emotion, depending on its nature and meaning for the person having it.

Work on human emotional scales can be found within the vast literature on human psychology with some basic scales adopted for marketing purposes. Good sources would include Izard (1977), Plutchik (1980), Damasio (1994), Mehrabian and Russell (1974), Russell (1980) and Liljander and Strandvik (1997).

As an example, Izard (1977) develops a 'differential emotional scale' which identifies 'distinct categories' of 'base emotions' such as interest-excitement, happiness-joy, surprise-astonishment, sadness-grief, interest-boredom, disgust-revulsion, fear-terror, contempt-scorn, shame-shyness and guilt-remorse. Plutchik (1980) defines emotions as 'distinct categories', including expressions of anger, fear, joy, surprise, acceptance, anticipation, disgust and sadness. Mehrabian and Russell (1974) take a 'dimensional' approach: they present that all base emotions can be attributed to three dimensions: pleasure, arousal and dominance. Russell (1980) develops a scale which attempts to explain and develop the interrelationships between the dimensional approach and basic emotions. We find that similar adaptations of these scales have been used in marketing and service studies (Liljander and Bergenwall, 2002; Liljander and Strandvik, 1997; Mano and Oliver, 1993; Oliver, 1997; Russell, 1980; and Palmer and Koenig-Lewis, 2009).

Berry et al. (2002, 2006) identify that several major organisations have used emotional scale methods to develop promotional campaigns: these include Proctor and Gamble, Unilever, World Bank, Heinz, United Healthcare, Xerox, Capital One and others. Zaltman (2003) acknowledges collaborations with several major corporations, including Coca Cola, Eastman Kodak, P&G, Gallo Wines, General Mills, World Bank, Alta Vista and General Motors.

In a study by Palmer and Koenig-Lewis (2009) they find that emotion may be a better predictor of future customer behaviour than, for example, satisfaction ratings. Similar findings are also presented by White (2010), Longbottom and Hilton (2011) and Longbottom and Modjtahedi (2013). Studies by Longbottom and Hilton (2011) and Longbottom and Modjtahedi (2013) suggest that base emotions (for example, happiness, sadness, anger, anxiety, etc.) tend to be of a short-term nature (and as a consequence may pass and have only a relatively small significance for overall behaviour patterns). Deep emotions, however, have a much more significant and long-term influence on behaviour.

For our purposes in discussing the role of emotion in a research context to better understand consumers, we will present examples of base emotions and deep emotions.

Base emotions

Base emotions may be relatively transient and short-term in nature. For example, if you receive poor service from an employee of an organisation where you are a regular customer, you may have immediate emotions of disappointment (about the lack of service), anger (at the way you were treated), and so on. However these emotions may well pass if later you judge that this was just a 'one-off occasion' and a 'poor employee' and that this was not 'typical' of the organisation you have dealt with in the past. In other words, your longer-term loyalty and decision making might be influenced not so much by base emotions but by deeper emotions and values. Table 4.1 presents example base emotions.

TABLE 4.1 Examples of base emotions

Happy	Sad
Joyful	Angry
Calm	Anxious
Safe	Fearful
Content	Curious
Satisfied	Dubious

Study exercise

Can you recognise base emotions?

There are several web-based games which you can use to test your ability to recognise base emotions from facial expressions. Test out your score.

From our own research we find that whilst simple base emotions may be easily recognised (for example, excited, happy, angry or scared), more subtle variations and themes are often not detected, and here the researcher needs to work hard on practising observation skills to pick up what may be important (if very subtle) variations.

Photo © YanLev. Image courtesy of Shutterstock

Photo © Vertes Edmond Mihai. Courtesy of Shutterstock

For the researcher the skill is in being able to recognise where emotions are being expressed. This might be evident in facial expression, body language or verbal expression. In verbal expression this may be explicit; for example, if the participant describes feelings of happiness or sadness. It may sometimes, however, be more hidden or implied and the researcher will need to probe to discover the emotion. For example, Zaltman and Zaltman (2008) present that emotions are often revealed through the expression of metaphors (some illustrative examples are shown in Table 4.2).

From our own research in relation to consumer attitudes to organisations and brands, we find base emotions to be relatively short-term in nature. Consequently they may be indicative of immediate experiences and useful in some respects (for example, assessing a particular service experience); however, they may not be good longer-term predictors of behaviour (for example, in predicting brand loyalty). For the longer-term perspective it may therefore be important to understand the nature of deep emotions.

Deep emotions

In contrast with base emotions, deep emotions relate to a collection of feelings and values that significantly influence the way we see ourselves and conduct ourselves.

Based on our research in this area we present three examples in the tables below. In the first example (Table 4.3), Zaltman and Zaltman (2008) identify seven deep emotions which they conclude typically influence our lives.

In relation to internal marketing within organisations, Longbottom and Modjtahedi (2013) find the following categories of deep emotion (Table 4.4).

In a study of the higher education sector within the UK, Hancock (2016) finds the following categories (Table 4.5).

Deep emotions are related to the values and drivers that define who we want to be, what we stand for. They are more long-term in nature (shaping our lives and decision making). In seeking to uncover these deeply held values the researcher may be uncovering real and important findings which lie below the surface, hidden, but which can be vital predictors of future behaviour intentions.

Interview skills are needed for the researcher to pick up on these emotional aspects, through careful interview planning, the use of deep questioning strategies and techniques, and careful observation. This will require lots of practice. In the next sections as we go through the research process, we will present examples of methods that may help you achieve the level of depth that we are describing here.

TABLE 4.2 Examples of metaphors

Rabbit out of a hat	Surprise
Bull in a china shop	Carelessness
Safe as houses	Safety
Over the moon	Happiness

TABLE 4.3 Seven deep emotions

Balance	How justice, equilibrium and the interplay of elements affect consumer thinking
Transformation	How changes in substance and circumstances affect consumer thinking
Journey	How the meeting of past, present and future affect consumer thinking
Container	How inclusion, exclusion and other boundaries affect consumer thinking
Connection	How the need to relate to oneself and others affects consumer thinking
Resource	How acquisitions and their consequences affect consumer thinking
Control	How the sense of mastery, vulnerability, and well-being affect consumer thinking

Source: Adapted from Zaltman and Zaltman (2008)

TABLE 4.4 Deep emotions (internal marketing perspective)

1. *Work/life balance:* To what extent do you feel that your work and working environment contribute to your feelings of 'well-being' and 'life balance'? For example, positive or negative feelings in relation to general health and fitness, social life, personal life. References to work/life balance, lifestyle, stability/instability, stress/calm, reciprocity (give/take).

2. *Personal development:* To what extent are changes in your work seen as having positive or negative impacts? For example, positive or negative feelings towards your job, career prospects, personal development. References to personal development, career, vision, plans, changing, developing, improving, maturing, growing, becoming better.

3. *Personal/organisation experiences:* What are your perceptions of your working experiences within your organisation, and what are your future expectations? For example, positive or negative feelings towards the past, the present, the future. References to events and experiences, a sense of direction, a work/life journey, a career pathway, work/life planning.

4. *Working environment:* To what extent do you feel that your organisation provides a positive place in your life, to which you belong? For example, positive or negative feelings in relation to personal safety, belonging and inclusivity, happiness and well-being. References to belonging in the organisation, being respected, being valued, being part of something, safe and secure, included/excluded.

5. *Working relationships:* To what extent do your organisation and your working conditions provide a positive environment to promote the development of working relationships? For example, positive or negative feelings in relation to immediate colleagues, line manager, customers. References to communications, networks, internal relations, teams, friends, connection to people, places and things, being part of something, attachment, belonging.

6. *Resources:* To what extent do you feel your organisation provides proper and sufficient resources to achieve your objectives? For example, positive or negative feelings in relation to tools, equipment, staff, training, education, skills, personal needs. References to supporting you, supportive work environment, supportive leadership, supportive structures and systems, provision of resources, the organisation as a resource to support you.

7. *Control:* To what extent do you feel comfortable and in control of events, or uncomfortable, vulnerable and out of control? For example, positive or negative feelings in relation to information, decision making and communication; job and working environment; personal needs. References to being considered, respected, internal communication, involvement in decisions, participation, awareness, trust, care.

TABLE 4.5 Deep emotions (from a study of the UK higher education sector)

Discovery	Feelings about who I am, what I want to be, how I get there.
Life style	Feelings about working hard and enjoying life, perspective, balance, health.
Future	Feelings about the future: prospects, job, family, home, destination.
Networks	Feelings towards friends and family, belonging. Deeper need for connection, extended family, lifelong friends. Belonging.
Security	Feelings of safety and security for the future.
Achievement	Feelings of achievement for self, family, friends. Paying back. Step change in transformation.
Motivation	Feelings of confidence and doubt. Will I be able to keep going or give up?
Management	Feelings about capability to manage day-to-day pressures.

Taking you through the research process stage by stage

In this section we will go over the main stages in conducting this type of research and in towards the end of the chapter we will show you a real example based on research we have conducted.

PROCESS BOX: MAIN STAGES AND ACTIVITIES FOR THE RESEARCH PROCESS

Stage	Activities (and key issues)
1	Selection of participants and sampling issues
	• Justify your selection
	• Choose an adequate sample size
2	Briefing participants and arranging collection of images
	• Individually or by group
	• Aim for six to eight images
	• Cover ethical issues
3	Interview planning
	• Create an interview plan
	• Identify depth level from Depth Gauge
	• Identify questioning strategies for depth
4	Conducting the interview
	• Allow 1–2 hours
	• Use audio (and possibly video) recording
	• Use questioning strategies for depth
	• Follow interview plan but allow for emerging themes

5	Analysis and data reduction
	• Transcript
	• Summary
	• Collage/montage
	• Cross-tab analysis
6	Presenting your data

There are, of course, variations that different researchers might like to use in the process to best suit their particular style (so use this as a guide only). The key issue with the process is to ensure (as far as is possible) that the research addresses key issues of reliability (can the results be repeated?), validity (do the results represent a true picture?) and bias (are the results free from false representations?).

The key for the researcher is to demonstrate that, as far is possible, consistency and rigour has been built into the process. A key question to keep in mind is: if the same research process had been followed by a different researcher, would the results achieved be very similar? These issues are related to what are common challenges for qualitative researchers: issues of validity, reliability and bias. Remember that the process is necessary for consistency and rigour, but also for achieving the deeper understanding of the mindset of the consumer.

Stage 1: selection of participants and sampling issues

The methodological approach we are presenting here is based on an interpretive philosophy:

- the participant is describing and interpreting events as they see them;
- the researcher is analysing by interpreting images and descriptions;
- the interested reader of the research is interpreting the outcomes for relevance to their own situations.

We are therefore looking to select a representative sample of people to participate in our study; for example, participants who are well informed or have practical experience of the subject we are researching.

So for example, in our case study of student perceptions of university our research was commissioned specifically to examine one university (the client/sponsor of the research). In this respect the university represents a case study (the results will be specific for it alone but may, subject to interpretation, have findings and conclusions which might apply to similar institutions). Within the case study university we decided to take a good sample of students from each stage in the undergraduate programme (years 1, 2 and 3) and some postgraduates.

Our study was to focus on 'business students' so they were all selected from our business programmes.

So the choice of participants must be justified to the research objectives: are the participants well informed and capable of addressing the research questions?

In some studies participants may be selected because they have special characteristics which make them a key to the study; for example, a case organisation might be chosen because it stands out from the literature review and secondary data analysis as having a particular speciality in the area we are studying. Similarly, certain individuals may stand out if they have expertise or hold significant positions relevant to our work.

With qualitative research the issue is about selection and justification, explaining why the organisation or participant was selected and is representative of the subject under review (unlike scientific enquiry where random sampling is preferred in order to achieve a measure of generalisability). Here we are concerned with the views of the particular respondent (and we are not seeking to generalise the results for a population. Our cause is not that the results are generalisable but rather that we are presenting depth and meaning (or what we might choose to call particularisable).

In scientific approaches to research (for example, questionnaire-based surveys) rules apply regarding random sampling and sample size in order to achieve levels of accuracy and statistical significance. In qualitative approaches the issues in sample selection concern the justification of relevant selection, and in sample size decisions we can refer to the principle of 'sample saturation'. Sample saturation is said to occur 'when new facts or information are no longer being added' (Yin, 2013). In other words the researcher reaches the point where clear themes and factors are emerging, common issues may be evident, and the researcher becomes satisfied that further interviewing will reveal little more new or important information.

The sample size can therefore vary depending on the nature of the subject under investigation. From our own experiences we have found that in organisation- or consumer-based studies saturation may typically be reached between 20 and 30 participants. In commercial studies we have been involved with however, clients often seek greater assurance and typically we have undertaken studies involving 100-plus depth interviews.

For students working on independent projects this presents a difficult dilemma; how many interviews is enough? Our advice would be to discuss this with your tutor and consult any regulations that your institution may provide. In independent study for undergraduate and postgraduate levels we believe that the primary purpose of the project is to demonstrate competence in evaluating, designing and undertaking a proposed methodology to a professional standard; and it would not normally be expected to achieve commercial level sample sizes. We would say four to eight would be enough to demonstrate competence and produce some interesting (if not conclusive) results.

In our case example which we present at the end of this chapter (part of a PhD-level study), 24 participants were selected, each for a 1–2 hour depth interview.

How many qualitative interviews is enough?'

The best guide we have found is in Baker and Edwards (2012) where the authors produce a report for the National Centre for Research Methods (NCRM). The report presents the perspectives of 14 'renowned social scientists' and '5 early career researchers' in answering the question 'how many qualitative interviews is enough?'. Our own reflections on this issue are presented in Chapter 2 (in particular see Table 2.4).

Stage 2: briefing the participant and the collection of images

Once the representative sample has been determined the participants are then briefed on the purpose and objectives of the study and what they will be asked to do. This can be done individually (in which case care needs to be taken to ensure that each brief covers the same content and is consistent across all participants) or might be done collectively (gathering all participants together). In our example case study of university students the participants were briefed collectively using a university classroom facility. This enabled some discussion and interaction which proved helpful for clarifying the brief.

Typically the briefing will describe the overall context and purpose of the research. For example, in our case study students were asked to consider 'your relationship with your university'. In our example, the researcher Charles Hancock briefed student participants to examine their relationship with their university and to select six to eight images which represented their thoughts and feelings towards the university. There was a request not to strictly select direct images of the university but rather to look more widely at images that had some personal meaning for the participant. The participants were given one week to consider, select and prepare their images (it is important to allow this time so that they can consider their choices very carefully and in an unpressured way).

It is important at the briefing to discuss ethical issues. This is particularly so in this type of research where interviewing may seek to discover deep thoughts and emotional responses. In our example the researcher followed the ethical code of practice established within the university. The code in full is made available to participants. Emphasis is given to issues of confidentiality (no individuals will be identified or reported without specific consent) and there is a right to withdraw from the research at any time.

Stage 3: interview planning

The images selected and presented by the participant provide the framework for the interview, the primary objective being to discuss the thoughts and feelings that lie behind the images. In this respect this may imply a less structured approach to the interview where issues will emerge from the discussion around the images (than perhaps would be evident in traditional depth interviewing where particular topics have been pre-identified by the researcher for discussion). It is, however, recommended that some pre-planning is conducted in order to identify and define criteria which are important for the overall objectives of the study. We would describe this as a semi-structured approach; key factors are identified but the researcher is alert to emerging factors that will develop directly from the discussion of the images.

In our example we present the study of university students and their relationship with their university. Prior to commencing the primary research a literature review was completed examining student–university relations and how the nature of these may be changing. Some critical issues were evident, for example:

- the changing nature of the student, and the development of 'customer-like' characteristics;
- the marketisation of higher education, with universities adopting 'marketing-like' approaches;
- changing student life, with high fees and debt burdens;
- pressures on students and on their family life;
- worries over future employability.

We were also mindful that the study objectives were to seek out issues which might inform future strategy for the university (particularly how it may add value and differentiate itself), develop the brand and provide creative inspiration for advertising and promotional campaigns.

We wanted to examine these issues within the interview process, but also be alert for emerging issues; for example, participants might identify areas or themes that we had not previously identified.

Our study was concerned to evaluate emotional elements in order to gain depth and meaning; for example, what are the issues and just how deeply important are these and how do they impact on student behaviour? The researcher must therefore be prepared and be alert to any emotional responses; these may be evident from emotional expression, in terms of either verbal expression of base or deeper emotions or observation of facial expressions or body language.

To accommodate both planned and emerging themes the interviewer needs to be flexible and have a plan which allows for comprehensive and consistent coverage of the main research themes, yet be open to new and emerging themes. We will call this a semi-structured approach to interview planning. An extract example from our case study semi-structured interview plan is shown below. The columns headed 'Depth Gauge level' and 'Question strategy' will be explained in stage 4 where we look at 'conducting the interview'. Table 4.6 presents the key stages and key themes (for an example interview plan).

TABLE 4.6 Interview key stages and key themes

Key stages and key themes to be covered	Depth Gauge level	Question strategy
Introduction		
Thank you for preparing these very interesting images of your relationship with the university. I would like to discuss with you each image and explore the meaning of the image in your relationship with the university, particularly your feelings, whether positive or negative.	1	Basic conversational
To start with, is there any particular order or image that you would identify as being particularly important?		
First image		
Please describe the image that you have chosen.	2	Basic describing
Prompts:	3	Move to:
	3 and 4	Means–end chain
• Why chosen?		Storytelling
• What does it say?		Critical incident
• Why is it important?		Empathy
• How does it make you feel?		Silence
Check for issues of:		
• metaphorical expression;		
• base emotions;		
• deep emotions.		
Repeat the process for:		
Second and subsequent images (for Images 2 to 6/8)		
Final stage/rounding up	1 and 2	Basic describing
Thank you for that very interesting discussion of all your images. Can we conclude this discussion by just reflecting on all of the images as a collection? Can you sum up what your overall relationship is with the university?	3 and 4	Move to Means–end chain Storytelling Critical incident Empathy Silence
Prompts:		
• Are you happy with you choice of university?		
• Are you happy that your university is adding value for you?		
• What would you like to see improved?		
• What does your university do well?		
• Has university life changed you as a person?		
• In what ways?		
Check for issues of:		
• metaphorical expression;		
• base emotions;		
• deep emotions.		

Stage 4: conducting the Interview

The methodological approach taken is inductive (where the researcher has only a semi-structure of themes and no individual set hypothesis), using a semi-structure of themes emerging from the literature. Whilst the researcher can follow the interview plan there needs to be flexibility to manoeuvre 'off-plan' for a time if the issues raised are important to the respondent and in context of the study.

Sticking to the plan?

A classic story often told in research seminars demonstrates how sticking too rigidly to an interview plan may distract the researcher from very important events.

© Everett Historical. Courtesy of Shutterstock

A famous broadcaster and commentator (at the time of this example in the very early stages of his broadcasting career) missed a rare opportunity during a live radio interview (on an unrelated topic) to pursue the story of an elderly man who revealed (in the process of conversation) that as a child he had survived the notorious and tragic sinking of the *Titanic* (in which both of his parents had tragically died).

Frustrated listeners were outraged that the interviewer was too inflexible and reading from scripted questions.

Having a good plan allows the researcher to simply use it as a checklist or guide as the interview progresses. There should be no need to make extensive notes; let audio/video technology record the event so that you can focus fully on the plan and look for verbal and non-verbal expression of emotions.

Interview strategy

The objective of conducting this type of research is to achieve depth and meaning, which perhaps conventional market research methods may lack. The use of images represents the starting point for discussion and may naturally lead the participant into deep areas revealing thoughts and feelings. We have found from our own research that this is often the case; many times participants are not fully aware at the outset of the full meaning of the image selected. It is only in conversation that stories behind the image emerge and begin to reveal emotions.

Images alone, however, may not be enough to explore hidden depths, and so the researcher needs to have an interview strategy aligned with questioning strategies to achieve the depth required. From our own research work in studies over many years we have developed a framework for thinking strategically about interview methods, which we are choosing to call the 'Depth Gauge'.

The Depth Gauge model has similarities with approaches often used in psychology. Earlier versions can be traced within marketing disciplines; for example, Cooper and Branthwaite (1977) identified different levels of engagement within

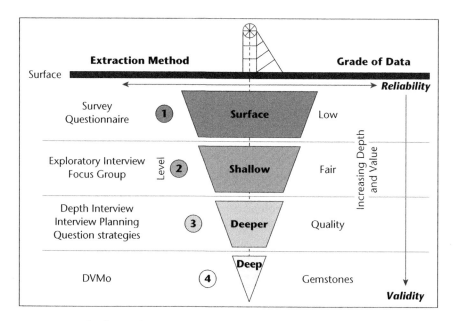

FIGURE 4.1   The deep value mining Depth Gauge

Source: Adapted from Hancock et al. (2015)

an interview setting, and proposed that researchers needed to be aware of the levels and develop strategies for dealing with them.

Our Depth Gauge model identifies four levels of depth, where extraction of information gets deeper and more difficult as we progress from level 1 to level 4.

Level 1   Surface mining: surface-level low-grade data

At the first level information is easily extracted; the participant comprehends what is required and is comfortable with the subject matter and is therefore easily able to present a coherent response. Most of this data may well be in the public domain.

These are relatively simple questions and usually illicit 'matter-of-fact' answers or description without the need at this stage for the participant to express opinion or preferences. Often they can be easily checked for supporting evidence such as available documents or records of events.

In the context of the interview, however, they may be important in establishing a rapport, getting the discussion started and putting the participant at ease.

Level 2   Shallow mining: shallow-level fair-grade data

At level 2 we begin to seek out opinion, particular points of view or preferences. Personal issues may be touched upon.

These issues are a little more sensitive for the participant and whist they are perfectly aware and able to present coherent responses they may feel some 'reluctance' to reveal their thoughts.

Think about the natural process of meeting people and making new friends. Initially we may exchange details such as name, place of work, hobbies, etc., which we would describe as level 1 data. At level 2 we might feel reluctant to go much deeper until we 'get to know' the person more and the 'friendship' begins to develop. Issues of 'trust' begin to arise before we are prepared to share more personal information.

In friendships these can be allowed to develop naturally and over a time frame that all are comfortable with. In interview situations, however, the researcher may be limited to a 1–2 hour slot or often even shorter time frame. So the researcher has to plan a strategy for building the relationship to a level where the participant feels comfortable and able to discuss level 2 data.

Simple ways can involve repeating the researcher's credentials; for example, years of experience, working with major clients, representing a creditable research organisation, conforming to an ethical code, and repeating that all issues discussed are confidential. Such credentials may be useful in building the trust element. Beyond this the researcher needs to think about questioning strategies which may elicit the deeper responses required.

Level 3   Deeper mining: deep-level quality-grade data

At level 3 we begin to encounter more serious difficulties for the researcher. Here the participant is aware and able to answer the questions but may not be willing to reveal what they perceive to be very personal thoughts and feelings. Perhaps they may even be tempted to answer in a way that misleads (for example, presenting answers which they feel may be considered more acceptable or what they perceive the researcher might want to hear but do not really reflect their own opinion or actions).

In a metaphorical analogy these may include 'skeletons in the cupboard'.

Participants may be reluctant to share inner knowledge (particularly if they do not know the researcher very well). So issues of trust and confidentiality are important credentials for the researcher to have established before attempting 'dives' into level 3.

At this level the researcher needs to be highly skilled and be able to draw on particular questioning strategies which may help to achieve these deeper dives.

Level 4   Deep mining: gemstones

This is the most difficult area, where we engage with the principle underpinning our notion of what market sensing is about. Here the participant may simply be unable to offer a valid response. For example, they might respond or behave in a certain way to events and stimuli but they themselves are not 'consciously aware' of this. So we are dealing here with issues that are below the level of the conscious mind.

Examples might include:

- subliminal reactions to certain people, or brands;
- personal traits or characteristics;
- subconscious or reflex actions to events;
- deeply held personal values or deep emotions.

We call these the 'gemstones' as it may be that we find significant things that we simply could not have anticipated. Such things might be critical in differentiating our strategy and brand.

In the example we are discussing here, we are making use of images to try to explore these hidden depths. As we have previously explained, studies from the fields of psychology and neurosciences suggest that people tend to think in abstracts and images. In selecting images they may not always be fully conscious of why they have chosen a particular image. They may have some reasons but the full extent of these may perhaps not become visible until engaged in an in-depth discussion.

We have found from our own research experiences that very often images elicit new insights and participants become very surprised and emotional during the discussions. Both participant and interviewer can become physically and emotionally exhausted at the end of a typical 1–2 hour session.

Summing up on interview strategy

Using the Depth Gauge to identify the four levels helps the researcher to plan in advance of the interview likely areas of difficulty and think about questioning strategies and other techniques which may help elicit meaningful responses from the participant.

If you refer back for a moment to the interview plan (presented in the previous section) you can see that in column 2 of the plan there is a 'level' indicator. Here the researcher is trying to anticipate areas of the interview within the plan that may give rise to deep and difficult issues. This can then be prepared for by considering what types of question and what methods might be used within the interview to deal with these issues, and this leads us to our next section which will consider some useful questioning strategies.

Questioning strategies

Over many years of conducting research involving depth interviews we have identified a number of useful questioning strategies, which are presented in Table 4.7

TABLE 4.7 Questioning strategies: some examples

Critical incident	Questions focus on a specific event or incident to gain rich insights into an actual example
Means–end chain	Questions move from understanding behaviour and instrumental values through to terminal values (moving from behaviour to deeply held values); sometimes called 'laddering'
Prisoner's dilemma	Introduces other evidence or opinion (often isolated from the participant) which may contradict what the participant is saying
Devil's advocate	Interviewer is well rehearsed on opposing point of view and takes on this role
Chief executive diary	Seeks to check out interview answers by observation of actual behaviour
Process	Seeks to gain depth by asking the respondent to talk through the process stage by stage
Storytelling	Similar to process where respondent is asked to talk through an example real or simulated
Silence	Use of prolonged and deliberate silences during an interview to tease out more comment
Perspective	Asks the respondent to look at the situation from another angle or other person's point of view
Projective	Asks the respondent to engage in creative thought or exploration of trends
Group (focus)	Introduces group opinion and dynamics into discussion
Empathy	Interviewer plays on building relationship with respondent and empathising with situation or events
Rank/rate scales	Useful for positioning opinion when answers not clear-cut
Metaphorical analysis	Based on theory that suggests 'deep emotions' are revealed in metaphorical expressions
Pressured probing	Interviewer continually repeats or returns to same subject area in attempt to 'grind out' responses; the 'third degree'

Whilst we have shown here in these sections an example of how to prepare an interview plan, consider interview strategy and prepare interview questioning strategies, the reader needs to be aware that whilst an understanding of these disciplines is very necessary for successful and deep interviewing, they can only really be effective in application and this requires considerable practice and skill. Planning is very useful but again, as we have said before, the interviewer must be alert for emerging themes and be able to respond intuitively with a relevant questioning technique. Interviewing is a skill which can really only be learned by rehearsal, practice and repeated evaluation of performance (use recording devices or peer observation). Like learning to drive a car this cannot all be done in a classroom or by reading books.

Study exercise

Watch out for broadcast interviews, either from a news format or featuring popular interviewers you know. Try to identify what questioning strategies they adopt at different phases of the interview.

Some modern classics available through YouTube include:

- Michael Howard being interviewed by BBC Newsnight's Jeremy Paxman (over alleged interference by a minister in dismissal of a senior official);
- Richard Nixon being interviewed by David Frost (over the Watergate impeachment affair);
- Russell Brand being interviewed by Jonathon Ross (over his views on certain celebrities);
- Lance Armstrong being interviewed by Oprah Winfrey (over allegations of drug taking).

Stage 5: analysis and data reduction

In quantitative analysis, rules for applying statistical and scientific methods can be applied and presentation protocols can be applied for analysis. In qualitative research, we are dealing with words, images and observations and these may not easily follow scientific rules. Some qualitative researchers use methods such as content analysis to analyse their data. This is a method which attempts to introduce some degree of science or objectivity into the process. An example would be counting (through the use of word codes, for example) the frequencies of occurrence of a particular word or theme in transcripts.

Content analysis can be useful to identify themes and show readers the evidence; for example by highlighting extracts from the transcript where these issues came up.

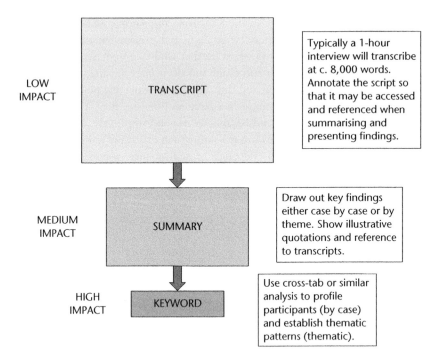

FIGURE 4.2 Data reduction process

Modern-day software is available to help in recording and structuring interview transcripts (effectively creating a database of transcripts for record keeping but also for searching key words, etc.). A popular example is NVivo.

Critics of the database approach argue that the researcher may become detached from the data; for example, seeing the exercise as more of a structuring and coding of data rather than a close interpretation of the discourse. This may particularly arise where transcripts are written up by someone other than the researcher. Paying someone to transcribe data can save researchers a considerable amount of time but issues of detachment may need to be carefully considered.

Whilst content analysis may be helpful, for example in spotting themes and trends, critics would argue that it is really an attempt to add scientific principles and may miss the vital issues of depth and meaning which are at the heart of qualitative and interpretive methods. In our practice we have tended only to use data bases for large-scale commercial projects (where sponsors wish to maintain records of data over a prolonged period).

For market sensing we would advocate a more traditional approach to analysis, which involves the stages of transcription, summary and keyword development (what we describe as the data reduction process).

In the next sections we present and describe the process of data reduction.

Transcripts

Good practice (and usually a requirement for higher degrees) is to transcribe interview data. Digital recordings of the interview are taken and transcribed with either a line-by-line numbering or paragraph numbering. This allows the researcher (in reporting back the findings and quoting extracts from transcripts) to make reference to the full transcript and location of the extract (the reader may then access this if they wish to view the wider context). Presentation in this way helps to add rigour into the process of analysis and shows the evidence on which the researcher has interpreted and presented the analysis.

With modern-day technology it is now relatively easy to edit recorded transcripts (either audio or audio video) into sections or locations. So, for example, the reference to an extract can refer to a location on a USB or similar device. In academic research for higher degrees, some institutions and examiners may accept this type of electronic presentation, which does save the need for full typed transcripts. Researchers considering this type of presentation should, of course, check out the requirements of their institution.

If transcribing, there are now several very good voice recognition software packages to speed up the process. In practice we find these are still not up to use in the actual fieldwork recording; we find that attempting to use them in situ leads to many translation errors and the technology does not yet cope easily with free-flowing conversation. It is likely that voice recognition software will advance in the coming years and this will be a considerable aid for researchers working in the field.

Reasonable results, however, can be achieved where the researcher dictates the transcripts after the event. There are several very good software packages; for example, Dragon software is a market leader within the UK.

Keeping close to the data is essential for the researcher. Reading and listening over and over again to transcripts is an important aspect of interpretation and rigour. We would always recommend that transcripts are written up or reviewed soon after the event so that issues are not lost with the passing of time.

Typically a 1–2 hour interview (normal, we would say, for gaining the required depth) will transcribe at around 8,000–16,000 words. Conducting and analysing qualitative work is a long and difficult process, but it is necessary to gain the depth and meaning that we are seeking in this type of research. We believe that the editing of transcripts using modern-day digital media for audio and video recordings will increasingly take over from typed transcripts.

Summarising the data

Clearly, when presenting research of this nature some form of data reduction is necessary; the reader is not likely to want to trawl through lengthy transcripts or view a 2-hour audio/video. The first stage is therefore to summarise the key findings emerging from the transcripts/recordings. There are two basic approaches to consider:

- case analysis;
- thematic analysis.

Case-by-case analysis may be preferred if it is an important aspect of the study to understand individual profiles; for example, in our study of student life we may wish specifically to build up student lifestyle profiles which we can feature in our promotional campaigns and materials.

Thematic analysis may be preferred if we are not primarily looking for individual profiles but are more concerned to see commonalities or themes running across a sample of respondents.

As a rule of thumb guide we would normally seek to reduce the word count in a summary by about 90% (so, for example, in a transcript of 10,000 words we would seek to reduce down to a 1,000-word summary). The important thing is that the summary must do justice and represent the main points being expressed. In summarising the data the researcher is interpreting participant responses; in this respect using extracted quotations is very necessary as these provide the evidence base for the interpretation. Further evidence to place the extracted quotations into context should be provided by referencing the extract to the transcript, effectively allowing the reader to access the full discussion and 'see for themselves'.

To add rigour to this process:

- gather documentary evidence to support what has been said;
- cross-check with the participant or with others for accuracy (is my interpretation accurate; is the participants' account accurate?);
- involve peer researchers or independent persons to review and interpret the data (do you hear/see what I hear/see?);
- create a theme board (involving the participant or peers).

Final stages and keyword analysis

Many qualitative research studies we have seen do not go beyond summary analysis. We feel that this is a shame and may miss the opportunity to give the findings real impact. We would therefore advocate further analysis of the data, moving into evaluation.

There are several ways to carry out further evaluation. The best source of further reading on this subject we suggest can be found in Miles and Huberman (2013).

Here we will describe a method that we often have used to good effect which makes use of cross-tab analysis. In this method we construct a table which compares participants against key themes. This enables the researcher to profile the individual respondent against all the themes (creating profiles or potential segments). It also enables analysis across all participants by theme (creating patterns of similarity or differences).

The data reduction process for images

In the illustrated case study featured at the end of this chapter, Charles Hancock develops and describes how the reduction process can be applied in the use of images (where words are reduced as we have already described, but also how images are data reduced). The process involves moving from case-by-case image collages to case-by-case image montages, then to thematic image collages, thematic image montages and through to the final tile/montage.

Mini-case 4.4

Using images to elicit student experiences in higher education

This involved 24 business students at the University of Derby who were asked to prepare images of 'your relationship with your university'.

In Part 1 we present an example of an extract from an interview with one of the students; this shows the images selected and some extracts from the interview.

In Part 2 the six images are shown collectively (as a collage).

In Part 3 the six images are shown as an arranged montage. The montage is co-constructed by the participant and the researcher (this is at a later date after the main interview and after preliminary analysis has taken place).

In Part 4 an emotional value map is constructed. This itemises issues of deep values, activity (doing) and feelings (emotions).

In Part 5 we show an example of an emerging theme (several participants' selected similar images).

In Part 6 we show further examples of emerging themes with possible implications for marketing strategy, branding, and advertising and promotion.

Finally, in Part 7 we show a diagrammatic representation of the visual data reduction process and the deep value mining process.

Authors' note

In the case study provided we have shown a brief extract of a single case to illustrate how images are presented as collages and montages. In presenting the research we would also add a written summary of the case, picking out key points, interpreting the data and giving extracted quotations from the interview transcript. For further discussion on presenting a summary analysis see Chapter 3 of this book.

PART 1: CASE STUDY

A study of student relationships with the University of Derby as exemplified by a first-year business management student

'Something I had always dreamt of'

Photo © MyMusick. Image courtesy of Shutterstock

'When I was a little girl, I always used to daydream, I used to spend hours looking at the clouds and used to tell everyone since I was six that I was going to come to university.'

'How does that dream look like now you're at university?'

'Scary, because I'm not six anymore!'

'Juggling home life and university was always going to be a challenge'

Photo © bikeriderlondon. Image courtesy of Shutterstock

'What do you think you'll feel once you have the degree?'

'A lot less stressed about where the next mortgage payment is going to come from, so more financial stability. My husband not working seven days a week, we'll spend more time together.'

'Look the same but all different!'

Photo © Denis Larkin. Image courtesy of Shutterstock

'I think for me, as students we're all tarred with the same brush. If I'm late because I've been dropping my daughter off, I get snide remarks from people. For mature students like me, that's something I find really challenging.'

'Has anyone else in your family come to university?'

'Sense of achievement upon graduating'

Photo © hxdbzxy. Image courtesy of Shutterstock

(continued)

(continued)

'No, I'm the first. I worked out yesterday that I have 77 cousins and I'm the first grandchild, for my Nan, to ever come to university.'

'How do you think this will change for your family?'

'I think it will give them the ability to believe that they can do it as well. People questioned why I was doing it.'

'I imagine that's how it's going to be, being amongst friends that have gathered along the way.'

'What do you think your parents will think?'

'I think as the years have gone on and I've got the grades and shown them what I'm doing, I don't think they'll ever understand why I've come to university at an older age. When I get my degree I think they'll understand slightly more.'

'New job to allow for new adventures'

Photo © Adriena Vyzulova. Image courtesy of Shutterstock

'I've always wanted to travel . . . now I have a family. Get a new job and take my daughter to see my world.'

'If I asked you to close your eyes and picture yourself there, how would you feel?'

'Like it was worth it!'

'That was me learning something new. I think although I had a lot of negative comments on coming to university the biggest issue was myself.'

'What do the unilluminated bulbs represent?'

'The light is now on!'

Photo © Brian A Jackson. Image courtesy of Shutterstock

'Friends and family.'

'Have you broken away from them?'

'Yeah definitely, I don't speak to a lot of people because some people just don't get it!'

'Has your husband seen a change in you?'

'Yeah, massively! Coming to university has made me do so much more. It's driven me to do more, I don't think I'd have done the weight loss if I hadn't come to university.'

PART 2: COLLAGE – the six images collectively

'I was always going to come to university'

'It was always going to be a challenge!'

(continued)

(continued)

'I have 77 cousins and I'm the first grandchild to go'

'Being amongst friends that I have gathered along the way'

'Like it was worth it!'

'The light is now on! The biggest issue was myself'

PART 3: MONTAGE – 'my university journey'

PART 4: EMOTIONAL VALUE MAP

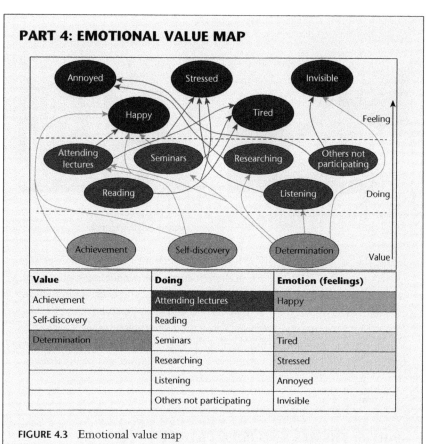

Value	Doing	Emotion (feelings)
Achievement	Attending lectures	Happy
Self-discovery	Reading	
Determination	Seminars	Tired
	Researching	Stressed
	Listening	Annoyed
	Others not participating	Invisible

FIGURE 4.3 Emotional value map

PART 5: COMMON THEMES

Photo © Rawpixel.com. Image courtesy of Shutterstock

Photo © hxdbzxy. Image courtesy of Shutterstock

(continued)

(continued)

Photo © Andresr. Image courtesy of Shutterstock

Photo © Wavebreakmedia. Image courtesy of Shutterstock

Across the 36 images chosen by the first-year students, two indicative picture choices were made: these illustrated graduation. The graduation pictures produced a deep level of understanding and value that the graduation was not only for them but also for their parents and siblings, often pioneering the way forward for their younger siblings. These graduation pictures were picked by four of the six candidates. They were not chosen by the second-year students but were dominant choices for both the third-year group and postgraduates.

PART 6: THEMES AND IMPLICATIONS

The light element in this picture is that of an illuminated light bulb: this is symbolic of starting afresh and 'switching on' (selected by a mature student).

The light bulb....

Photo © Peshkova. Image courtesy of Shutterstock

The light in this image is the sun shining from behind a cloud; it is in the distance and suggests that the end goal is some way away.

Every cloud has a silver lining

Photo © Happystock. Image courtesy of Shutterstock

A phrase used by many; once again this represents the end goal as being the light of joy at the end of the tunnel. A first-year student is seeing the university journey as relatively long and arduous but that there is light at the end of the tunnel.

Light at the end of the tunnel

Photo © Arsgera. Image courtesy of Shutterstock

This picture represents a very bright future and the expectation of great things at the end of the university journey. The student is rising towards the light and the elevation represents the raised level of expectations.

(continued)

(continued)

Ascending towards the light

Photo © Leigh Trail. Image courtesy of Shutterstock

The gateway is slightly open and in the distance there is a bright future. For the student who selected this image, the gateway had been closed but it was now open, with a refreshed brighter horizon available.

Gateway to a lightened horizon

Photo © Klemen Misic. Image courtesy of Shutterstock

This image symbolises the mature student seeing the light of commitment and having to stick at something. The picture was chosen because he realised that he needed to change his ways and commit to something: this commitment is to his studies and attending lectures and seminars and completing assignments.

The light of commitment

Photo © Art_girl. Image courtesy of Shutterstock

PART 7: PROCESSES INVOLVED

These are our representations of the visual data reduction process and the deep value mining process.

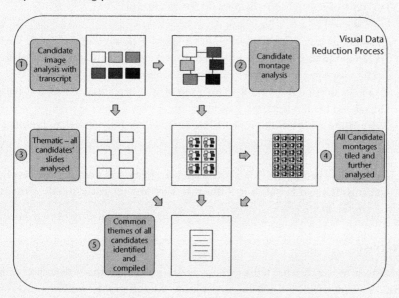

FIGURE 4.4 The visual data reduction process

Source: Hancock (2016)

(continued)

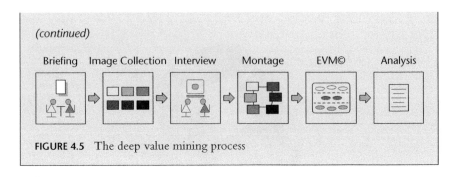

(continued)

Briefing   Image Collection   Interview   Montage   EVM©   Analysis

FIGURE 4.5   The deep value mining process

Summary

This chapter has demonstrated how images may be used in research in order to provide a framework around which an in-depth interview can be based. Images may allow the skilful researcher to delve below the level of the conscious mind, revealing deeper thoughts and meaning.

In analysing interviews on images, the researcher should play close attention to expressions of emotion, and be able to interpret both base and deeper emotions. Deeper emotions have been found to be a strong predictor of future behaviour intentions, and consequently are valuable insights for marketers.

This type of research may help marketers in areas of:

- marketing strategy: providing visual images of how customers relate to the organisation and strategy, and helping marketers to 'see' the potential for a value proposition and differentiation in strategy;
- brand evaluation: providing a visual representation of how customers see the brand and brand values;
- advertising and promotion providing creative images, collages and montages, which may be inspirational in designing and developing a communications strategy;
- internal marketing: providing a visual representation of how customers see the organisation and brand so that this may be communicated to staff within the organisation.

Exercise

A classroom exercise that works well is to try out the methods described in this chapter. Whilst it is not possible to replicate the full process within a classroom session of, say, 2 hours, it does allow students to experience some of the important disciplines and issues associated with this type of method.

Students should prepare (at least a week in advance) a collage of six to eight images which visualise their relationship with a familiar brand of their own choice.

Working in groups of three:

- one person takes the role of interviewer;
- one person takes the role of interviewee;
- one person takes the role of observer.

Before the interview, the interviewer should prepare an outline interview plan and identify (using the Depth Gauge) suitable questioning strategies.

A group and/or class discussion can be conducted at the end of the session.

We have sometimes found it useful to video record selected interviews for later discussion and analysis.

References

Anderson, J. C., Narus, J. A., and van Rossum, W. (2007). 'Customer Value Propositions in Business Markets'. *Harvard Business Review* 84, no. 3, pp. 90–9.

Baggozzi, R. P., Gopinath, M. and Nyer, P. U. (1999). 'The Role of Emotions in Marketing'. *Journal of the Academy of Marketing Science* 27, no. 2, pp. 184–206.

Baker, S. E. and Edwards, R. (2012). *How Many Qualitative Interviews is Enough?* Southampton: National Centre for Research Methods.

Berry, L. L., Carbone, L. P. and Haeckel, S. (2002). 'Managing the Total Customer Experience'. *MIT Sloan Management Review* 43, no. 3, pp. 85–8.

Berry, L. L., Wall, E. A. and Carbone, L. P. (2006). 'Service Clues and Customer Assessment of the Service Experience: Lessons from Marketing'. *Academy of Management Perspectives* 20, no. 2, pp. 43–57.

Cooper, P. and Branthwaite, A. (1977). 'Qualitative Technology: New Perspectives on Measurement and Meaning through Qualitative Research'. *Proceedings of the Market Research Society Conference 1977.*

Damasio, A. (1994). *Descartes' Error: Emotion, Reason and the Human Brain.* London: Vintage.

Hancock, C. (2016). 'Using Images and Deep Emotions in Marketing Strategy in Higher Education'. Doctoral thesis completed March 2016, University of Derby.

Hancock, C., Longbottom, D. and Banwait, K. (2015). 'Seeing through the Strategy Illusion: Uncovering Images and Deep Emotions for a Marketing Strategy in Higher Education'. *Proceedings of the Academy of Marketing Conference, Limerick, July 2015.*

Izard, C. (1977). *Human Emotions.* New York: Plenum.

Jackson, M. (2003). *Systems Thinking: Creative Holism for Managers.* Chichester: John Wiley.

Liljander, V. and Bergenwall, M. (2002). 'Consumption-Based Emotional Responses Related to Satisfaction'. Occasional Paper, Swedish School of Economics and Business Administration, Department of Marketing, Helsinki.

Liljander, V. and Strandvik, T. (1997). 'Emotions in Service Satisfaction'. *International Journal of Service Industry Management* 8, no. 2, pp. 148–69.

Longbottom, D. and Hilton, J. (2011). 'Service improvement: Lessons from the UK Financial Services Sector'. *International Journal of Quality and Service Sciences* 3, no. 1, pp. 39–59.

Longbottom, D. and Modjtahedi, A. (2013). 'Can Emotional Scaling Methods Improve Quality in Services?' *International Journal of Quality and Service Sciences* 5, no. 4, pp. 364–81.

Mano, H. and Oliver, R. L. (1993). 'Assessing the Dimensionality and Structure of the Consumption Experience: Evaluation, Feeling and Satisfaction'. *Journal of Consumer Research* 20, no. 3, pp. 451–66.

Mehrabian, A. and Russell, J. A. (1974). 'The Basic Emotional Impact of Environments'. *Perceptual and Motor Skills* 38, pp. 283–301.

Miles, B. M. and Huberman, A. M. (2013). *Qualitative Data Analysis*. London: Sage.

Oliver, R. L. (1997). *Satisfaction: A Behavioural Perspective on the Consumer*. London: McGraw-Hill.

Palmer, A. and Koenig-Lewis, N. (2009). 'A Longitudinal Study of Emotions and Satisfaction as Predictors of Behavioural Intention'. Academy of Marketing Conference, published proceedings, Leeds, July 2009.

Piercy, N. (2008). *Market-Led Strategic Change*, 4th edn. Oxford: Butterworth Heinemann.

Plutchik, R. (1980). 'A General Psycho-Evolutionary Theory of Emotion', in R. Plutchik and H. Kellerman (eds), *Emotion: Theory, Research and Experience*, pp. 3–31. New York: Academic Press.

Rose, G. (2014). *Visual Methodologies: An Introduction to Researching with Visual Methods*, 3rd edn. London: Sage.

Russell, J. A. (1980). 'A Circumplex Model of Affect'. *Journal of Personality and Social Psychology* 39, no. 6, pp. 1161–78.

Seddon, J. (2008). *Systems Thinking in the Public Sector: The Failure of the Reform Regime and a Manifesto for a Better Way*. Axminster: Triarchy Press.

Symon, G. and Cassell, C. (2012). *Qualitative Organisational Research: Core Methods and Current Challenges*. London: Sage.

White, C. J. (2010). 'The Impact of Emotions on Service Quality, Satisfaction, and Positive Word-of-Mouth Intentions over Time'. *Journal of Marketing Management* 26, no. 5, pp. 381–94.

Womack, J., Roos, D. and Jones, D. (1990). *The Machine that Changed the World*. New York: Rawson Associates.

Yin, R. K. (2013). *Case Study Research: Design and Methods*. London: Sage.

Zaltman, G. (2003). *How Customers Think: Essential Insights into the Mind of the Market*. Brighton, MA: Harvard Business Press.

Zaltman, G. and Zaltman, L. (2008). *Marketing Metaphoria: What Deep Metaphors Reveal about the Minds of Consumers*. Brighton, MA: Harvard Business Press.

Bibliography

Bryman, A. (2012). *Social Research Methods*. Oxford: Oxford University Press.

Bryman, A. and Bell, E. (2012). *Business Research Methods*. Oxford: Oxford University Press.

Denzin, N. K. and Lincoln, Y. (2012). *The Sage Handbook of Qualitative Research*. London: Sage.

Marshall, C. and Rossman, G. B. (2010). *Designing Qualitative Research*. London: Sage.

Saunders, M., Lewis, P. and Thornhill, A. (2012). *Research Methods for Business Students*. London: FT Prentice Hall.

Silverman, D. (2013). *Doing Qualitative Research: A Practical Handbook*. London: Sage.

5

DISCOURSE ANALYSIS

Analysing talk and text

Lesley Crane

FIGURE 5.1 David Cameron, UK Prime Minister 2010–16

Source: Photo © 360b. Courtesy of Shutterstock

Purpose

This chapter introduces discourse analysis as a theoretically grounded methodology for the analysis of talk and text as the topic of interest and study in its own right. Discourse is approached as the site in which human action is accomplished.

The analysis of discourse as action-orientated, functional and consequential allows us to approach words as actions which do things. The chapter particularly focuses on discursive psychology as a methodology that can reveal insights which are unavailable to more conventional research methodologies.

Context

With its origins in the 1950s and 1960s, discourse analysis is a thriving field which is increasingly seen as a valid and robust method of studying diverse topics. Its values for and potential contribution to modern marketing should be obvious: in everyday conversation people routinely and mostly implicitly perform often highly complex, delicate and consequential actions in managing their stake and interest, their accountability, their version of events, their construction of the social world as it is – for them. The discourse analyst seeks an understanding of what version of the world and its contents speakers orient to in their talk and text, how, and with what effect.

Learning outcomes

At the end of this chapter, the reader will possess an appraisal of what discourse analysis is, its core concerns, its focus and how it approaches talk and text, also its potential and limitations as a research methodology.

THEORY BOX

Philosophy: interpretive

- ontology: speakers construct versions of reality in their talk and text in interaction;
- epistemology: knowledge is approached as socially constructed in discourse in interaction.

Approach: variable

- approaches vary between the different types of discourse analysis;
- discursive psychology, for instance, is an observational science which is not necessarily inductionist;
- discourse analysis in general does not place particular importance on indicative research questions;
- the aim is to understand the particular, rather than to impose meaning on the general.

Strategy:

- discursive psychology focuses on the in-depth analysis of everyday talk and text, taking any format or topic relevant to the researcher's sphere of interest;
- acquisition of sufficient amounts of recorded talk and/or written text to facilitate the demands of analysis and study objectives;
- the concern is with how and what versions of events speakers themselves construct as live concerns in social interaction.

Design:

- The 11-action guide to discourse analysis includes literature review, research questions, sample selection, data collection, interviews, transcription, coding, analysis, validation, report writing and application.

Analysis:

- in discursive psychology, there is no set of established rules for the analysis of discourse;
- analysis has a focus on what discursive actions speakers deploy, and on how and with what effect for both speakers and recipients;
- analysis should recognise and reflect on the researcher's role in every aspect of the analysis;
- importantly, analysis is grounded in the extant literature.

Presentation:

- there is no prescription for the presentation of research findings, although researchers are advised to include extracts from their data to substantiate research claims and to enable the reader to formulate their own interpretation.

Introduction, origins and core concerns

In a scene from the film *The Imitation Game* a young Alan Turing observes to his friend that when people speak, their meaning does not always lie explicitly in what they say, but rather depends on the hearer's knowledge of some commonly shared 'code' which allows them to de-code and understand what is really meant. His problem, he explains, is that he does not know the code. Following this metaphor, none of us 'know the code' in the sense of being able to put it directly into words. But most speakers tacitly know how to use it.

This chapter introduces a radical alternative to the traditional experimental paradigms used in mainstream research: it is called discourse analysis (hereafter 'DA').

- DA's core concern is the study of language as action-orientated, locally situated and functional;
- discourse is approached as the topic of study in its own right;
- DA represents a rapidly growing and important method in the study of human action and of how the social world is constituted, and it has a flourishing literature of theory and research.

Used extensively in investigating the social construction of organisational and inter-organisational phenomena (Phillips and Di Domenico, 2009), discursive research is taking on a major role in, for instance, driving debates in organisation and management theory (Hardy, 2001). Within the broader topic of organisation research, DA studies have focused on leadership (e.g. Clifton, 2012, 2006); trust (Crane, 2016); workplace identities (e.g., Sveningsson and Alvesson, 2003); workplace meetings (e.g. Svennevig, 2012) and other forms of institutional meeting (e.g. Potter and Hepburn, 2010); healthcare workers (e.g. Marshall, 1994); advice-giving in the workplace (e.g. Stubbe et al., 2003); and emergency helplines (e.g. Hepburn and Wiggins, 2005). Interestingly, as a theoretically grounded methodology, DA appears to have made little appearance in the marketing literatures.

Origins

Discourse as the topic for the study of human action has antecedents in the 1950s and 1960s with an increasing interest in language as social performance (Willig, 2003). Influential works include John L. Austin's *How to Do Things with Words* (1962) and Searle's *Theory of Speech Acts* (1969). Both introduce the idea that 'people do things with their words'. For Austin, statements are more than just descriptions of versions of affairs: they can be performative in the sense of 'to state something is to do something'. Recall the younger Alan Turing's observation on what people do with their talk. These sorts of ideas can be seen in significant works in many different disciplines: for instance, Thomas Kuhn's *The Structure of Scientific Revolutions* (1996); Michel Foucault's *Archaeology of Knowledge* (1972); Michael Polanyi's account of *Personal Knowledge* (1962); the research work of Harvey Sacks in *Conversation Analysis* (see Wooffitt, 2005, for a concise introduction); Alfred Schutz's *The Phenomenology of the Social World* (1967); Harold Garfinkel's project of ethnomethodology (e.g. 2002); Ludwig Wittgenstein's *Philosophical Investigations* (e.g. 1986); and latterly in Derek Edwards and Jonathan Potter's contribution to social psychology, *Discursive Psychology* (1992). These ideas lit the fires of a different kind of scientific enquiry spanning a range of disciplines including psychology, sociology, linguistics, literary studies and philosophy (Potter and Wetherell, 1987).

In social psychology the 'turn to talk' starting in the 1970s and 1980s (Potter, 1998a; Marshall, 1994) evolved as a critical reaction against conventional positivist experimental methodologies (Wooffitt, 2005) and their adherence to laboratory methods of investigation (e.g. Silverman, 2007; Antaki, 2000; Wood and Kroger, 2000; Wiggins et al., 2001). The use of laboratory methods to simulate real life, often using students as research participants, is strongly criticised on many fronts: in its inappropriateness to its subject matter (Wood and Kroger, 2000) for example, and as possessing the unrealistic goals of generalising its findings to the 'real' world (Antaki, 2000). In social psychology DA offered the means to drive what Potter describes as the re-specification of its topics. The debate referred to here centres on nothing less than the constitution of knowledge and reality and the nature of language.

Core common concerns

There are many different types of DA (Wood and Kroger, 2000) and a confusing use of the term 'discourse' (Alvesson and Karreman, 2000), indicative of a multi-disciplinary development (Potter and Wetherell, 1987). In general though, they share an analytic concern with how discursive accounts display an orientation to action, their function and effects, and their variability (Wooffitt, 2005: see Potter and Wetherell for a discussion of six principles of DA). Additionally, they share a common assumption that language is the means by which we make sense of the world (Zajacova, 2002). Stainton-Rogers gives a useful definition of the term from the perspective of constructionist social psychology: '. . . a discourse is defined as the product of constructing and the means to construct meaning in a particular way' (2003: 81).

Nonetheless, the proliferation of types of DA has resulted in what Potter and Wetherell describe as the potential for two books on the same topic with no overlapping content. For these reasons, the present discussions are contextualised in social psychology with a particular focus on discursive psychology (hereafter 'DP'). In overview, DP adopts a constructionist position in which speakers' accounts, reports and descriptions construct versions of their world and in which those accounts are themselves 'fabricated in occasions of talk' (Potter, 1998a).

We begin with a brief review of some other popular DA methodologies – conversation analysis, membership categorisation analysis and critical discourse analysis – before exploring DP in more detail. This is followed by an appraisal of some points of criticism of DA in general. The majority of the chapter focuses on a practical step-by-step introductory guide demonstrating how to analyse discourse drawing on DP, using as an example a controversial speech delivered by the Rt Hon. David Cameron in his role as the UK's Prime Minister. The chapter concludes with a recommended activity.

What does discourse analysis do?

By far the dominating methodology in the DA field is conversation analysis, originally developed by Harvey Sacks and his colleagues in the 1960s and 1970s, although note that Wooffitt (2005) differentiates between conversation analysis and

DA. Conversation analysis is concerned with how the organisation of talk-in-interaction is accomplished, what normative rules are deployed and how speakers display their understanding of others' utterances, thus underlining the jointly accomplished nature of talk (Stubbe et al., 2003). Analysts seek to discover and describe the 'architecture of the structure of verbal communication' (Wooffitt, 2005: see Wooffitt for a comprehensive discussion and comparison of conversation analysis and DA). In other words, it seeks to uncover and render explicit that part of Turing's 'code' which tells us how to understand what rhetorical actions are being done.

By contrast, membership categorisation analysis, described by Stokoe (2012) as a 'milkfloat compared to conversation analysis' juggernaut, and also originated by Sacks, is concerned with the categorical or topical rather than the sequential unfolding of discourse (see Stokoe for a comparison between MCA and conversation analysis). So, for instance, the researcher might be interested in how and what effect the category of 'mother' or 'office worker' has in discourse. Finally, critical discourse analysis, most associated with Fairclough (e.g. 2001), is concerned with how political and social inequalities are produced, maintained and sustained, even developed, in discourse. Importantly, Fairclough and Wodak (1997) emphasise the dialectical relationship between discourse and the events, institutions and social structures within which it is enacted. By 'dialectical' Fairclough and Wodak refer to what they perceive as the two-way relationship between a discourse event and the world in which it takes place: discourse both shapes the world and is shaped by it. Consequently, and in part, critical discourse analysis focuses on the relations between discourse and other phenomena, notably power.

Discursive psychology draws on ideas from DA, conversation analysis, rhetoric and ethnomethodology (Potter, 1998). It takes its theoretical and analytical origins from, for instance, the pioneering work of Gilbert and Mulkay in sociology (e.g. Mulkay and Gilbert, 1982; see Potter for a detailed account). It is concerned with the action-orientation of language (talk and text), specifically the rhetorical construction and organisation of versions of affairs, their social organisation – how it works – and what it is designed to do (Edwards and Potter, 1992). To paraphrase Edwards and Potter, DP is concerned with descriptions and explanations, how reports are constructed as factual while managing one's own stake and interest in particular versions of affairs: in short, its interest lies with how matters of knowledge, cognition and reality are made live as speakers' concerns. Its core assumption is that language is constructive/constructed, functional, consequential and locally situated, and thus variable.

Key insight

> Rather than seeing the study of discourse as a pathway to individuals' inner life, whether it be cognitive processes, motivations or some other mental stuff, we see psychological issues as constructed and deployed in the discourse itself (Edwards and Potter, 1992: 127).

This perspective raises a particularly important point. By locating psychology in language, it makes possible the direct study of the processes of thinking (Billig, 2001). Contrast this with the traditional experimental method which, by comparison, is reduced to the study of secondary or indirect phenomena. This difference is significant: DP studies psychological phenomena as constructed in everyday talk and text, and as oriented to by both speaker and recipient, while conventional methods treat discourse as the representation of inner mental thought (Edwards and Potter, 1992). This latter inevitably treats phenomena as second-hand. The kinds of questions that DP focuses on are then how the account is constructed to appear, for instance, factual and objective; what resources are used and with what function (Edwards and Potter); and how these connect to topics in social psychology (Potter, 1998).

In other words, DP is not concerned with why speakers perform certain actions in certain situations. From a DP perspective, concerns with 'why' questions, which are the hallmark of traditional research methods, implicate discourse as a report of thought. For instance, consider a typical marketing survey questionnaire: participants are generally asked to rate their opinion or attitude towards a particular set of statements. Such an approach assumes an honest report, unbiased by the question, the researcher, what the participant has read that morning, the opinions of others, and so on. DP, by contrast, analyses what a speaker does with their words, what actions they perform, how and with what effect.

Mini-case 5.1

Doing authenticity

A recent study by the present author (Crane, 2016) shows how speakers in a routine, regular project team meeting in a software services consultancy firm use reports of what 'others say' to work up persuasion and to construct their version of affairs as accurate, trustworthy and authentic. In this particular instance, two speakers who adopt opposing positions on a topic use the same reports of what others have said to script their opposing versions as more authentic and trustworthy than the other. The way that they do this is fascinating: one speaker reports what others have said in the format of an eye-witness account (a device shown to be effective in invoking accounts as trustworthy and as warranting entitlement to opinion – see Hutchby, 2001), while the second speaker downgrades what others say as being 'what they always say', thus scripting this as inconsequential and beneath notice. The analysis shows how this works particularly to set a trajectory of one speaker undermining the competency and trustworthiness of another.

Mini-case 5.2

Focus on social media

There is considerable interest in applying a DA approach to the study of social media contexts, often referred to as 'computer mediated communications'. One study, for instance, focuses on product review sites investigating how contributors work up their accounts as trustworthy in the absence of visual/ body language cues. Otterbacher (2011) examines how contributors use structural (e.g. profile information about the writer), textual features and persuasive writing to gain prominence 'in the crowd', finding that the latter two are the most salient tactics.

Studies have also uncovered some unexpected findings: for example, Stommel and Koole's (2010) study of an online support forum for people with eating disorders finds that, contrary to expectations, the threshold for joining (that is, being accepted and responded to by others) is actually quite high, and that the expected norm of advice offered being accepted and adopted by the recipient is not always in evidence.

The significance of this latter finding stems from conversation analysis' 'adjacency pair': this is the term used to describe two individual 'turns at talk' which naturally and inevitably form a pair. An example of an adjacency pair is 'question – answer': in constructing an utterance as a question, a speaker places an almost unavoidable imperative on another speaker to respond with an answer. The giving of advice, similarly, usually places an imperative on the receiver to accept this, with the implication of intention to follow it. The finding from Stommel and Koole's (2010) study suggests that advice giving does not function in the same way in the context of an online discussion forum.

Grounds for criticism

As an interpretive methodology DP is not immune to criticism on the grounds of the subjectivity of the researcher's analysis. For sceptics, this might imply the potential for a lack of methodological rigour (Zajacova, 2002). On this point, van Dijk (2001) claims that there can never be an unbiased interpretive analysis of discourse, and consequently the role of the researcher should and must be considered as part of the analysis. As Stubbe et al. (2003) point out, any transcript-based analysis of meetings or interviews is potentially subject to bias in how the analyst 'notices things' in the text and interprets linguistic transactions, in the analyst's choice of what is included in the analysis, and what is left out, to give just a few examples.

The question of how to measure the quality of qualitative research methods is also a topic of some debate, and relevant to studies drawing on DP. Yardley

(2000) and Elliott et al. (1999) offer some useful guidelines for dealing with this issue, whilst noting that a consensus approach is yet to be reached (also see Smith, 2003, for an outline summary of the debate). The issue boils down to the view that the traditional 'measures' of quality in conventional studies – bias, reliability and validity – are irrelevant to qualitative studies, particularly those adhering to a DA approach.

At the heart of this particular debate is the issue of validity. From a pragmatic perspective, as an analytic account can only ever represent one of possibly many alternative interpretations, it can never be judged as either right or wrong (Wood and Kroger, 2000), which renders the traditional measure of 'validity' invalid. Potter (1998) offers a useful summary of four considerations: (1) analysis should pay attention to speakers' own understanding as displayed in discursive interaction (and not just the analyst's interpretation); (2) the adequacy of a claim can be assessed against any 'deviant cases' in the data; (3) analysis and claims should be grounded in previous studies, and (4) the inclusion of data extracts will allow the reader to form their own interpretations and judgments. However, Potter notes that none of these considerations works as a guarantee of validity, but questions whether such 'bottom-line guarantees' can ever be provided for – no matter what methodology is applied.

Practical guide to discourse analysis

A first point to note about the DP methodology is that '[T]here is no single simple recipe for analysing discourse' (Potter, 1998: 239). This can be seen as both a challenge and an opportunity: it is challenging because analytic skills must therefore be learned through time and practice. Fortunately, there is a range of books designed to assist the novice analyst in getting started (see References section at the end of this chapter). As an opportunity, there are least two positive aspects: first, this is a comparatively new discipline, meaning that there is considerable scope for significant contributions to be made. Second, there is an equally considerable scope for creativity in interpretation, providing that the researcher stays within the 'golden rule' of paying attention only to what speakers themselves orient to or index as live concerns.

In terms of the nearest there is to a 'recipe' for doing DP, the reader is referred to Edwards and Potters' (1992) discursive action model which they present as a conceptual scheme that synthesises various features of discursive action and the relationships between them. It is organised into three principal themes: action (e.g. a focus on action rather than cognition), fact and interest (e.g. negotiating the dilemma of stake and interest) and accountability (e.g. the speaker's displayed sense of accountability in reports). It establishes some useful guiding principles as well as some potential areas on which to focus research (such as, for instance, how speakers construct and manage their remembered accounts of past events as factual and authentic). Lester and Paulus's (2011) study of public displays of knowing in an undergraduate's online discussion forum is a good example of using the discursive action model to inform and frame research.

The aim of this section is to walk the reader through some of the more contextually relevant stages of DA using an example of real data. The objective is to demonstrate how this methodology can yield fascinating and valid research findings with valuable contributions to the understanding of the social world. As a starting point, we will draw on Potter and Wetherell's (1987) useful 10-action guide to discourse analysis. Not all of these actions are relevant to the data example used here, so a generic description is presented for each (see Table 5.1). To this list, we have added a further action – literature review – which is presented both as a first step in research work, but also, importantly, as an ongoing action through the research project as a whole.

TABLE 5.1 Action guide to discourse analysis

Literature review	This is presented as a first action in research as well as an ongoing, iterative part of the research. This point is developed below.
Research questions	Not all DA/DP studies adopt research questions to drive the focus of their investigations. If research questions are used, these should be framed around 'what' and 'how' questions, avoiding 'why' questions.
Sample selection	Unlike traditional research methods, the size of any given research sample does not determine the success of research outcomes. Generally, there is a preference for 'naturally occurring talk', which can include, for instance, contributions to social media forums. The key point is that the researcher is not present/does not contribute/ does not influence the data in any way. Otherwise, the selection of samples is, like conventional methods, driven by the nature of the research enquiry.
Data collection	In DA studies, the researcher should adhere to the same ethical principles and considerations as the conventional researcher.
Interviews	Where interviews are used in DA studies it is particularly important that the questioner, whether this is the researcher or someone else, is considered to be a participant, with their utterances or contributions in the data subject to analysis.
Transcription	Audio data has to be transcribed in such a way as to realise a written version that is as representative as possible of the spoken word. Researchers typically use a standardised set of transcription conventions originally developed by Gail Jefferson (see, for instance, Potter, 1998 for an explanation).
Coding	This action refers to the sifting of the transcribed data, audio recordings and written text data for instances of interest either to the study's research question, or whatever phenomena the researcher judges to be relevant.
Analysis	This is probably the lengthiest, most complex of all actions. Analysis can involve many iterations between the source audio data, the transcriptions and relevant literatures. Depth of analysis can vary but the guiding principle is to seek to relate analytic claims to wider phenomena.

Validation	Potter's (1998) four validation procedures arguably provide an adequate set of criteria to which studies should adhere, the key elements of which can be seen in the analysis below. Accordingly, analysis should focus on what understandings speakers themselves display in their discourse; be alert for any cases which are deviant from the apparent discursive patterns; be grounded in existing published works; and include extracts from the data to enable the reader to formulate their own analysis.
Report writing	Whilst there is no mandated structure for report writing, researchers should generally work within the accepted format of:

- locate the study;
- identify and justify the area of interest;
- describe the methodology and research design, paying particular attention to validation procedures;
- describe the analysis, including examples from the data;
- either include discussion in the body of the analysis or include this as a separate section;
- draw some conclusions, explaining how these are grounded in the findings, and implications for future research.

	In some cases, it may also be useful to include a discussion on how the role of the researcher is addressed.
Application	This action centre-stages a question that most if not all researchers should address: what real-world application does the research have?

This guide is referred to here as an 'action guide' to avoid this being seen as an incremental stepped process: the order in which these actions are engaged is entirely dependent on each specific research case.

In the next sections, we draw on an example of real-world data in the form of a written version of a speech given by the United Kingdom's Prime Minister to heads of state of member nations of the European Union in 2013. This is selected because, as a monologue, available both as full written text and video, it is a simpler piece of text to work with than a dialogue between two or more speakers. There is also no need to use transcription conventions (unless one chooses to use the video version). The text, nonetheless, is a fascinating example of rhetoric delivering what many would see as a highly controversial message to an audience expected to be less than receptive and supportive. Each of the action guides, as relevant, is addressed in terms of how it relates to the data, and how it can be applied. We start with the literature review.

Literature review

As with any research project, an important step towards developing prospective avenues of enquiry for research, and in formulating research questions, is researching the relevant literature. This has two practical outcomes: first, it enables the researcher to understand how particular topics are dealt with, and to identify any gaps in the literature. Secondly, it enables the researcher to ground analysis in existing research. Both support the drive for coherence because, as Potter (1998) points out: 'a study which is couched within, adds to and builds on existing research is more acceptable and plausible than one which stands apart'.

It is also recommended that relevant literatures be continuously re-visited and reviewed, with new studies sought, throughout the lifecycle of the research project. Such a discipline brings a number of advantages including:

- The project remains current with the latest publications.
- As the project develops, and inevitably encounters challenges, a re-appraisal of existing literature can often help to elicit alternatives for thinking about, and addressing such challenges.
- As the researcher becomes more familiar in 'living with' the existing literature, your own project and research implicitly becomes more embedded to this.

With respect to the present data, the early development of some indicative research questions is driven by the data itself, and this in turn directs the directions for the literature review.

Research questions

In DP the use of research questions is more a matter of opinion and preference than prescription. Some are persuaded that even indicative research questions are unnecessary and potentially limiting to the analysis at hand. They may, for instance, restrain the researcher's analytical focus and vision to the exclusion of potentially interesting phenomena beyond their boundaries. Where they are used, Willig (2003) advises that these should be related to how speakers go about the business of managing their accountability (that is, how they deal with matters of answerability, liability and responsibility in utterances) and stake (their personal interest in particular versions of accounts). In their extensive studies of discourse, Edwards and Potter (2005) find that speakers routinely work up accounts as 'disinterested', even contrary to their personal desires and beliefs in order to inoculate against others' claims of self-interest. Accordingly, DP asks 'what' and 'how' questions rather than the 'why' questions which are the hallmark of experimental methods.

The data used here is the text of a controversial speech given by David Cameron in January 2013, in his role as Britain's Prime Minister, to the European Union (EU) Member heads of state. In essence, the text does three things: (1) it critically constructs the EU as an institution in need of serious and far-reaching reform; (2) it establishes an imperative for Britain to have a re-negotiated treaty of EU membership; and (3) it announces a forthcoming referendum in which the British electorate will be given a simple choice of staying in or leaving the EU. From these perspectives, it can be seen as a 'loaded speech'. Consequently the indicative research question focuses on what and how linguistic strategies are used, and with what effect, in delivering this controversial message.

FIGURE 5.2   David Cameron delivering a speech

Source: Photo © 360b. Courtesy of Shutterstock

Wooffitt's (2005) analysis of how people issue, receive and deal with invitations from others reveals how particular linguistic devices can serve to work up inoculation of both one's own face and that of others. In the present analysis, the indicative research questions prompt an investigation of four rhetorical strategies used in the text to mediate accountability and stake:

- conjuring jointly shared cognitive states;
- scripting jointly faced threats;
- creating a 'them and us' differentiation;
- and the demonising of the EU as an institution separate from its members.

These are discussed with reference to the text below. As background, the reader is referred to Chilton's (2004) analysis of 'inflammatory' political speech-making.

Selection of sample and data collection: 'the data'

The size and content of any sample selection is driven by the research question. Potter and Wetherell advise that '[F]for discourse analysts the success of a study is *not* in the least dependent on sample size' (1987: 161; italics in original). The analyst's priority is an interest in the language itself, how it is used and what it accomplishes, not the speakers. Most DA research generally samples a corpus of data from different sources, or from similar sources (e.g. Wooffitt's 2001 study of verbal interaction between mediums and their clients finding 'reported speech' to be a commonly used linguistic device which, he claims, works to invoke 'favourable assessments' of the psychics' authenticity).

When collecting data, many of the same principles of conventional research methods are relevant: a consideration of ethics, for instance, and ensuring the appropriate permissions are gained (see Ethics Box below). Such practical matters can, of course, complicate the life of the discourse researcher where the preference is often for using naturally occurring language in interaction (that is, with the complete absence of the researcher), which means recording conversation in everyday domestic situations, for instance (e.g. Wiggins and Potter's 2003 study of evaluative talk), or business meetings to give another example (e.g. Potter and Hepburn, 2010). The use of surreptitious recordings would, for instance, be ethically questionable.

For simplicity, the example text uses the 'written not spoken' version of Cameron's speech. (Note that published reports should focus on more than one political speech to avoid potential limitation, but a single speech suffices for our purposes here). The speech is available (in both text and video format) on the website of the UK government. All content from this website is available under the Open Government Licence v3.0 giving free rights to 'copy, publish, distribute, transmit, adapt and exploit' the content provided that the source is acknowledged.

ETHICS BOX

Any research project, of whatever nature, should be designed and carried out in accordance with your university's ethical requirements. Generally, these advocate:

- submitting a proposal to the university's ethics committee prior to research;
- providing all participants with a briefing note and a consent form which should be signed prior to engaging in research;
- this consent form must state the terms under which participants can withdraw from the study at any time;
- it is good practice to offer participants the opportunity to receive a post-research briefing;
- consideration should be given to the ethics of, for instance, using publicly available online discussion forum data (see Crane, 2016 for a discussion).

In the present case, the data is available for use under the terms of the UK's Open Government Licence, a reference to which is sufficient in meeting the requirements of ethical standards.

Be prepared to justify and defend your choice of data sample from an ethics perspective.

Transcription

While the text used here did not involve transcription (an advantage of using such texts) a few words on transcription would be useful. Transcription as a preparatory step to analysis involves transforming spoken texts into written form suitable for analysis. It also involves annotating the transcript with symbols indicating pauses (often including duration), intakes of breath, rises or falls in tone, increase or decrease in volume, over-talk, laughter, speech repairs and so on. The aim is to produce a written version that is, as far as the research aims require, as accurate a representation as possible of the spoken words while acknowledging that a literal rendering is impossible (Wood and Kroger, 2000). Most 'how to' books and many published research papers reference or include a key to transcription conventions, the most popular of which is that developed by Gail Jefferson (see Wood and Kroger for an example). The transcription's level of detail will be determined by the research question (Potter and Wetherell, 1987). As a guideline, a formal conversation can take around 10 hours to transcribe per hour of talk, while informal talk, potentially involving far more transcription detail, can take up to 20 hours per hour of data (Potter and Wetherell, 1987).

All that was done to the text used here was to sequentially number each line of the text, which is a common procedure in discourse analysis and which facilitates references to the text's contents in the written up analysis.

Coding

Not to be confused with the application of transcription symbols nor with the analysis itself, coding is the process by which the researcher searches for and selects instances in the transcript relevant to the research question or theme under investigation (Potter and Wetherell, 1987).

The research question here has a particular interest in how the text manages stake and interest in delivering a controversial message, and with what effect. People routinely work to 'inoculate' their versions of accounts against criticism of self-interest (Edwards and Potter, 2005) and 'face threatening acts' to both self and others (Wood and Kroger, 2000: see Myers (1989) for a study of how scientific writers mitigate against 'Face Threatening Acts'). So we are interested in instances where the text works up consensus with the audience, jointly faced threats, or instances of a 'them and us' formulation, for instance.

Having collected instances of the phenomena of interest, which Potter and Wetherell (1987) advise should be as inclusive as possible, one is ready to begin analysis.

Analysis

The core principle is that the topic of interest is language itself (Potter and Wetherell, 1987; Edwards and Potter, 2005). It is the difference between studying a text for what someone says as an expression of opinion or attitude, and analysing it for what participants are doing with their text and with what effect (see Crane, 2012 for an example of an analysis of how online forum contributors construct identities as expert in what is scripted as a competitive context). Although there are no set procedures for doing analysis, there are some key questions to be borne in mind: why am I reading the text in this way, what are the features which lead to this way of reading it (Potter and Wetherell, 1987)? One is specifically looking for both patterns and variation in the data (Edwards and Potter, 1992).

As preparation, recall the indicative research question's focus on what and how linguistic strategies are used, and with what effect, in delivering this controversial message.

Jointly faced threats

Extract 1: Jointly faced threat

28. The map of global influence is changing before our eyes. And these changes are

29. already being felt by the entrepreneur in the Netherlands, the worker in Germany, the

30. family in Britain.

In extract 1 the text scripts a world changing 'before our eyes', conjuring the sense of passive observation. Bearing in mind that the text deliverer and his audience are all national leaders, the inference of the sphere of 'global influence' changing beyond their control suggests that these are troubled times.

The peoples of Europe are equally impacted by these events, scripted as the proto-patients to whom things are done (Chilton, 2004), adding to the sense of change happening beyond the control of those who might normatively expect or be expected to have some control. A particular linguistic device often used by politicians is the three-part list (Edwards and Potter, 1992: lines 29–30: '. . . entrepreneur . . .', '. . . worker . . .' and '. . . family . . .'). These are shown to be effective in scripting states of affairs as factual and are implicated in doing persuasion (Edwards and Potter, 1992; Wood and Kroger, 2000). It is suggested that the text here is orienting to persuasion, in conjuring a mutually faced threat scripted as authentic – it is being experienced by real people across Europe. It cannot be ignored nor denied. Thus, it works on the level of empiricist warranting: a description of events 'happening out there' as a neutral and available record (Edwards and Potter, 1992). A 'warrant' acts as an excuse for something – some opinion or action (Willig, 2003) – so the question then is: what is the text excusing?

Scripting 'the others'

Extract 2: 'The others'

75. Some might then ask: why raise fundamental questions about the future of Europe

76. when Europe is already in the midst of a deep crisis?

77. Why raise questions about Britain's role when support in Britain is already so thin.

78. There are always voices saying 'Don't ask the difficult questions'.

Here we see the first invoking of 'the others' ('Some', line 75 and 'voices', line 78), which becomes a recurrent action throughout the text. These vague 'others' are not specified but are scripted here as problematic in questioning Britain's role in the EU and criticising Britain (as a nation) for asking 'difficult questions'. There are interesting parallels here with Chilton's analysis of another political speech in which the speaker also invokes an unspecified agent whose actions are responsible for (undesirable) things being done to the 'patient' (the native British people): the sense of this depends on the hearers' '. . . ability to make an appropriate inference on the basis of whatever background knowledge they have of the political world' (Chilton, 2004; 123). As Chilton notes, the use of an unspecified agent device effectively shifts responsibility onto the hearer for any inference drawn. Similarly to Chilton's data, these agents are not specified anywhere in the present text. The effect, though, is to implicate these 'others' as a group ('them') distinct from the 'EU Members', to which group ('us') the text-deliverer belongs.

What can be heard then is a 'them vs. us' demarcation. These 'voices' have persistence (line 78: they are 'always' there), which upgrades (Potter, 1998) their potential. This reflexively orients (Locke and Edwards, 2003) to both the necessity of asking difficult questions, and in not being 'shut up' by these voices. Note the use of reported speech indicators in line 78: the spoken equivalent to the parentheses used here would be expressions such as 'you said' or 'he said' (Wooffitt, 2001). What the voices say is thus constructed as '. . . a reproduction or quotation of the (exact) words initially uttered by another speaker in another context' (Wood and Kroger, 2000: 103), with the text scripting a role as a first-hand witness to what has been said.

A further context invoked by the text is the nature of Britain's support (line 77). Note the construction of 'support in Britain is already so thin', with the implication that the object of support is the EU itself. The intensifier ('so thin': Schegloff, 1997) upgrades the ante: Britain's support cannot get any thinner without vanishing. There is also a sense that the cause of the troubling nature of Britain's support is attributed (Wooffitt, 2005) to the 'voices', who both question Britain's role and urge against asking difficult questions. This works up 'the others' as unreasonable and as claiming rights that they will not sanction in others. So the discourse in extract 2 accomplishes three actions: (1) the status of Britain's support serves as a warrant (Silverman, 2007) for asking difficult questions; (2) that the cause of this status lies elsewhere with the implication that it is 'the others'; and (3) it is left to the audience/reader to interpret who or what is meant by 'some' and 'voices', which deflects responsibility for such interference from the text itself (Chilton, 2004).

Thus, the context evoked and made relevant in this text is Europe's troubles (line 76: 'deep crisis'), which are made even more difficult by these 'others' ('them vs. us'). There is also the implication that the audience know who the text is referring to. Further, the fragile status of Britain's support serves as a warrant for asking 'difficult questions' allied to the construction of consensus (Abell and Stokoe, 2001) with the audience. This upshot has consequences for managing stake (Wetherell, 2001) and face (Benwell and Stokoe, 2012) in what is conjured as a challenging environment. But how does the text accomplish the business of preserving the deliverer's position, authority and stake in the act of giving a contentious speech to an audience likely to challenge it?

Mitigating against criticism

A number of rhetorical devices and strategies are shown to mitigate against criticism and challenge, two of which are investigated here: (1) the invocation of a memory-emotion construct and, (2) the demonising of the EU as an entity distinct from EU Members.

Invoking memory and emotion

Extract 3: Activating psychological states

2. But first, let us remember the past.

3. Seventy years ago, Europe was being torn apart by its second catastrophic conflict in

4. a generation. A war which saw the streets of European cities strewn with rubble. The

5. skies of London lit by flames night after night. And millions dead across the world in

6. the battle for peace and liberty.

7. As we remember their sacrifice, so we should also remember how the shift in Europe

8. from war to sustained peace came about. It did not happen like a change in the

9. weather. It happened because of determined work over generations. A commitment to

10. friendship and a resolve never to re-visit that dark past – a commitment epitomised by

11. the Elysée Treaty signed 50 years ago this week.

In line 2 the inclusive pronoun, combined with a call to action, invokes consensus (Abell and Stokoe, 2001). Thus, early on, the text works to script consensus with its audience with a call to an activation of 'collective' memory. What is interesting about the extract is that not only does the text invoke collective memory, but it does this by effectively issuing instructions. People often 'issue instructions' on how recipients should interpret their utterances: Wooffit (2005), for instance, describes how people wrap their account of some extraordinary event with 'doing being ordinary', such as 'I was just coming in to the kitchen when . . .' (see also Smith, 1978, for a more explicit account of using 'instructions' to direct the recipient on how to understand what is about to be related). Here the text instructs on how and what to remember.

The audience comprises leaders from nations all across Europe – they can all be assumed to have different memories and experiences (first- or second-hand), even political positions over events in Europe seven decades ago. The text treads a fine line: on one side, it could be seen as working up a truth warrant (Edwards and Potter, 1992) on the basis that if everyone can remember it thus, it must be true – truth through consensus. On the other, the veracity of the account to be 'remembered' by everyone implicitly depends on the moral position and assumption that no one will dispute this version of past events. But this is only part of the action.

The emotion work is done through negative evaluation in lines 3–6 ('torn apart', 'catastrophic conflict', 'strewn with rubble', 'skies lit by flames' and 'millions dead'), contrasted with positive evaluation work in lines 8–10 (the positive shift from war to 'sustained peace', 'determined work', 'friendship and a resolve'). Both conjure vivid accounting, giving the impression of perceptual re-experience (Edwards and Potter, 1992). The contrast is further underpinned by the surrealistic cinematic proportions assigned to the negative evaluation. On one level, this extract stands as a pattern for the text as a whole: the continuous contrasting of constructions of the extreme with the common-sense. Wiggins and Potter (2003) propose that people use evaluative expressions to work up entitlement to express opinion. Here, emotive evaluations work to invoke shared emotion with hearers: that is, they work to underpin the version of 'remembering' that the text instructs on as true and undeniable – the moral position referred to earlier. Collectively what these actions accomplish is the scripting of a warrant for what follows: all this work which took sacrifice and generations to achieve is under grave threat – the jointly faced threat in extract 1.

There is a line in this extract which stands out as a curiosity: 'It did not happen like a change in the weather' (lines 8/9). This metaphor does not seem to fit in the context of the surrounding utterances, suggesting a line added at the last moment, perhaps by someone who did not write the rest of the text. Wood and Kroger (2000) suggest that idioms or metaphors are difficult to challenge because they invoke 'taken for granted' shared knowledge. However, this metaphor is unusual: in its place, one might expect something like 'This wasn't like a walk in the park'. So what it is doing? Arguably, this utterance can be heard as invoking the notorious British obsession with the weather – is the text trying to invoke humour? Humour – like metaphors – generally relies on shared understanding. But it would surely be foolish to inject a call to humour in the midst of what is otherwise the scripting of historic tragedy and national loss. It is speculated here that what this utterance does is conjure the pre-existence of relationships between the text-deliverer and at least some members of the audience with whom this topic of humour has been exchanged in the past. One interpretation would then suggest that the text-deliverer is activating support within the audience.

An alternative, perhaps more simple, interpretation suggests that things cannot be left to the vagaries of the natural environment, which activates the context for the subsequent utterance concerning things 'changing before our eyes' (line 28). Thus, a threat is manifest on an epic scale which must be faced together, and the warrant is established for the controversial message to follow.

The demonising of the EU: 'them vs. us'

As touched on in a previous section, the text scripts unnamed 'others' as the ones challenging Britain's actions, and which are conjured as unjust. Moreover, these others are distinct from the EU leaders present. In transferring responsibility for inferring who these 'others' are to the hearer, the text is consequently liberated to construct negative evaluative assessments of the (shared inferentially) 'EU', using a 'them vs. us' structure. Such evaluations are characteristically polarised in political discourse. Extract 4 serves as an example:

Extract 4: demonising the EU

190. The EU must be able to act with the speed and flexibility of a network, not the

191. cumbersome rigidity of a bloc.

This part of the speech reflexively constructs the EU as being slow to act and inflexible, scripted as weaknesses, while simultaneously constructing the opposite qualities for the text-deliverer and the audience members: thus polar opposites are brought into action. Most telling is the negatively charged comparison between the EU and the 'cumbersome rigidity of a bloc' (line 191), which serves to conjure the old Soviet Bloc.

This notion of the dictatorial Soviet Bloc is earlier activated in the text, shown in the following extract:

Extract 5: tearing down the Iron Curtain

61. In more recent decades, we have played our part in tearing down the Iron Curtain and

62. championing the entry into the EU of those countries that lost so many years to

63. Communism.

In this earlier extract, the text works up the positive side of 'tearing down the Iron Curtain', and the heroic role of Britain ('championing') in saving whole countries from the imprisonment of Communism. Thus, 'we' are framed as the 'good guys' while later on, the EU is sided with the evils of Communism (extract 4: line 191). Note the powerful association of the 'Iron Curtain' which imprisons but which can be torn down, and the 'rigidity of a bloc' which cannot act with speed or flexibility – but which can also be torn down. If the EU cannot change from the 'rigidity of a bloc', then it must be torn down. In this way, Britain's 'thin support' (line 77) is further warranted: it would be irrational for a nation to play 'our part in tearing down the Iron Curtain' yet support another entity comparative to the fabricator of the 'Curtain' – the Soviet Bloc. This works as an unchallengeable rhetorical construction.

Extract 6 offers an equally hard negative assessment of the EU:

Extract 6: the EU as dictator

201. Some Members, like Britain and France, are ready, willing and able to take

202. action in Libya or Mali. Others are uncomfortable with the use of military

203. force.

204. Let's welcome that diversity, instead of trying to snuff it out.

This extract is drawn from the 'visionary' section of the text, in which the principles for a new EU are laid out, the implication being that the current institution is broken and unfit for the twenty-first century. Having already aligned the EU (the 'others') with the worst features of a Soviet bloc, now the EU is conjured as a dictator which seeks to 'snuff out' (line 204) diversity. This works in contrast to the positive, action-orientated characteristic of the EU Members referred to in lines 201–203.

This is a particularly interesting move: on the one hand, the text orients to partnership and shared interests ('Some Members, like Britain and France . . .', line 201) with 'let's' working to fabricate a collective which balances its strengths with its weaknesses (line 202). This is contrasted with others who are 'uncomfortable', but note the downgrading work that this description does: here the contrast is not made judgmentally or negatively, but reasonably and acceptably, and as an example of 'diversity'. This is then directly contrasted with the implied negative work of the EU in acting against its own members ('them vs. us') and the diversity these represent. Thus the EU is further demonised but, importantly, differentiated from 'us' (Member States) and 'our' common interests. This is a recurring pattern throughout the text which serves to accomplish criticism of the EU whilst simultaneously working to protect the 'face' of its Member States by divorcing them from the EU actions. In this way the text works to mitigate challenges to mutual face. According to politeness theory (Brown and Levinson, 1987: as cited in Benwell and Stokoe, 2012), people will always work to preserve their own esteem or face, as well as that of other interactants.

Summary

The indicative research question is interested in linguistic strategies in the context of delivering a controversial message. This is a subtle and clever piece of political rhetoric, with the analysis of the three themes of 'joint threats', scripting the 'others' and 'mitigating against criticism' showing a range of linguistic strategies in action. One can observe the issuing of warrants, for instance, for asking difficult questions; the construction of consensus invoking support for the message being delivered; polarised assessment, using extremes to work up the reasonableness of one scripted position or assessment compared with an extremist alternative.

Perhaps the most interesting characteristic of the text is the scripting of Britain with an identity of 'champion', who helps to tear down the Iron Curtain thus liberating many nations (some of which are now Members of the EU); who persists in asking difficult questions in the face of unreasonable demands (by the 'voices') to desist; and who joins with other Member States to pursue the liberation of others even where it involves military force, and who is understanding of those Members who choose not to contribute because of their 'discomfort'. Contrast this identity with that scripted for the EU: an entity characterised by faceless and nameless voices with the inference of their disavowal of accountability; which is as intransigent and cumbersome as the old 'Soviet Bloc', responsible for the Iron Curtain which 'lost' nations for so many years; and which acts like a dictator in insisting on 'snuffing out' any diversity between nation Members, with the implication that far from being unwanted wrinkles in the fabric of Europe, such diversity is to be valued, and whose loss would be significant. In all of this, the Member States themselves are exonerated, and scripted as apart from the EU. One cannot help but feel that if the 'EU' could be pulled down or sacked, then what is left – the Member States – would be a far better and more productive community.

Application

Application is probably the most undervalued and the least addressed of these stages of DA. What this refers to is the potential for the practical application of research findings. If no attention is given to this, the researcher runs the risk of producing analysis for analysis' sake, and producing findings with little relevance beyond a potentially narrow academic audience. With respect to the analysis included here, an obvious use for such analyses and findings would be in the context of public speaking training courses, or courses for script writers, for instance. They might also be of interest and use to political analysts and journalists, who may find access to such discursive analysis of use and interest in their own analysis.

On a final note, becoming adept in the application of discursive psychology – or indeed any form of discourse analysis – opens the door to an understanding and perception of language as more than words, but as actions which do stuff. It might have helped the younger Turing in learning to understand what people are doing with their words.

Summary

This chapter has demonstrated how the analysis of discourse can be used to investigate psychological phenomena in action by approaching discourse as the site of research interest in its own right. Based on the approach that people 'do things with their words', this methodology is shown to be capable of revealing phenomena that might otherwise be unavailable to traditional research methods. It is further proposed that discourse analysis allows the direct study of human cognition and action.

In the discussion of 'how it works' and through the example given in the 'practical guide', talk and text is shown to be:

- indexical and reflexive;
- action-orientated and performative;
- functional and consequential;
- constructed and constructive;

- locally situated and influenced by perception of contextual particulars;
- variable according to situation;
- the means of making sense of the world and its contents.

Exercise

There are two suggested seminar activities, both of which would involve accessing and downloading the full text of the speech from the UK government's website: https://www.gov.uk/government/news/david-camerons-eu-speech--2

1. In the analytic section on 'Mitigating against criticism', there is a reference to several rhetorical devices and strategies used in the text of the speech, two of which are included in the example analysis. Using the full text of the speech, what other devices and strategies are constructed? Perhaps split the class into several smaller groups, each tasked with analysing a different part of the text. After one hour, re-assemble the class and engage in a compare and contrast discussion.
2. The indicative research question used here specifically focuses on linguistic strategies in the context of delivering controversial messages. What other research questions might be considered in relation to this text? Task two or more groups with different research questions and allow them to engage in an analysis of the text, coming together for a compare and contrast exercise at the end.

Acknowledgements

This article 'Contains public sector information licensed under the Open Government Licence v3.0': https://www.nationalarchives.gov.uk/doc/open-government-licence/version/3/.

References

Abell, J. and Stokoe, E. (2001). 'Broadcasting the Royal Role: Constructing Culturally Situated Identities in the Princess Diana *Panorama* Interview'. *British Journal of Social Psychology* 40, pp. 417–35.

Alvesson, M. and Karreman, D. (2000). 'Varieties of Discourse: On the Study of Organisations through Discourse Analysis'. *Human Relations* 53, no. 9, pp. 1125–49.

Antaki, C. (2000). 'Simulation versus the Thing Itself: Commentary on Markman and Tetlock'. *British Journal of Social Psychology* 39, pp. 327–331.

Austin, J. (1962). *How to Do Things with Word*, in J. Urmson and M. Sbisa (eds), 2nd edn, Cambridge, MA: Harvard University Press.

Benwell, B. and Stokoe, E. (2012). *Discourse and Identity*. Edinburgh: Edinburgh University Press.

Billig, M. (2001). 'Discursive, Rhetorical and Ideological Messages', in M. Wetherell, S. Taylor and S. Yates (eds), *Discourse Theory and Practice: A Reader*. London: Sage.

Chilton, P. (2004). *Analysing Political Discourse: Theory and Practice*. London: Routledge.

Clifton, J. (2006). 'A Conversation Analytical Approach to Business Communication: The Case of Leadership'. *Journal of Business Communications* 43, no. 3, pp. 206–19.

Clifton, J. (2012). 'A Discursive Approach to Leadership: Assessments and Managing Organizational Meanings'. *Journal of Business Communication* 49, no. 2, pp. 148–68.

Crane, L. (2012). 'Trust Me, I'm an Expert: Identity Construction and Knowledge Sharing'. *Journal of Knowledge Management* 16, no. 3, pp. 448–60.

Crane, L. (2016). *Knowledge and Discourse Matters*. New York: Wiley.

Dijk, T. van (ed.). *Discourses as Social Interaction*. London: Sage

Edwards, D. and Potter, J. (1992). *Discursive Psychology*. London: Sage.

Edwards, D. and Potter, J. (2005). 'Discursive Psychology, Mental States and Descriptions', in H. Molder and J. Potter (eds), *Conversation and Cognition*. Cambridge: Cambridge University Press.

Elliott, R., Fischer, C. and Rennie, D. (1999). 'Evolving Guidelines for Publication of Qualitative Research Studies in Psychology and Related Fields'. *British Journal of Clinical Psychology* 38, pp. 215–29.

Fairclough, N. (2001). 'The Discourse of New Labour: Critical Discourse Analysis', in S. Yates, S. Taylor and M. Wetherell (eds), *Discourse as Data: A Guide for Analysis*. London: Sage.

Fairclough, N. and Wodak, R. (1997). 'Critical Discourse Analysis', in T. van Dijk (ed.), *Discourses as Social Interaction*, Volume 2. London: Sage.

Foucault, M. (1972). *The Archaeology of Knowledge*. New York: Vintage.

Garfinkel, H. (2002). *Ethnomethodology's Program: Working Out Durkeim's Aphorism*. Oxford: Rowman & Littlefield.

Hardy, C. (2001). 'Researching Organizational Discourse'. *International Studies of Management and Organization* 31, no. 3, pp. 25-47.

Hepburn, A. and Wiggins, S. (2005). 'Size Matters: Constructing Accountable Bodies in NSPCC Helpline Interaction'. *Discourse and Society* 16, no. 5, pp. 625–45.

Hutchby, I. (2001). '"Witnessing": The Use of First-Hand Knowledge in Legitimating Lay Opinions on Talk Radio'. *Discourse Studies* 3, no. 4, pp. 481–97.

Kuhn, T. (1996). *The Structure of Scientific Revolutions*, 3rd edn. London: University of Chicago Press.

Lester, J. and Paulus, T. (2011). 'Accountability and Public Displays of Knowing in an Undergraduate Computer-Mediated Communication Context'. *Discourse Studies* 13, no. 6, pp. 671–86.

Locke, A. and Edwards, D. (2003). 'Bill and Monica: Memory, Emotion and Normativity in Clinton's Grand Jury Testimony'. *British Journal of Social Psychology* 42, pp. 239–256.

Marshall, H. (1994). 'Discourse Analysis in an Occupational Context', in C. Cassell and G. Symon (eds), *Qualitative Methods in Organizational Research*. London: Sage.

Mulkay, M. and Gilbert, G. (1982). 'Accounting for Error: How Scientists Construct their Social World when they Account for Correct and Incorrect Belief'. *Sociology* 16, pp. 164–83.

Myers, G. (1989). 'The Pragmatics of Politeness in Scientific Articles'. *Applied Linguistics* 10, no. 1, pp. 1–35.

Otterbacher, J. (2011). 'Being Heard in Review Communities: Communication Tactics and Review Prominence'. *Journal of Computer-Mediated Communication* 16, no. 3, pp. 424–44.

Phillips, N. and Di Domenico, M. (2009). 'Discourse Analysis in Organizational Research: Methods and Debates', in D. Buchanan and A. Bryman (eds), *The Sage Handbook of Organizational Research Methods*. London: Sage.

Polanyi, M. (1962). *Personal Knowledge: Towards a Post-Critical Philosophy*. Chicago: University of Chicago Press.

Potter, J. (1998). 'Discursive Social Psychology: From Attitudes to Evaluative Practices', in W. Stroebe and M. Hewstone (eds), *European Review of Social Psychology*. London: Wiley.

Potter, J. and Hepburn, A. (2010). 'A Kind of Governance: Rules, Time and Psychology in Institutional Organization', in J. Hindmarsh and N. Llewellyn (eds), *Organization, Interaction and Practice*, pp. 49–73. Cambridge: Cambridge University Press.

Potter, J. and Wetherell, M. (1987). *Discourse and Social Psychology: Beyond Attitudes and Behaviour*. London: Sage.

Schegloff, E. (1997). 'Whose Text? Whose Context?' *Discourse and Society* 8, no. 2, pp. 165–87.

Schutz, A. (1967). *The Phenomenology of the Social World*, 2nd edn. Illinois: Northwestern University Press.

Searle, J. (1969). *Speech Acts: An Essay in the Philosophy of Language*. Cambridge: Cambridge University Press.

Silverman, D. (2007). *A Very Short, Fairly Interesting and Reasonably Cheap Book about Qualitative Research*. London: Sage.

Smith, D. (1978). '"K is Mentally Ill": The Anatomy of a Factual Account'. *Sociology* 12, no. 23, pp. 23–53.

Smith, J. (2003). 'Validity and Qualitative Psychology', in J. Smith (ed.), *Qualitative Psychology: A Practical Guide to Research Methods*. London: Sage.

Stainton-Rogers, W. (2003). *Social Psychology: Experimental and Critical Approaches*. Maidenhead: Open University Press.

Stokoe, E. (2012). 'Moving Forward with Membership Categorization Analysis: Methods for Systematic Analysis'. *Discourse Studies* 14, no. 3, pp. 277–303.

Stommel, W. and Koole, T. (2010). 'The Online Support Group as a Community: A Micro-Analysis of the Interaction with a New Member'. *Discourse Studies* 12, no. 3, pp. 357–78.

Stubbe, M., Lane, C., Hilder, J., Vine, E., Vine, B., Marra, M., Holmes, J. and Weatherall, A. (2003). 'Multiple Discourse Analyses of a Workplace Interaction'. *Discourse Studies* 5, no. 3, pp. 351–88.

Sveningsson, S. and Alvesson, M. (2003). 'Managing Managerial Identities: Organizational Fragmentation, Discourse and Identity Struggle'. *Human Relations* 56, no. 10, pp. 1163–93.

Svennevig, J. (2012). 'Interaction in Workplace Meetings'. *Discourse Studies* 14, no. 1, pp. 3–10.

Wetherell, M. (2001). 'Themes in Discourse Research: The Case of Diana', in M. Wetherell, S. Taylor and S. Yates (eds), *Discourse Theory and Practice: A Reader*. London: Sage.

Wiggins, S. and Potter, J. (2003). 'Attitudes and Evaluative Practices: Category vs Item and Subjective vs Objective Constructions in Everyday Food Assessments'. *British Journal of Social Psychology* 42, pp. 513–31.

Wiggins, S., Potter, J. and Wildsmith, A. (2001). 'Eating your Words: Discursive Psychology and the Reconstruction of Eating Practices'. *Journal of Health Psychology* 6, no. 1, pp. 5–15.

Willig, C. (2003). 'Discourse Analysis', in J. Smith (ed.), *Qualitative Psychology: A Practical Guide to Research Methods*. London: Sage.

Wittgenstein, L. (1986). *Philosophical Investigations*, 3rd edn. Oxford: Blackwell.

Wood, L. and Kroger, R. (2000). *Doing Discourse Analysis: Methods for Studying Action in Talk and Text*. London: Sage.

Wooffitt, R. (2001). 'Raising the Dead: Reported Speech in Medium–Sitter Interaction'. *Discourse Studies* 3, no. 3, pp. 351–74.

Wooffitt, R. (2005). *Conversation Analysis and Discourse Analysis: A Comparative and Critical Introduction.* London: Sage.

Yardley, L. (2000). 'Dilemmas in Qualitative Health Research'. *Psychology and Health* 15, pp. 215–28.

Zajacova, A. (2002). 'The Background of Discourse Analysis: A New Paradigm in Social Psychology'. *Journal of Social Distress and the Homeless* 11, no. 1, pp. 25–40.

6

CONSUMER ETHNOGRAPHY

Ian Churm

Purpose

This chapter explores how consumer ethnographers gain depth in research through immersion into consumers' lives and activities.

Context

Understanding consumer behaviour is vitally important for modern marketing; for example, to inform marketing strategy, brand development, promotion and advertising. Predicting how consumers might behave is extremely difficult and complex; the consumer ethnographer seeks to gain insights by studying actual behaviour at the point where it occurs. Traditional research methods such as surveys and focus groups simply do not go deep enough to understand consumer minds and behaviours. As a consequence organisations may miss vital signals which may have serious consequences for their future.

Learning outcomes

At the end of this chapter you will be able to confidently design, plan, conduct and present a research project based around the use of consumer ethnography to gain deeper insights into the mindsets of consumer participants.

THEORY BOX

Philosophy: interpretive

- ontology: no single reality, results are subject to interpretation;
- epistemology: knowledge and meaning derived from the study of social interactions in social and organisational settings at the point at which they occur by observation and immersion.

Approach: inductive

There is no pre-determined hypothesis; theory development emerges from the research.

Strategy:

Observation and immersion into consumer behaviour at the point at which it occurs.

Design:

Immersion into consumer behaviour by accompanying, observing, studying, examining consumer processes and decision making. Audio and video recording of events and activities in the field.

Analysis:

- by case: images and transcripts; data reduction obtained by case-by-case summaries; cross-tab analysis of cases and emerging themes;
- by theme: images and transcripts; data reduction obtained by theme-by-theme summaries; cross-tab analysis of themes and cases.

Presentation:

- by case: images and annotations by case; discussion and key findings, implications for strategy, branding and promotional activity;
- by theme: images and annotations by theme; discussion and key findings, implications for strategy, branding and promotional activity.

Why ethnography?

Ethnography is not new. Far from it, for as long as mankind has sought to understand the behaviours of his fellow humans, direct observation has played an integral part of acquiring that understanding.

As marketers we like to think we understand consumer behaviour. We do, after all, spend enormous amounts of time studying them, researching their buying behaviour, understanding their reasons for wanting products and then convincing them our product is the ultimate satisfier of their deepest needs, wants and desires. We know vast amounts about our fellow human beings, gleaned primarily from wide-ranging traditional market research activities which detail the behaviours of consumer segments and tells us all we need to know to market to those sectors . . . or does it?

The problem with consumers is that they are fickle, they change. Or, more correctly, the contexts of their lives change as the environment in which they

FIGURE 6.1 Understanding how we live

Source: Photo © glenda. Courtesy of Shutterstock

consume products and services changes over time. The question therefore is whether the tried and trusted assumptions that underlie our marketing efforts still hold as true today as they did even as recently as a year ago. Do we really understand the reality of our customers' lives and the way day-to-day reality influences the purchase and use of products? Our tried and tested market research techniques may seemingly give us all the answers we need, but do they? Are we missing things that are important to our consumers and by missing them leaving our brands uncompetitive? Are there hidden meanings in the way that consumers actually choose to buy and use our products? The reality is that change is ubiquitous and 'facts' about the marketplace and the consumers within it have an increasingly short shelf life.

Business and corporate managers like to work with facts. They are understandable, in the main quantifiable and therefore provide managers with easy justification for corporate decision making. With managers continually looking to justify their positions in the light of potentially expensive decisions on new product development or corporate strategy, 'traditional' research techniques have become the research methods of choice. Stemming almost universally as they do from the scientific tradition of positivistic research they have been seen as the safe decision making option, and certainly less career threatening than a reliance on seemingly less 'objective' observational techniques. Pie charts and statistical analyses may provide an easy rational for management decisions . . . but do they actually provide any real depth and understanding of customers' motivations? The scientific approach might be argued to be capturing the words . . . but does it effectively capture the deeper meanings behind those words?

The natural world generally obeys rational laws. Scientists seek to define and understand those rational laws. Action and reaction are inextricably linked. The problem with human (consumer) behaviour, however, lies in its very unpredictability. While our bodies may operate in largely predicable ways our minds and the actions that stem from our thought processes are far more irrational. Behaviours, particularly in terms of the way we structure our lives, the way we interact with families and friends, the way we think and, most importantly for marketers, the way we select, purchase, use and even discard the products and services that make up our day-to-day life experiences are all consequences of the environment in which we live. Background, upbringing, education, experiences, to say nothing of bigotries and biases fostered by years of contact with other human beings, all contribute to our view of the products and services we use.

If traditional research, in its attempts to measure and quantify reality, actually fails to capture the deeper insights of human lives and experiences, what research techniques can we use that will? Unlike *The Hitchhiker's Guide to the Galaxy* (Adams, 1979), ethnography may not be able to provide the answers to 'Life, the Universe and Everything'. If what is important is gaining a deeper contextual understanding of consumer behaviour towards your brand and products, ethnography is one of a number of observational techniques worthy of consideration. Why? Because ethnography attempts to dig beneath the surface and identify those unarticulated contextual behaviours inherent in the way consumers really lead their lives. Altheide and Johnson (1994) expressed it thus: 'Ethnography aims to make sense both of understanding and experiences people articulate and the non-discursive ones that are implicated by people as they perform their everyday lives!'.

Author's note

'Ethno-' literally means folk (the study of folk); '-graphy' means description (through living with, observing, experiencing).

Background to consumer ethnography

It is worthwhile at this point taking a brief look at the history of ethnography as a research tool. The scientific observation of behaviour really came into widespread use at the start of the twentieth century when sociologists and particularly anthropologists such as Frans Boas, Bronislaw Malinowski, Ruth Benedict and Margaret Mead developed the technique as a means of studying civilisations. Initially their studies tended to look at the more exotic civilisations such as South Sea Islanders (Malinowski, 1922) and Samoan cultures (Mead, 1928) but this slowly extended into more prosaic studies of contemporary Western life in cities such as Chicago (Wirth, 1956 [1928]).

Irrespective of the society being studied, the technique employed remained the same. The researcher embedded him- or herself into the society by moving in and living with its members over an extended period of time, anywhere from five to ten years not being uncommon. While in that community they lived the way the community lived, they shared in the day-to-day trials and tribulations of the community and they became an accepted part of it. The more integrated they became the less they were seen as an outsider and the more the villagers behaved naturally. The barriers between researcher and those being observed had been broken down and real functioning of the society could be discovered. This classical concept of ethnographic research through long-term involvement of the researcher has become the accepted domain of anthropologists and sociologists, and they rightly protect that domain fervently.

FIGURE 6.2 Studying tribal lifestyles

Source: Photo © J. F. Rock, *The National Geographic Magazine.* Courtesy of Wikipedia

By the 1980s, however, business was also looking at ways to apply ethnographic techniques to consumer and market research. The need for valid information on which to base new product development and marketing strategies is fundamental for any business and 'learning about consumer behaviour, emotions, consciousness and language in relation to brands and product categories offers a point of departure for the marketing adventure' (Hirschmann, 1989).

The problem for business (rather than anthropological research) is that companies looking to find marketing solutions in a rapidly changing cultural environment need answers in far shorter timescales. Embedding a researcher in the company's target markets for years on end is simply unrealistic where decisions on a new product launch or committing to production of an expensive advertising campaign needs to be made in a matter of weeks, or at the very best months rather than years. Consumer ethnography (in a business/marketing context) therefore relies much more on the use of teams of researchers making focused observations over relatively short periods of time. In marketing, weeks rather than years are the order of the day.

Author's note

In marketing we use the term 'consumer ethnography' to differentiate this from pure or traditional ethnography. In consumer ethnography, immersion has to be achieved in much shorter timescales and involves greater focus on particular events. There is also a need to use modern-day technologies to record events for later review and analysis (often by a team).

Note that if the researcher has practical or work experience within a particular company or with particular customers this can help contribute to justifying the principle of immersion.

The commercial imperative of business is to provide products and services that meet the requirements of consumers. Get that right and you will have a successful business, so companies spend vast sums of money trying to discover exactly what boxes need to be ticked to make their product the 'must-have' product for a generation of consumers. What prospective consumers really want from a product and discovering the ultimate truth behind their needs, wants and desires is precisely what consumer ethnography seeks to do. By getting as close to the consumer as possible and breaking down the artificial barriers that traditional research methods can unwittingly create, ethnography tries to discover the true thoughts and feelings of consumers towards products.

What are those unwitting barriers that we need to bypass in order to gain the depth of understanding we are looking for?

The design of 'traditional' market research techniques, such as consumer surveys, focus groups and in-depth interviews, largely assume a scientific approach, with respondents being treated in essence as commodities or as lab rats. They are selected (or even self-selected, which in itself brings in another set of issues), brought into an artificial situation, asked questions deemed relevant by the researcher and their responses recorded for later analysis. Each element of the approach takes the respondent further away from their natural environment. A focus group, for example, even if not conducted in a formal laboratory, will more than likely take place in an unfamiliar room or office. Those taking part are unlikely to be known to each other and they are then asked to operate in an unfamiliar environment well outside their normal comfort zone. At the very least the whole scenario is likely to engender a degree of anxiety within them and at worst lead participants to possibly behave, either consciously or unconsciously, in totally unrealistic ways. Since no one likes to look a fool or be seen to be acting in an unusual or provocative way, responses can tend towards an affirmation of what they believe the researcher is looking for rather than what they truly believe and, by so doing, unconsciously invalidate any subsequent research findings.

Obviously, much time and effort is given by researchers in trying to eliminate these errors of situation but the argument remains that artificial situations potentially lead to artificial responses. Ethnography, on the other hand, seeks to eliminate the problem by conducting research in the very environment the product will be used in and one the subject is comfortable with. For consumer products this will be the respondents' own homes with the research taking place as they perform the everyday tasks of normal life. How do they really behave as they cook the evening meal? What constraints make family life more difficult than it need? What products do they actually use regularly and what are never used? These and the answers to an infinite range of other questions are the forte of ethnography. Answers to the often unspoken questions are the deep insights that ethnography (alongside many of the other techniques that form the content of the book) seeks to provide, be that for corporate strategists, product designers, market planners, advertisers or indeed anyone seeking deeper insights into consumer motivations and behaviours.

'Corporate ethnography isn't just for innovation anymore. It's central to gaining a full understanding of your customers and the business itself' (Anderson, 2009). At the time Anderson worked as an ethnographer for Intel, the manufacturer of the computer chip that lies at the heart of so many PCs in businesses and homes all round the world. He goes on to explain that Intel's philosophy is to listen and observe their consumers in a non-directional way. 'Our goal is to see people's behaviour on their terms, not ours.'

Ethnography and the cultural dimension

The concept of culture cannot be divorced from ethnography. Culture underlies all human behaviour, but the way culture fashions those behaviours is by no means always obvious. If we accept Spradley's definition of culture as 'the acquired knowledge that people use to interpret experience and generate social behaviour' (Spradley, 1979), then we start to get a feeling for its power to influence consumer behaviours. 'Culture' is acquired through years of immersion in our environment and is therefore deeply entrenched in our brains. It triggers feelings, sensations

FIGURE 6.3 Understanding our culture

Source: Photo © Wikimedia Commons. Courtesy of Creative Commons

and emotions about the way we live our daily lives and impacts directly on the way we see products and assess their value to us as consumers. A well-executed ethnographic study can highlight and explains these cultural intricacies. This is particularly true where clients are looking for comparative market research across different countries or even across different ethnic groups within a single country.

Mini-case 6.1

Ethnography and the cultural dimension of laundry

Ethnographic research company QualiData was asked to undertake a multi-cultural study of laundry behaviour across a number of Western European and Middle Eastern countries. To their surprise they found a number of significant differences between typical laundry practices of Western European countries and those of Islamic nations. Men's and women's clothing, for example, were nearly always washed separately in Islamic households. Likewise special care and attention was devoted to the washing of socks. Why? What makes socks so special in Islamic households and why go to the trouble of separating male and female clothing?

Ethnographic insights into the cultural dimensions of Islamic society provided the answer. The profound sexual segregation characteristics of Islamic culture accounted for the absolute necessity to keep male and female clothes apart. To do otherwise is an anathema to their religious beliefs; as it was with the socks, where the removal of shoes and the cleanliness of feet has a direct connection with prayer.

Adapted from Mariampolski, 2006

(continued)

(continued)

Photo © Antonio Guillem. Courtesy of Shutterstock

Mini-case 6.2

Ethnography and consumer rituals: chaotic breakfasts

In the late 1960s and early 1970s Kellogg's became concerned about lagging sales for some of its major breakfast cereal brands. Even Cornflakes was not immune from these trends. What was happening?

The Leo Burnett advertising agency finally identified the answer for Kellogg's through an early application of consumer ethnography. With Kellogg's existing advertising approach clearly no longer working, the agency decided it needed to look beyond simply the product itself (breakfast cereals) and consider more closely consumers' actual use of the product. Was there some sort of social change occurring that was affecting demand for breakfast cereals? To answer that question they needed to understand the reality of the typical American breakfast table and see what was actually happening during that crucial hour or so before the start of the working day. They needed to become part of the 'family' and observe at first hand the reality of the 1960s/1970s breakfast. Ethnography was the obvious approach to take and the Leo Burnett agency elected to run an ethnographic study into the breakfast rituals of typical American homes. Despite being of relatively small scale (only 12 homes were actually observed in their study) the results from Kellogg's perspective were enlightening.

Breakfast in the typical American family unit had changed. Rather than the family all sitting down together to a common cooked breakfast, each family member was now doing their own thing in the morning. Busy lifestyles meant each family member was eating slightly different breakfasts at different times as they sought to get out to work, college or school and sharing a few moments of family time with whoever happened to be around. The traditional family bonding round the breakfast table was a thing of the past (at least during the working week), and confined to weekends . . . if at all.

Photo © Creatista. Courtesy of Shutterstock

Ready-to-eat breakfast cereals had now become the obvious choice for these busy individuals in the morning rush to work and this change – spotted through ethnographic observational research – became the basis for a new advertising campaign for Kellogg's. 'A Kellogg's Kind of Morning!' struck a chord with customers' lifestyle experiences and saw Kellogg's' sales rise and stimulated the development of a range of new breakfast cereal products to meet the 'new' customer demand.

Adapted from Plumber (2006)

Consumer ethnography applications

So the question now arises: when is consumer ethnography an appropriate research technique to consider? Clearly, with suitable research design ethnography can be used for almost any type of research where a deeper cultural and contextual understanding of consumers is required, but currently the most common uses it is put are decisions affecting new product design, product usage analysis and for gaining insights into retail navigation. We will therefore spend a little time looking at these issues in more detail.

New product design

First let us recall the basic idea behind businesses needing to embrace a marketing orientation. Long gone are the days when a business could sell whatever it chose to offer to its customers without any thought as to what those customers might actually need, want and desire (Levitt, 1961).

To be successful it is not enough for businesses to rest on their laurels and assume customers will remain faithful to their existing products. New products need to be continually identified or old products adapted to meet customers' expectations. The question becomes: what are those expectations? Many corporate managers mistakenly believe that customers are ever eager to express their dissatisfaction with their company's current products and tell them of the need for new products. In reality such open and constructive dialogue with customers rarely occurs. Complaints or dialogues may not always be forthcoming (consumers cannot be bothered and just migrate away).

Most customers do not actually analyse their use of existing products or the need for new ones rationally but rather adapt to the product they have, accepting suboptimal end results with comments such as, 'Well, it's best you can expect . . . for the price'. Most people do not even recognise their own unhappiness with products and see themselves as being a cut above the rest by the ability to apply their own creative solutions to bypassing products' inherent faults. They can even gain a sense of pride by making a virtue out of 'beating' an imperfect product.

The real route to successful business, of course, is to design products that eliminate the imperfections of the current offerings . . . but how do we identify those less than ideal elements when users themselves do not even recognise them?

The value of consumer ethnography for new product development (or existing product redesign) lies not in what is openly said but in the unspoken clues that consumers unwittingly leave behind when they use similar products and services. The job of the ethnographer is therefore to try and spot behaviours that suggest new products are needed.

Mariampolski (2006) suggests six typical behaviours that are indicators of the need for new product development.

Combining existing products

This is where no one single product does the job. The example given by Mariampolski is that of stain removal from a carpet. Having tried various proprietary brands of carpet stain remover without success the housewife mixes one of the stain removal agents with her normal soap powder and uses the resultant mix. It works! She is proud of her creative solution and this becomes her established 'mix' whenever she has to address a stain removal issue in her carpets. In observing the housewife some months later she automatically used her technique and even explained to the researcher how she 'discovered' her pet solution. Since this particular housewife is unlikely to be the only person to have this particular problem, this observation and the respondent's clear pride in her solution to the problem should immediately trigger thoughts of new product developments.

Don't know how to do it: self-blame

The product fails dismally but the user blames him/herself for failing to achieve the results expected. This can apply in any situation but an example close to many (generally) older people's hearts could be setting up digital recording of TV programmes. People of a certain age may even make a joke out of their inability to work their digital recording device while to a younger generation it may seem frustratingly obvious. The age element, however, is not necessarily the real issue. To the ethnographer such an observation speaks of a badly designed (or at least badly explained) piece of electronics and a need to either simplify the functionality of the unit or rewrite the operating instructions (probably both).

Indifference to the product

Spotting either indifference or a willingness to accept indifferent results during an observation can be a clear indicator of the need of a new product. The kitchen cleaner that gets things 'clean enough' or comments such as 'it's the best you can expect', 'it's good enough for me', all shout out that either the product is being used incorrectly or that a new product is needed. Either way, something in the product or the consumers' understanding needs to be addressed!

Alternative ways round the problem

We have already mentioned this but consumers who are observed to be finding their own ways round a problem give a clear indication of a new product opportunity.

Avoidance

In some ways an extension of the previous point but in this case the respondent, having no product available to do the job at hand simply postpones the task until all the easy-to-accomplish tasks have been completed . . . or even leaves it until another day. *Mañana*!

The perfect product that just doesn't exist

During an observation, possibly through frustration at things not going as well as hoped, the respondent articulates, either verbally or through gesticulations and demonstration, his conception of the ideal product. A study looking at mobility issues for arthritis sufferers might, for example, observe their constant struggles to do even simple household tasks such as switching on and tuning a radio. Combine that with an unsolicited comment of 'Why can't I just tell it I want to listen to Radio 4 . . . and it just do it!' would be a prime indicator that the application of voice activation technology could be a real winner with this particular consumer group, plus offering wide-ranging new product opportunities across other consumer groups.

Mini-case 6.3

From Hoover to Dyson

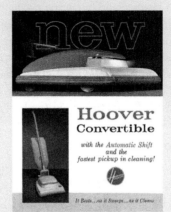

Photo © Wikipedia. Courtesy of Creative Commons

Photo © Wikipedia. Courtesy of Creative Commons

Hoover were traditional market leaders in the carpet vacuum cleaning market in the UK; indeed their very name 'Hoover' became 'hoovering'.

Observing household rituals, in the 1980s the innovator James Dyson identified that the traditional vacuum cleaner was 'just not up to the job' and did not address the needs of 'busy people' for a quick but clean solution. The Dyson vacuum raised the bar in home cleaning technology and captured the market leader position in just a few years after its launch. Customers were willing to pay a premium price for this convenience and effectiveness (the Dyson came to market at nearly four times the price of the beleaguered Hoover).

The continuing challenge for Dyson is innovation, as consumers move away from traditional carpet floors to new, smooth surfaces, and demand even more convenience and flexibility.

Ethnographic studies are an excellent way for innovators to keep track of household rituals and behaviours.

Photo © Wikipedia, Courtesy of Creative Commons

Product usability

An area frequently forgotten by companies in their bid to sell more of their products and services is the functional interaction between consumers and products – the applied science of usability. Particularly in today's age of rapidly changing technologies new product design can almost have a life of its own as companies seek to take advantage of consumers' desire for the latest lifestyle-enhancing gadgets. Technologists and scientists are often the worst offenders as their enthusiasm for new technologies is given free rein by corporate managers desperate for that elusive competitive advantage over their rivals.

The marketers equally like the added marketing opportunities that new technology in products gives them, but it is their job to also bring a degree of consumer reality to the table. When it comes to long-term viability of products (and thus corporate profitability), usability is an area that cannot be ignored.

Usability refers to the understanding of how consumers actually use the products they are being asked to buy. What are the problems they face? What barriers make using the product or service difficult or even impossible? Bluetooth, for example,

FIGURE 6.4 Product usability: fit for purpose?

Source: Photo © Richard Masoner in Flickr. Courtesy of Creative Commons

is now incorporated widely into technological products. It adds functionality to everyday products by allowing their interactive use – but does it automatically make those products more satisfying, exciting or easy to use? To some it is clearly an exciting bonus; to others, however, it is simply adding layers of complication and confusion that outweigh any added benefits claimed by the manufacturers, and sales to that group of consumers will suffer.

Designers alone cannot necessarily be trusted to anticipate the problems typical users might face when encountering a new (or even not so new) product. They can become so engrossed in the technology itself and their desire to incorporate it into products that functionality and usability for the end-user gets left out of the equation. With an aging society who typically find new technologies more difficult to access and an increasingly powerful 'grey pound', usability is a dangerous thing to ignore.

Indeed, usability studies (Norman, 1990) showed that today's consumers expect products to have a degree of functionality and for that functionality to be visible, i.e. they expect to be able to use those products without reference to tedious instruction manuals. Arguably this is one of Apple's strong points. Ask almost any user of Apple products what they like most about Apple products (above and beyond the kudos of the brand itself) and comments such as 'it's so easy to navigate', 'everything is so intuitive' and 'you can use it straight out of the box without thinking' are common themes.

The applied science of usability has become an increasingly important area of study and one where ethnographic observations can be used to provide powerful insights into people's real use of products.

Retail navigation

FIGURE 6.5 Designing a navigable layout

Source: Photo © Wikimedia Commons. Courtesy of Creative Commons

Consumer ethnography can also play a major role in retail navigation. For many firms the company's store (or in today's increasingly online world, 'virtual' store) is the organisation's showcase to the consumer. Making the store environment accessible and inviting to the consumer is an essential precursor to trading successfully and profitably.

Any retail store environment is a complicated mix of elements, each important in its own right but, when brought together, a combination of elements that dictates the success or failure of the company. What elements actually compose a typical retail store environment and therefore what are the areas about which we might wish to understand consumers' attitudes? Location, accessibility, stock of goods and services, display of those goods and services, signage, point of purchase displays, lighting, sounds, smells, size and orientation of shelving, product adjacencies, colour blocking, customer routings through the store . . . to name but a few! The job of the ethnographer is to observe customers' (and potentially staff) behaviour as they navigate the retail store environment and to then decode the meaning and consequences of those behaviours in order to maximise the performance of the store.

How is this done? In larger store environments such as the major supermarkets and department store chains, time-lapse photography/video using cameras mounted around the store is frequently used. The primary advantage from the research point of view is that it avoids direct interaction between the researcher and the consumer and thus eliminates the likelihood of researcher bias being inadvertently introduced. It was this type of observational technique that led Underhill (2000: 76) to identify a natural tendency of shoppers entering a store to steer to the right as they navigate the retail environment. A simple observation, but one with major implications for store managers seeking to maximise the impact of store layout and draw consumers into and around their store.

An alternative approach suggested by Mestel (1998) is the use of what he termed the 'accompanied walk through'. In this case, rather than the researcher remaining isolated from those being observed, the researcher and the respondent circulate around the store environment together. By doing so the respondent is able to express their thoughts directly to the researcher at the point the issue is actually being experienced. A point worthy of note here is that, as with any ethnographic study, it is observing the respondent's natural reactions and behaviour that matters. With any direct interaction it therefore becomes imperative that the researcher does not lead the respondent in any way with those interactions.

In reality most ethnographic studies combine a mixture of both active and passive forms of data collection. An example of this might be for purposes of category management (the management of shelf space and resources) within a retail merchandising environment. The aim here is to maximise the effectiveness of store layout for a particular store's customer base by understanding the interaction between typical customers' browsing habits and elements of store design such as shelf layout, stock locations, pricing and the impact that specific sales promotion displays that might have on customers' propensity to put goods into their shopping trolleys (Corstjens, 1995).

Guerrilla ethnography

A more controversial approach to ethnography and one deemed by many researches to border on the unethical, guerrilla ethnography involves the combined observation of consumer behaviour while actively engaging them in conversation. In its own right, a mix of observation and direct interaction with a respondent is not a problem and one that any well-designed ethnographic study would embrace as a means of gaining deeper understanding of consumer behaviour patterns. The controversial (ethical) element comes from the fact that in guerrilla ethnography the researcher fails to emphasise his/her researcher role and simply engages in apparently innocent chat with the consumers as they go about their natural activity. Proponents of the technique argue that the 'spontaneous' nature of the interaction minimises the social distance between the researcher and subject and the barriers of formality inherent in traditional research are eliminated. The result therefore is claimed to be a more natural response from the consumer and thus giving a greater validity of findings.

The counter-argument centres on whether such an interaction can be perceived as an invasion of privacy (and therefore unethical) and the potentially manipulative nature of such an intervention.

These questions aside, guerrilla ethnography is frequently used as a pilot research technique to gain initial insights prior to designing such things as focus groups or more formal surveys.

The practice of consumer ethnography

Before starting we need to ask ourselves a fundamental question: is consumer ethnography the most appropriate research tool to use? The underlying issue is: are we using ethnography because it is the right method to use or simply because it's trendy? Being fashionable is not justification.

Over the years consumer ethnography has waxed and waned in terms of its popularity. In 1988 Mariampolski was hailing the revival of ethnography as a serious market research tool (Mariampolski, 1988), while over 18 years later it was still only said to be 'becoming popular and fashionable in market research' (Nafus, 2006). This waxing and waning of ethnography in the market research context has led to questions as to whether it is in fact the powerful research tool claimed by many people or merely a research fad appealing to those marketers and research directors wishing to differentiate themselves from others and wanting something new and unusual to talk about (Boddy, 2009). Many research companies, when approached by company marketing directors looking for new vibrant approaches to their market research, have claimed an expertise in consumer ethnography not borne out by its application. Such companies, having sold it as a fashionable addition to their portfolio, have left marketing managers wondering why they were talked into spending considerable time and effort to achieve results that could have been gained far more cheaply and quickly by more traditional methods. This is not to say the technique is at fault but unimpressive results produced by agencies more driven by fashion than ability has been a major reason for the rise and fall in consumer ethnography's popularity over the last forty years.

Being trendy is not, therefore, sufficient justification for the use of consumer ethnography. Simply being different from the normal gamut of traditional research tools does not mean it is the appropriate tool to use in your planned study. So, having satisfied yourself that you are doing it for the right reasons, Mariampolski (2006) suggests a list of criteria to help assess whether consumer ethnography may actually be an approach worth considering. His suggestions are to consider whether one or more of the following applies to your proposed research:

- Cultural: Are you seeking to identify underlying patterns within an organisation or community, perhaps to define an intervention strategy or investment opportunity?
- Environmental: Is the location of the event critical? e.g. is it specific to a workplace location, a store environment, a consumer's home, a bathroom, kitchen, garden, etc.?

- Holistic: Do you need to understand the 'bigger picture' to gain the information you need? Are the influences of lifestyle, hopes, aspirations, family or work interactions fundamental to developing the insight you need?
- Engagement: Can you get close to the consumer to get an unfettered view of their reality? Rich insights come from unfiltered access.
- Visual documentation: Will visual images (photo/video diaries, etc.), combined with consumer written and verbal reports, add a significant extra dimension to your analysis?

Additionally, consumer ethnography (as distinct from classic anthropological ethnography) comes into its own wherever a deeper understanding of consumer behavioural issues are likely to impact on brand and business development. If your client is interested in achieving any of the following (Mariampolski, 2006), then consumer ethnography becomes an appropriate research technique to consider.

- stimulating new product ideas;
- identifying product modification opportunities;
- increasing the understanding and operational use of products;
- improving product handling and practices for storage and packaging;
- gaining insights into the effect of culture and lifestyles on product selection and usage;
- stimulating improvements in corporate work practices and brand communication;
- identifying emerging trends in consumer attitudes and behaviours.

Overriding all those considerations, however, it must always be remembered that the practical employment of ethnography in a business/marketing context (as distinct from classical anthropological techniques) is always likely to be constrained by the commercial realities of budgets and time frames. In the business environment ethnographic studies need to provide results within weeks (or at most a few months) if they are to remain commercially relevant. Obtaining deep insights into consumer behaviour without excessive long-term immersion into your consumers' lives and while keeping your research within tight commercial budgets may at first seem impossible balancing acts, but they are the commercial realities within which consumer ethnographic research is required to operate.

The danger in trying to balance those various constraints is in ending up with a cheap and nasty telephone survey which, while satisfying the cost issue, provides little or no depth or understanding of the consumers' reality. An immediate task, therefore, is to educate your client to the limitations of what you can and cannot do. 'On that budget we can do (this)'; 'To gain the information you are asking for will take (this) amount of time'; 'The geographical extent of our work would be (this)', and so on. The client needs to understand and expectations need to be managed. Then, with understanding established, we can go on to design a consumer ethnographic study with a realistic expectation of delivering the outcomes sought by the client.

Project design issues

Overriding any other considerations, before we start designing any ethnographic research activity we must keep in mind the issues of reducing bias, preserving objectivity and authenticity, and providing continual respect and consideration for respondents. Failure to respect any of these will seriously impact the validity of your research. So to what extent can we actually control these issues?

Bias

Be open-minded, avoid pressures of expectation or any pre-assumptions about the results expected. This may sound obvious but in the commercial environment a client's desire to achieve the 'right answer' can be difficult to resist. A chief executive who has already put his reputation on the line by approving an expensive new corporate strategy is not going to take kindly to you saying that they have got it all wrong!

Objectivity

Ethnographic research should not start from a premise of trying to prove something. While there will undoubtedly be pressures from clients (and in reality it will be almost impossible to remain totally dispassionate, they are after all the ones who are paying you) you do have an obligation to be realistic with them. You need to make them fully aware of the limitations of ethnographic research, explain what you can and cannot do and consequently exactly what they can and cannot expect from you. Good companies will understand, but operating as they do in a competitive environment they will almost invariably have an 'agenda' (hidden or openly stated) behind the research you are being asked to perform. Total objectivity may therefore be an impossible target but be pragmatic and always ensure your client is fully aware of any potential issues with what they are asking you to do.

Authenticity

For its validity, ethnography relies on the research being conducted in 'its natural environment'. Do not, therefore, knowingly design a study that disrupts that natural environment. The problem is fundamental – the simple act of being observed tends to make people behave unnaturally . . . and your job is to observe the natural!

Underhill (2000) stated: 'It's crucial [to consumer ethnography] that shoppers don't realise they're being observed. There's no better way to be sure that we're seeing natural behaviour'. While true in a pure observational research sense there is an equally valid approach, that of participatory philosophy where instead of trying to 'hide' from participants they are treated as allies and taught how to be effective respondents by sharing information and experiences.

Respect and consideration

Always treat respondents with respect and consideration. Respondents are human beings with feelings and emotions and if made to feel uncomfortable will make poor research subjects. Before research starts, think about likely points of embarrassment or invasions of privacy, try to eliminate them and make sure that respondents who feel uncomfortable in any way know that they can refuse to participate or withdraw from the research at any point.

Designing a consumer ethnographic study

Where do we start?

A successful consumer ethnographic study begins by defining the extent of the fieldwork we are about to undertake and dealing with the so-called sufficiency questions; i.e. what is sufficient to achieve a successful study? Having defined our area of interest the first consideration is the selection of suitable sites, both in terms of location and the number at which we will be conducting our research. Since with ethnography we are looking for depth rather than width there is no specific requirement for a 'minimum' number of sites. The extent of our study is usually determined not by statistical requirements but by what is required to achieve the depth of understanding sought.

Sites themselves can be extremely varied. In a traditional social ethnographic study a site would typically be geographic-based but in marketing/consumer ethnographic research sites have a much broader meaning. A shop, high street, home, office, factory or any other location where the issue being studied is actually performed can represent an appropriate site for ethnographic research. Or in the case of consumer netnography, in digital and social media.

> **Author's note**
>
> Consumer netnography has grown in popularity in recent years with the increased use of social media and digital networks. In netnography the researcher engages (and becomes immersed for a period) with a digital community to study talk and text over an extended period.
>
> The advantages of such an approach include the ease of data collection and availability of data. Disadvantages may include the authenticity of the data.
>
> A good discussion of netnography can be found in Kozinets, 2015.

In the home, for example, if we were looking at food preparation or cooking utensil design our research site could be the family kitchen, or in the case of a study looking at outdoor barbecuing, respondents' back gardens. In the UK there has recently been a noticeable shift in food shopping habits away from large weekly or monthly shops at out-of-town supermarkets to more frequent convenience shopping at smaller local food outlets. For major companies such as Tesco, with very large property holdings and a strategy traditionally built around ever-larger out-of-town shopping complexes, this poses a potentially serious problem. Why should UK food shopping habits be changing so dramatically? Why are continental 'imports' such as Aldi and Lidl with their much narrower product ranges suddenly proving so much more successful than the 'full service' offerings provided by traditional UK supermarket giants such as Tesco, Asda, Sainsbury's and Morrisons? Finding answers to these questions are ideal subjects for consumer ethnography but what might represent suitable sites for conducting such research? Supermarket stores would seem the obvious choice but another possibility could well be the homes of shoppers. This latter choice would look more holistically at the whole food shopping experience of families and contextualise the study around their lifestyles and environments.

How many respondents do we need to consider and who should they be?

Again, as the researcher you need to consider the issues being looked at and make decisions accordingly. In the example of changes to UK food shopping behaviour an argument could easily be made for looking at the female head of the household (traditionally the primary food shopper) but not only could that bring in potential sexist and selection bias issues but it could also ignore other likely influences. In many households (including my own) the husband does all the food shopping and, depending on the make-up of the household, do we also need to bring children into the equation? Pester power can be incredibly influential in what appears in the kitchen cupboards!

A little thought around issues such as these will guide your decision on the respondents to be targeted. If the choice is the whole family then how many families would be needed to gain the insights you are seeking? Is one family enough? Clearly the wider the range of families that can be observed the more relevant and widely applicable your results are likely to be but the choice you make needs to be rationalised against the time and expense of wider and more extensive research involvement. A good discussion of relevant sample size can be found in Chapter 2 of this book; in particular see Table 2.4.

When should the research be conducted?

Yet again, there are no hard and fast rules. The choice is partly dependent on the issue being researched but elements such as time of day, day of the week, the season and even the weather need to also form part of your design/thought process. For example, researching snowboarding clothing during the height of summer or visitors to an outdoor garden centre on a day of torrential thunderstorms may not be particularly fruitful. It can be done, but getting good results will take a little more creative thinking on your part!

Time actually spent on site taking observations is usually a more pragmatic than scientific decision. As noted already, the major difference between traditional anthropological ethnography and marketing/consumer ethnography lies in the commercial imperatives surrounding the research. Too much time and the commercial window of opportunity has passed, too much expense and the profit benefit disappears. Consumer ethnography is therefore a fine balance and you, along with your client, need to assess the balance between academic rigour and commercial viability then design your study accordingly. Field times are invariably dictated by client time scales and budgets. While anthropological ethnographic field research is often to be measured in years, even fairly extensive commercial ethnographic studies are unlikely to involve more than four to eight weeks on site, just to meet the commercial imperatives of the client. A student consumer research project might equally be undertaken in as little as a few hours. Remember that the objective of student projects for independent study or dissertation is not to produce samples and sizes for commercial use but primarily to demonstrate that as a student you have mastered the particular marketing research technique and can apply it.

The ethnographic encounter itself and the collection of data

This is the sharp end of the research and an opportunity to conduct your consumer ethnographic research in one of three alternative ways (Whitehill, 2009).

Pure observer

This is the classic dispassionate observer role where your job as researcher is to simply record what you see for later analysis. It is a largely undifferentiated approach where those being observed are effectively self-selecting by the simple fact of choosing to be in that particular location at that particular moment in time. Since they are not usually identified as individuals there is no clear requirement to gain explicit consent for their cooperation, tacit agreement being assumed by their entering the store (potentially reinforced by the presence of notices to the effect of 'this store is being monitored for research purposes'). Numerous methods of data collection can be used here. Written notes or dictation into some form of voice recorder are frequently used but with today's plethora of digital recording technology available the most usual method employed is HD digital photography or video recording: the advantages are that the quality of image produced is high and the researcher is able to perform more detailed analysis at a later date, including the identification of important behavioural patterns possibly overlooked in the original observation.

Observer plus a participant role

This is typically used when you wish to assess a service encounter from the customers perspective – say, the simple act of buying a coffee in a café. What is the process, the attitude of staff, the ambiance of the place, the comfort level, the reactions of other customers as they proceed through the coffee buying process, etc.? In this instance you, the researcher are also acting as a participant and therefore have first-hand understanding and involvement in the experience. It also provides the opportunity to ask questions of those you are observing, perhaps asking them why they came into the store, their opinion of the service provided or possibly introducing them to alternative coffee experiences available and observing reactions.

Participant as observer

In this case the subject observes their own behaviour, records their observations in some way (video diaries being a typical method used) and then passes this information on to the researcher.

Author's note

Whatever the data collection method you choose to use (video diaries, notes, voice recording, still photography, etc.) you should always try to ensure your data collection is conducted as unobtrusively as possible. In the presence of cameras or microphones people often become self-conscious and behave unnaturally. Your job as an ethnographic researcher is to avoid the unnatural and tease out consumers' natural responses and the real-life behaviour patterns that lie behind them.

People and the way they behave are endlessly fascinating. Consumer ethnography is a way to discover that diversity of human behaviour and hopefully use that understanding to make our everyday lives better.

Seminar discussion questions

1. Guerrilla ethnography. What are the major arguments for and against its use? Is it ethical to research people without their knowledge or agreement and how would you rationalise this against the use of hidden cameras in (say) a supermarket research scenario?
2. How about mystery shoppers? Do they suffer from the same ethical limitations? Construct an argument for their use.
3. Underhill (2000) stated that 'It's crucial to [consumer ethnography] that shoppers don't realise they're being observed. There's no better way to be sure that we're seeing natural behaviour'. How does this square with the alternative participatory approach where participants are treated as allies and taught to be effective respondents? When would one be preferable to the other and why?
4. Identify studies that might be good potential for ethnographic research. Consider contemporary cases that are in the news. Consider projects that might fit within the criteria above identified by Mariampolski (2006).

Seminar exercise

FIGURE 6.6 Out-of-town supermarket

Source: Photo © JuliusKielaitis. Courtesy of Shutterstock

You have been asked by a large out-of-town UK supermarket to look at the parking habits of customers as they visit the retail complex of which their store is a major element. On the same site are a number of other well-known high street retail outlets, all of whom share the very large parking area within the complex. While this variety of retail shopping experiences undoubtably brings greater footfall to the complex as a whole the supermarket has seen a drop in its own customer footfall over the last year and is looking to find and address the source of its problems. While general changes to food shopping behaviour in the UK are known to be the primary cause, other elements, more within the control of individual supermarkets, are thought to be detrimental to regaining customers and parking is thought to be one of them.

Parking per se is not the issue. It is indeed the entire premise of out-of-town shopping: provide lots of parking convenient to the store and shoppers can load their trolleys with ever more groceries, wheel them out to their cars and drive off into the sunset happy in the knowledge that the weekly task of feeding the family has been completed with the minimum of tedium. But while the interior of stores has received considerable attention over the years as managers sought to keep the cash registers busy through innovative changes to store layouts, product ranges and sales promotions, car parking has been the neglected child of the supermarket package. It's just there! What more do people want than a space to park their car?

With the cash till beginning to fall silent it finally been decided that the outside should be reviewed and you have been asked to undertake some observational research into the parking behaviour of shoppers at your local store.

Your task is to design and undertake a suitable ethnographic study to identify the behaviour of shoppers during the period they are *outside* the store: i.e. from the moment they enter the supermarket car park until they enter the store and then again from the moment they leave the store, return to their car and leave the car park on their way home.

In small teams, consider all the elements necessary to design a study of the car park usage of a local supermarket near to your college or university.

- Is ethnography an appropriate technique to employ and if so would a purely observational approach be likely to give you enough data to useful results and insights or would you need to expand your study to include either self-participation or direct contact with members of the general public? (If the latter, be sure to carry documentation explaining that what you are doing is a student research project and, most importantly, that they have the right to refuse to participate or withdraw at any point should they wish. You should also seek the approval of the store manager before you begin.)
- What will be your chosen site, where will you position yourself? (You need to be able to gain an appropriate vantage point to make your observations.)
- When will you make your observations, during the day or in the evening? At what time, during peak periods or during quieter periods?
- Will you gather data as a team or take turns so as to gather a wider spectrum of results?
- How will you collect the data? Would video be the most appropriate technique?
- What exactly will you be looking to measure? Is it car park space, is it the size of bays? What about trolley parks? Are they appropriately located?
- Are there particular areas of frustration for customers as they negotiate the spectrum of parking and getting to the store entrance? (Don't go with pre-conceived ideas, but having some ideas of what you might see will allow you to think of likely issues to watch for.)
- Having gathered sufficient data, how do you foresee that data being analysed?

These are by no means all the design issues you need to consider. Work as a team and get the best ethnographic design concept that you can come up with. Then, when everyone is happy with the approach you are suggesting, go and do it for real. See what insights you can come up with and, if appropriate, suggest a redesign of the car park layout that maximises the use of that expensive piece of real estate to the benefit of customers . . . and therefore the store. Enjoy!

Bibliography

Adams, D. (1979). *The Hitchhiker's Guide to the Galaxy*. London: Pan.

Altheide, D. L. and Johnson, J. M. (1994). 'Criteria for Assessing Interpretive Validity in Qualitative Research', in N. K. Denzin and Y. S. Lincoln (eds), *Handbook of Qualitative Research*. Thousand Oaks, CA: Sage.

Anderson, K. (2009). 'Ethnographic Research: A Key to Strategy'. *Harvard Business Review* 87, no. 3, p. 24.

Arnould, E. J. and Price, L. L. (2006). 'Market-Oriented Ethnography Revisited'. *Journal of Advertising Research* (September), pp. 251–62.

Boddy, C. (2009). 'The Faddish Breakout of Ethnography'. *International Journal of Market Research* 51, no. 1. The Market Research Society.

Cayla, J. and Arnould, E. (2003). 'Ethnographic Stories for Market Learning'. American Marketing Association. *Journal of Marketing* 77 (July), pp. 1–16.

Corstjens, J. and Corstjens, M. (1995). *Store Wars: The Battle for Mindspace and Shelfspace.* Hoboken, NJ: Wiley.

Desai, P. (2007). *Viewpoint. Ethnography and Market Research*, Special Issue on Ethnography. Market Research Society, September 2007.

Hammersley, M. and Atkinson, P. (2007). *Ethnography: Principles in Practice.* London: Sage.

Hirschmann, E. C. (1989). *Interpretive Consumer Research.* Provo, UT: Association for Consumer Research.

Holloway, I., Brown, L. and Shipway, R. (2010). 'Meaning not Measurement: Using Ethnography to Bring a Deeper Understanding to the Participant Experience of Festivals and Events'. *International Journal of Event and Festival Management* 1, no. 1, pp. 74–85.

Kozinets, R. V. (2015). *Netnography: Redefined*, 2nd edn. London: Sage.

Levitt, T. (1961). 'Marketing Myopia'. *Harvard Business Review.* July–August.

Malefyt, T. (2009). 'Understanding the Rise of Consumer Ethnography: Branding Techno Methodologies in the New Economy'. *American Anthropologist* 111, no. 2, pp. 201–10.

Malinowski, B. (1922). *Argonauts of the Western Pacific.* London: Routledge

Mariampolski, H. (1988). 'Ethnography Makes a Comeback as a Research Tool'. *Marketing News* 22, no. 1, p. 32.

Mariampolski, H. (2006). *Ethnography for Marketers: A Guide to Consumer Immersion.* New York: Sage.

Mead, M. (1928). *Coming of Age in Samoa.* New York: William Morrow Paperbacks.

Mestel, A. (1998). 'Avarice'. *New Scientist*, 28 March, pp. 38–9.

Nafus, D. (2006). 'Who Needs Theory Anyway?' at www.aqr.org.uk. Association of Qualitative Researchers.

Norman, D. A. (1990). *The Design of Everyday Things.* New York: Currency/Doubleday.

Plumber, J. T. (2006). Editorial, *Journal of Advertising Research*, September 2006.

Sangasubana, N. (2009). 'How to Conduct Ethnographic Research'. *The Qualitative Report* 16, no. 2, pp. 567–73.

Spradley, T. (1979). *The Ethnographic Interview.* Austin, TX: Holt, Rinehart & Winston.

Underhill, P. (2000). *Why We Buy: The Science of Shopping.* New York: Simon & Schuster.

Whitehill, C. H. (2009). 'Is Ethnography a Dirty Word?' Introduction to *International Journal of Marketing Research* Special Issue on Ethnography. Summer 2009.

Wirth, L. (1956). *The Ghetto.* Chicago: University of Chicago Press [1928].

Zaltman, G. (2003). *How Customers Think: Essential Insights into the Mind of the Market.* Boston, MA: Harvard Business School Press.

7

SOCIAL MEDIA NETWORKS

Rich online data sources

Annmarie Hanlon

Text
@the_risk_man We're always here to help when you need us, Darren. Enjoy the rest of your weekend. ^Gareth
@rie_barbara Hi Barbara, if you're on standby, you'll need to check in at the airport on one of the kiosks. ^Gareth
@BriannaStubbs You made it, Brianna! It was a close call, but you had a couple of minutes to spare. ^Gareth
@HuntyPeter It's definitely not deliberate, Peter. We know how frustrating delays are and we're working hard to reduce them. ^Gareth
@philadams We're sorry we couldn't offer you a seat in the cabin you booked, Phil. We do hope our ground staff assisted you. ^Gareth
@marcusbonfanti We'd love to recognise them individually, Marcus, if you can complete this form: https://t.co/22cnREayH6 ^Gareth
@LibertyLndnGirl Don't be disheartened, Sasha. We have every faith in you that you'll return to Silver. ^Gareth
@EducatingRachel We can help you, Rachel. Please DM your reference, contact details and the change you're wanting to make. ^Gareth
@mopimpim Hi Mo, it's only the check-in closure time that's changed. This is 45 minutes for short haul and 1 hour for long haul. ^Gareth
@gameposession We're sorry for any misunderstanding. Infants don't get a seat unless you purchase a child's ticket. ^Gareth
@Crustyfur Hi Chris, I'm afraid this can't be taken further. We can only apologise for the way this was handled. ^Gareth
@the_foad Hi James, we're working really hard to improve our punctuality. We hope the @GBRowingTeam have a great flight. ^Gareth
@ZeroMoment1 You didn't catch his name did you? If you did, you can leave some personal feedback here: https://t.co/22cnREayH6 ^Gareth
@TabzzK We do hope you may change your mind and give us a chance to redeem ourselves, Tabrez. ^Gareth
@BillyStirling3 We're following you if you want to DM us. Sorry again for the inconvenience caused by the delay. ^Gareth
@tiiffiinnii We're sorry your journey was disrupted, Tiffinni. Can you tell us some more about what happened? ^Gareth
@London_Photog We've got that covered, Richard. ^Gareth
@jogga84 We're glad you've managed to reschedule, Joanne. Can't promise an upgrade though. We hope you're coping ok with the floods. ^Gareth
@mehinix We're so pleased you like the A380, Radu. We do try to offer as much legroom as we possibly can. ^Gareth
@lozzercozzer We understand the changes we made were disappointing, Laurent. We appreciate your feedback regarding this. ^Gareth
@simon_rp84 Thanks for the information, Simon. This has been reported internally. We're sorry for any discomfort you experienced. ^Gareth
@Julesdcc Hi Julian, we've recently changed our hand luggage policy to reduce the problems you've raised. This should improve soon. ^Gareth

FIGURE 7.1 Example of Twitter data

Source: Author's own data extraction

Purpose

This chapter illustrates how social media networks can be harnessed for research to highlight the feelings, behaviour and opinions of customers. This is a new area of research and will include discussions on data mining and thematic analysis.

Context

Social media networks were initially perceived to be a fad. Their ability to attract large volumes of customers has altered this perception and marketing managers have since recognised their place within the marketing mix to inform new product development, deliver customer services, provide business development and facilitate brand management. One advantage of social media networks is the ability to conduct research quickly and adapt promotional offers and customer service messages and to include customers within the product development process.

Learning outcomes

At the end of this chapter you will understand the research opportunities available within social media networks and be better able to plan the management of research via social media.

THEORY BOX

Philosophy:

- Research studies using social media may come in different guises depending on either the personal preferences of the researcher or perhaps the nature and objectives of the study.
- A positivist philosophy involves the predetermining of a theory (or hypothesis); here the researcher develops a hypothesis from previous knowledge (for example, drawn from a literature review). The researcher then sets about searching and testing data which will either prove or disprove the hypothesis. This approach is also sometimes called a scientific approach, and often involves applying measurements and statistics. In this chapter the author presents the research process based on the positivist perspective.
- An alternative might be an interpretive philosophy. Here the researcher has no predetermined hypothesis as such but rather enters the field of research in order to discover and interpret new data.
- Ontology (positivist perspective): there is an objective reality and we can understand it through the laws by which it is governed.
- Epistemology (positivist perspective): employs a scientific analysis and measures derived from the epistemologies of positivism and realism.

Approach:

Experimental and deduction. The hypothesis is seeking to prove evidence of positive or negative content.

Strategy:

Thematic analysis based on data mining.

Design:

Data capture via social media platform based on specific search terms (organisation or product names, descriptive words, keywords).

Analysis:

- By theme: topics, words and phrases; data reduction is by thematic analysis.

Presentation:

- By theme: words and phrases presented by theme as tree graphs and diagrams.

Introduction, background and context

In this chapter we will be exploring how social media can be used to provide information to researchers and businesses. Our focus is on content created by consumers, rather than the numerical aspect of social media network visit duration and/or least and most successful posts and updates.

Marketing is moving at a faster pace than ever before. In our 24/7 always-on world, customers seek responses to questions within minutes; they share feedback instantly which can go viral, sometimes before businesses have had the opportunity to respond. Consequently positive or negative comments online can build or break businesses. Much of this communication takes place online via social media networks (SMNs) which have been present since 1997, with the earliest SMN recognised as the now defunct SixDegrees (boyd and Ellison, 2007). The most dominant current SMN in the USA and Europe is recognised as Facebook, launched in 2004 and today comprising over one billion active users.

As noted by boyd and Ellison (2007: 11), 'Social media network sites provide rich sources of naturalistic behavioural data'. This is especially evident within Facebook. Its format has evolved to encourage users to share great amounts of significant personal data, which includes:

- personal identifiers: names, date of birth, place of birth, home town;
- relationship material: relationship status, linked relationships, family members, friendship groups, significant dates;
- work and education records: places worked, where studied, education levels;
- interests: religious affiliations, political views, hobbies, preferred music, films watched, favourite brands;
- behaviour: pages liked, comments added, downloads performed, purchases made, actions taken.

This data is available anonymously to advertisers to more closely tailor and target their offers. In a social media context, 'anonymously' means without names and addresses. It is also available to Facebook partners who develop applications (known as apps) where the primary purpose is to extract data from Facebook to incorporate the information into the business's own customer relationship management databases and subsequently deliver customised marketing offers. This is one of the primary reasons for companies to develop 'apps': to discover more detailed information about their fans or friends, to understand how and when they engage online and to facilitate marketing opportunities.

Other SMNs have started to follow Facebook's lead as they start to gather more user data. As an example, Twitter is trying to enrich its user data by obtaining dates of birth, not directly but through the use of a celebratory hashtag #HBD inviting users to share their birth date.

 Adding a hashtag symbol (#) 'tags' a word, making it easier to index and find through search engines such as Google. This was initially started outside Twitter, by a technology expert keen to group content through Twitter and needing a common search prefix.

User data from the SMNs such as Facebook and Twitter is available to its advertisers and partners, as well as to researchers. Additionally, as SMNs have advanced and become more sophisticated, there is a move towards capturing more than the user profile (gender, age, location) and widening the data sets to include the user content; the updates, posts, tweets and other information which has been shared publically.

For example, Twitter is blazing a trail in gathering extant public posts and has indexed and made searchable every public tweet since the microblogging platform's launch in 2006. At one time it provided free access to researchers! This has since ended, although data is available via third party suppliers for a fee and with restrictions.

The SMNs therefore provide a rich source of data; from personal opinions to relationship circumstances; location data to individual behaviours; employment records to political persuasion, as well as content created.

FIGURE 7.2 Example of hashtag usage in Twitter

Source: Author's own

What can you research via social media?

Social media offers researchers real insights, often in real time, for many aspects of data, including:

- users – behaviour and opinions;
- networks – size, scale, topics, connections, tie strength;
- content – comments, images, video, hashtags;
- companies – brand sentiment, product launches, product testing, customer services, feedback.

Furthermore, data collection and research via SMNs afford additional advantages, including less administration, reduced costs and rapid response rates (Laskey and Wilson, 2003). Unsurprisingly, there are also some disadvantages.

Disadvantages of conducting research via social media

Challenges with collecting data from social media networks include:

- The required target population may not use social media.
- The data is anonymised therefore demographic details are limited.
- It can be difficult to access the data (see Ellison and boyd, 2013; Morstatter et al., 2013).
- The messages available are public not private, which can limit the study (see Hong et al., 2011).
- The messages tend to be shorter and contain less detail than other sources.

This mini-case provides an example of how social media has been used to test behaviour.

Mini-case insight 7.1

Use of Twitter to test behavioural responses to advertising messages

As an example of how Twitter user behaviour can inform social media advertising, Jilin Chen (Chen et al., 2015) and others are working on targeting ads across social networks based on personality type.

(continued)

(continued)

They created a Twitter account @TravelersLikeMe and focused on Twitter users visiting New York, because they found this city to be among the most popular destinations mentioned on Twitter. Where they found Twitter users who said they were planning to visit New York in the near future, the @ TravelersLikeMe account sent a reply tweet recommending various activities and encouraging a sign-up to a web link. If the user followed them back, they sent them a direct message.

The research methodology involved surveys and field studies and showed that this specific targeting has had an impact on the open rates.

The concept is that organisations could profile Twitter users and start conversations, based on their personality type.

TravelersLikeMe
@TravelersLikeMe

travel connoisseur, food expert, wine enthusiast, fine living coach, travel concierge for creating and delivering individualized experience

⚲ Silicon Valley
𝒮 travelerslikeme.org
🗓 Joined June 2013

Use of social media research in mainstream marketing research literature

The literature regarding the use of social media as a research tool is an emerging area. Although the history of social media has been well-documented (O'Reilly, 2005; boyd and Ellison, 2007; Kaplan and Haenlein, 2010) and the concepts of SMNs and social media have been widely reviewed in the literature (Kozinets, 2002; Muñiz and Schau, 2007; Adjei et al., 2009; Kaplan and Haenlein, 2010; Mangold and Faulds, 2009; Stephen and Toubia, 2010), special issue papers and research agenda have concluded unsurprisingly that social media requires further research (Leeflang, 2011; Kietzmann et al., 2012; Kane et al., 2014).

As a newer marketing discipline, which was initially perceived as 'simply another channel', a factor noted by scholars (Rowley, 2004; Weinberg and Pehlivan, 2011), interest in SMNs is starting to grow.

One of the challenges within the research area of SMNs is that this domain crosses several research areas beyond marketing and often extends into technology, healthcare and education. The references used in this chapter also span several disciplines as the domain of marketing does not contain all the material needed.

User research

User behaviour as shown in mini-case 7.1, as well as opinions, can be researched in social media. This section looks at two popular areas: electronic word of mouth and sentiment.

Electronic word of mouth (eWoM)

Word-of-mouth marketing is possibly the oldest form of marketing communication and has been studied in traditional marketing communications for many years (see for example, Dichter, 1966; de Matos and Rossi, 2008) and is accepted as an effective method of marketing for business. 'Research generally supports the claim that WOM is more influential on behaviour than other marketer-controlled sources' (Buttle, 1998). Social media marketing has been identified as a form of word-of-mouth marketing (WoMM) using professional techniques to influence consumer behaviour (Berthon et al., 1998; Kozinets et al., 2010; Abrantes et al., 2013). eWoM communication can be described as 'any positive or negative statement made by potential, actual, or former customers about a product or company, which is made available to a multitude of people and institutions via the Internet' (Hennig-Thurau et al., 2004: 39).

Positive word of mouth can create sales and negative word of mouth can be costly for companies. Positive reviews have the potential to convert a consumer from 'not purchasing' to 'purchasing' by reassuring him/her that the product is of good quality and/or the company is reputable; uncertainty is thereby reduced. Conversely, negative reviews can 'squelch the "buy"' (Mangold and Smith, 2012) and unsurprisingly there is much research taking place into managing negative reviews (Brunner and Ullrich, 2014; Williams and Buttle, 2014). eWoM influences consumer buying behaviour and perceptions of brand (Amblee and Bui, 2011; Abrantes et al., 2013) and is therefore an essential element within market sensing.

The concept of eWoM has evolved and researchers Canhoto and Clark (2013: 522) refer to 'brand-related online conversations – also called electronic word of mouth (eWoM)'. One of their research projects adopted a snowball sampling approach to gathering online data, by posting invitations across SMNs and inviting respondents to share the invitation with others. They conducted analysis manually, which was possible with a population of 44.

Chu and Kim (2011: 50) suggest there are three aspects to eWoM: 'opinion seeking, opinion giving and opinion passing'. All can be explored within the data, in terms of the content provided, as well as the sentiment within the content which can impact brands positively and negatively. The next section considers part of this, known as sentiment analysis.

Sentiment analysis

Another aspect of eWoM is sentiment analysis, which is also referred to as opinion mining. This is an aspect of natural language processing and measures polarity classified in basic terms as positive, negative, neutral and mixed valence. It enables organisations to see their customers' comments and thoughts, which could be used to inform new product development, improve customer services, identify business development opportunities and facilitate brand management.

As Lima et al. (2015: 757) suggest, 'Polarity determination can be made at different levels: document, sentence, word, or attribute'.

There are two primary techniques used to conduct sentiment analysis, both based on data mining.

- lexicon-based, which considers the polarity of terms which may be extracted from an online system such as SentiWordNet;
- machine-based using software for predictive modelling.

Several researchers (see for example: Prabowo and Thelwall, 2009; Chamlertwat and Bhattarakosol, 2012; Cotelo et al., 2015) propose combinations of these techniques.

Challenges involved with sentiment analysis

Mining data for sentiment analysis is not without challenges. The first is the volume and velocity of data. As an example, in the summer of 2015 Twitter was recording over 6,000 tweets per second, or 350,000 posts per minute. This nature of the data can benefit from automated processing although this has gained mixed responses for various reasons, including the way Twitter permits data collection (as an example, see Pew Research Center, 2013).

Secondly, the lexicon used may incorrectly ascribe a positive comment as a negative and vice versa. Schweidel and Moe (2014) discuss this in their work and also provide examples. There are recognised issues where natural language processing does not recognise sarcasm, irony and humour (see for example, Chamlertwat and Bhattarakosol, 2012).

As an example, consider the tweets shown in Figure 7.3. Based on the content of the language, would they be machine-coded negatively or positively?

Thirdly, there can be duplication in the data downloaded. If downloading tweets and retweets, the same core content may be retrieved several times.

Finally, the rules on data collection from the SMNs can change. Twitter initially provided open access to data for researchers, although this has now been limited.

ItsJustJayNow @ChocnessMonsta · 57s
Twitter is **like** the singer that ruins their best song with one too many "woo-woo's" or "mmmyeah's!" when they perform it live. #RIPTwitter

Daniels Nation @CaptainSDaniels · 9m
Thanks again delta. 😠😠😠 looks **like** I'm stuck in Tokyo again

FIGURE 7.3   Examples of issues with sentiment analysis

Source: Author's own

More information

For a comprehensive guide to research in microblogging, see Cheong and Ray (2011). Marc Cheong has researched Twitter extensively and his work in this area is worthy of review. Okazaki et al. (2014) provide very useful procedural guidelines on opinion mining whilst Huang and Xu (2014) have written an insightful paper on exploring social data.

Researchers using social media can also download their own personal data from most social media networks. This can provide useful insights to understand what is available.

For more in this area, there are academic papers by several scholars, including: 'Word-of-Mouth Communications in Marketing: A Meta-Analytic Review of the Antecedents and Moderators' by de Matos and Rossi (2008) and 'What We Know and Don't Know About Online Word-of-Mouth: A Review and Synthesis of the Literature' by King, Racherla and Bush (2014).

Study exercise

Go to your Facebook page:

- select Settings;
- select General Account settings;
- download a copy of your Facebook Data.

Or go to your Twitter account:

- select Settings;
- select Your Twitter data;
- scroll to the bottom of the page and select Twitter archive;
- download;
- request your archive;
- you will receive an email when the archive is ready;
- click to download and follow the instructions.

- Was it easy to find the information?
- How long did the process take?
- What did you discover?

Network research

Understanding the size and scale of networks as well as the topics, connections and tie strength are areas of interest to both academics and practitioners. Since Granovetter's seminal work on 'The Strength of Weak Ties' in 1973, which heralded the need for a social media network like LinkedIn, tie strength has evolved and comprises new areas such as blogger outreach programmes, enabling organisations to identify opinion leaders who will share their stories. This is where understanding the network, its size, scale and scope, can better inform practitioners as well as researchers.

Technical applications can calculate the tie strength of the SMNs. The Facebook application programming interface (API) facilitates data access and advises users about the data which they are sharing. Spiliotopoulos and Oakley (2014) provide a useful description of this process and Groeger and Buttle (2014) visually illustrate network ties in their research.

 An API (application programming interface) provides the building blocks for computer programmers and developers to access software systems, following their guidelines. Most SMNs share their API with developers.

Content research

Content research explores a variety of formats; from words and images to video and symbols like hashtags. The benefits of researching content allow organisations to shape their customer messaging, as well as managing issues and developing more effective advertising programmes.

To assess future content potential, in the form of predictions, Suman Kalyan Maity and colleagues are exploring a social media question and answer site (Quora) and have analysed the prediction of question topics (Maity et al., 2015). They gathered data over four years using web-based crawling techniques to understand topic dynamics and their popularity.

Business research

Businesses conduct marketing research into many areas, such as new product development and customer services, which we will discuss here.

New product development

Historically, new product development could take years to generate ideas, starting with idea generation, then the creation of prototypes, followed by gaining initial customer feedback and finally bringing the products to market. With social media, this entire process can be significantly reduced, with the target audience being involved in the process of co-creating the product or service. There is value in involving the customer in the process of new product development, as shown in research by Fang et al. (2008: 322):

> Customer participation affects new product value creation by improving the effectiveness of the new product development process, by enhancing information sharing and customer–supplier coordination and by increasing the level of customer and supplier specific investments in the product development effort.

Several companies have used SMNs, in particular Facebook, as a new product development research platform. This is a phenomenon known as crowdsourcing: this can be defined as harnessing the skills of many to deliver a solution. The solution ranges from ideas and suggestions, to finance and practical help (Surowiecki, 2004).

Mini-case insight 7.2

Use of Facebook to develop new products: Walkers Crisps

This well-known company uses a social media network as an element of its new product development. Their research process for new product development takes place via Facebook. They use crowdsourcing and ask their fans on Facebook to recommend new product ideas. The process is usually followed by short-listing, mass voting and subsequently a winner is selected. The entire process takes place and is shared on Facebook.

Customer services

Market sensing works in a dyadic way; customers seek information from companies and companies seek information from customers. As customers moved online and communicated with brands across a 24/7 environment, several companies had to move their customer services into the social media space. In some cases there was no prior research to advise that social media was a customer services environment, simply a sense of need and urgency created by customers.

Developing a customer services offer online has long been identified (Walsh and Godfrey, 2000) and using social media networks such as Twitter has been embraced by consumers who have realised that comments in public generate faster responses (Canhoto and Clark, 2013).

One of the management issues for companies is the lack of control over content, timing and frequency of information, which generates its own challenges: '[firms] are struggling to navigate the emerging complex, consumer-empowered environment' (Gallaugher and Ransbotham, 2010: 197).

Mini-case insight 7.3

Use of Twitter as a customer services tool: British Airways 1

Social media networks (SMNs) act as research tools in a dyadic format; for both organisations and customers. A public example of a company which was forced, by customers, to harness Twitter as a customer service tool, is British Airways.

British Airways did not consider Twitter as a research platform and was not listening to its customers' comments online. When British Airways joined Twitter in 2008, it was a monadic redirection system. Its function was to sign-post customers to the official website. This use of Twitter for British Airways changed in 2013, when customers demanded a dyadic approach.

One customer (known as @HVSVN) flying with British Airways was unhappy when his luggage was lost and he could not achieve the desired response from the company. To gain redress he publicly described the poor customer service. In each comment (tweet) he referenced British Airways' Twitter name. When no formal acknowledgement was forthcoming, he spent $1,000 on Twitter advertising and promoted his comments across the SMN (British Airways, 2014). The comments gained widespread attention and raised fundamental questions about the use and management of social media for businesses.

Several companies, including British Airways, now use social media as part of their integrated marketing research process.

Mini-case insight 7.4

Use of Twitter as a customer services tool: British Airways 2

Using social media networks (SMNs) for ongoing customer research can enable businesses to manage specific processes. An example of good practice in marketing through SMNs includes a UK train company, London Midland.

Their Twitter home page explicitly demonstrates their adoption of the purpose of the SMN, as evidenced by their biography: 'Here to help from 7am to 7pm (8am to 4pm weekends & Bank Holidays). Please try to be polite if things have gone wrong – we're real people just trying to help!' This shows leadership by stating their rules of engagement and enabling a consistent and authentic voice, where staff share real names and add personality to updates.

(continued)

(continued)

For examples of how corporations use Twitter as an engagement tool, read Mamic and Almaraz (2014).

Study exercise

- Identify one example of best practice of customer service via a social media network.
- Does the organisation state its 'rules of engagement?'
- How quickly does the company respond to negative feedback?
- Is the brand voice corporate (like British Airways) or personal (like London Midland)?

ETHICS BOX

The social networks have eyes and ears as well as a host of data that you can extract. At this stage it should be noted that there are debates about whether it is ethical to use online data.

There are two major ethical considerations in data mining, the first being permission to use the data and the second being permission to gather the data.

Ethics – Permission to use data

Individuals may tweet publicly but be unaware that their posts may be used after publication. From an ethical stance it is unclear where posts on social media networks (SMNs) are public or private behaviours. Tweets may be made publicly but considered private content to be shared within a network.

Another issue is how the researcher has access to the network. Some researchers are part of specific networks and could potentially use the data for their own research. For example, internet message boards by mothers sharing ideas and support, such as Mumsnet in the UK and Babycentre and Essential Baby in Australia, are available to any expectant mother who could also be a researcher.

Simply following an organisation on Twitter enables the researcher to see all their tweets, as well as comments made about the organisation.

At the same time, membership of all SMNs is optional. Organisations and individuals can select whether or not to join a special network. They can also decide whether their content is private (locked) or public.

Ethics: permission to gather data

The social media platforms allow researchers the facility to gather data, but have rules about the volume of data captured and the timescales. See for example, https://support.twitter.com/articles/160385-twitter-api-limits and https://www.facebook.com/terms.php before embarking on studies.

Some platforms also have dedicated data resellers, such as Gnip which sells Facebook and Twitter data.

The 'gold standard' of ethics policies is widely accepted as that used by the British Psychological Society (see www.bps.org.uk/what-we-do/ethics-standards/ethics-standards for the full list of options).

Taking you through the process stage by stage

In this section we will go over the main stages in conducting this type of research.

PROCESS BOX: MAIN STAGES AND ACTIVITIES FOR THE RESEARCH PROCESS

Stage	Activities (and key issues)
1	Selection of platform and topics • justify your selection; • agree your topic focus.
2	Sampling • to test the dataset availability.

(continued)

(continued)

3	Selection of data mining method
	• by machine, manually or third party intervention;
	• cover ethical issues.
4	Conduct the data mining
	• data extraction;
	• data processing.
5	Thematic analysis
	• six-step process.
6	Presenting your data

Stage 1: selection of platform and topics

The methodological approach we are presenting is based on a positivist philosophy:

- the data source is based on specific platforms;
- the data is selected based on predetermined topics, words or organisations;
- the researcher is analysing by thematic analysis;
- the interested reader of the research is interpreting the outcomes for relevance to their own situations which could change business practice.

The data source is based on SMNs which facilitate data access and allow researchers to capture data. This currently includes the world's major social media networks, such as Facebook, Twitter, Tencent Weibo, Sinar Weibo, Tumblr, Google+, YouTube and Instagram.

The selection of data source will be dependent upon:

- the target audience;
- the research objectives and topics;
- the skills of the researcher in terms of technical ability and languages spoken.

The target audience

Different individuals and organisations use different SMNs. The latest social media research from the US advises that Facebook is used by over 70% of adult internet users, Twitter is popular with those aged under 50 and 54% of its users live in households earning more than $50,000. Instagram is popular with those aged 18 to 29 and Pinterest is mainly used by women (Duggan et al., 2015). The key is understanding the target audience and identifying the most relevant SMN.

The research objectives and topics

The data to be analysed emanates from user-generated content which has been publicly shared online. This comprises, for example:

- posts, tweets or comments which users have added to an organisation's Facebook, Twitter or other social media network page,
- posts or comments about an organisation, added to the user's social media network page.

The first step is deciding the type of information required or 'unit of analysis' (Okazaki et al., 2014). Several researchers have classified different categories of online content, with examples shown here. Their papers discuss the classifications in detail:

Secondly, the researcher has to decide whether the topic is about an organisation, a subject as denoted by a hashtag or other specific words, including product names. This is for several reasons. As one example, the volume of data can be overwhelming, therefore a focus is required. Also, when using machine methods (see stage 3) data can only be extracted when specific terms are provided. It is difficult to search for 'feelings about brand X' whereas 'negative feelings (including the words, dislike, unhappy, terrible) about brand X' can be obtained, as the search terms have been elucidated. This positivistic approach has been adopted by companies such as DataSift (see http://datasift.com) who have developed 'Curated Stream Definition Language'. Effectively they have built (as have others) their own lexicon. This is a paid-for service and outside the financial scope of most researchers.

The skills of the researcher

Skills at this stage are required in terms of technical ability and languages spoken. Some of the larger social media networks, such as Tencent Weibo and Sinar Weibo which are widely used instead of Twitter in China, are in simplified Chinese. Xing

TABLE 7.1 Categories of tweets and of influence

Categories of tweets (Bruns and Stieglitz, 2013)	Categories of tweets (Sriram et al., 2010)	Categories of influence (Cha et al., 2010)
Original tweets	Neutral News	Indegree influence
@mentions	Personal News	Retweet influence
Genuine @replies	Opinionated News	Mention influence
Retweets	Opinions	
Unedited retweets	Deals	
Edited retweets	Events	
Tweets containing URLs	Private Messages	

mainly occurs in German, and Japanese users of Twitter, unsurprising, predominantly communicate via Kanji. This means language ability would be required for analysis in some geographical areas, as not all social media networks converse in English.

The additional skill required can be technical. There are options, discussed in stage 3, about data mining methods.

Stage 2: sampling

To test the potential dataset, sampling is required. This could take place manually (if machine mining will be used for the main survey), to understand if the required data is available.

There are several free options to conduct the sampling. For instance, to search for hashtags include, for example, the website Tagboard (see tagboard.com). This allows searching via hashtag and enables any user to perform a simple search, such as the one shown here, using the hashtag #travel.

A similar tool is TweetArchivist (see www.tweetarchivist.com) which displays the results in a different format and enables the viewer to see limited details about the topic.

This is supported by additional data options, such as the top users, most frequently mentioned words associated with the hashtag and the language in which the content was provided.

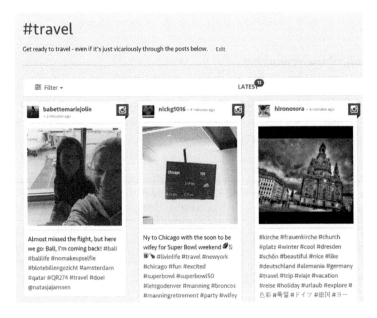

FIGURE 7.4 Example of data from Tagboard using the hashtag travel in Twitter

Source: Author's own

FIGURE 7.5 Example of data from TweetArchivist using the hashtag travel in Twitter

Source: Author's own

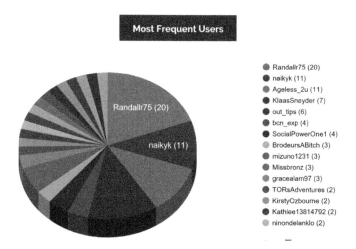

FIGURE 7.6 Example of data sources from TweetArchivist using the hashtag travel in Twitter

Source: Author's own

To obtain more detailed data from TweetArchivist requires a paid account, which starts at $14.99 per month.

Twitter can also provide samples. There are fees involved and some form filling. Initially, an estimate for the data can be obtained via a form at http://gnipinc. formstack.com/forms/data_rofr and approval is also required.

TABLE 7.2 Some methods of data mining

Method	Advantages	Disadvantages
Machine mining	• Quick to capture the data • Captures large amounts of data quickly	• Expensive • Can require third party input (technical help or software) • Demographic details may be missing • Machines cannot see sarcasm or humour!
Manual mining	• Less expensive as it involves the researcher's time • Can interpret nuances such as sarcasm or humour	• Time to capture the data • Time to copy and paste into other software (such as a spreadsheet) for analysis
Third-party intervention	• Other people follow your instructions and carry out the tasks	• Clear instructions needed • Only available in certain countries • Costs can mount up • Questions of data reliability and bias need to be addressed

Stage 3: selection of data mining method

There are different methods of data mining and, based on the research question, timescales and budget, there are several options available.

Machine mining

Machine mining ranges from ready-to-use paid-for options to building data extraction applications. Twitter provides access to its data via several options, the most popular being via its API (application programming interface) which enables developers to extract raw data. This includes data such as the message content, time of message and geo-location information. Marc Cheong's thesis 'Inferring Social Behaviour and Interaction on Twitter by Combining Metadata about Users and Messages' contains useful background to Twitter data extraction using technology (Cheong, 2013).

Other machine mining methods include a range of paid-for tools provided through SMN partners such as Gnip, DataSift and others.

A paper by Watne, Cheong and Turner is a good example of using machine mining in Twitter (see Watne et al., 2014).

 QSR NVivo coding software includes N-Capture which, when installed as an extension on your browser, will enable automatic retrieval of tweet, Facebook and LinkedIn data, direct from the page. Some NVivo training may be required.

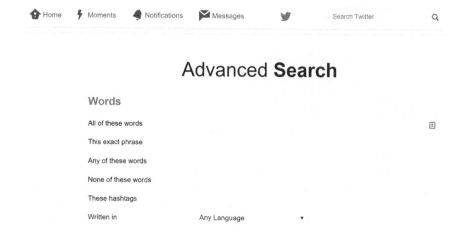

FIGURE 7.7 Example of Twitter advanced search options

Source: Author's own

Manual mining

Manual extraction of data takes considerable time and patience. This is achieved by identifying a search term, such as #travel, and using Twitter's advanced search feature (see twitter.com/search-advanced).

This allows the researcher to specify the exact search terms, whether the data is about certain organisations, geographically centred, within certain dates and whether the tweet was positive or negative (determined vaguely with use of emoticons and language, but not failsafe).

The search results are based on the defined terms and the researcher at this stage could manually copy and paste the posts from the screen into an Excel sheet. This takes some time, depending upon the required sample size and research question.

Third party options

As a result of the time required for manual data mining, a range of alternative third party options have been created, known as micro-tasking. This includes the largest in this field, Amazon's Mechanical Turk (MTurk) as well as others such as Microworkers.com and Clickworker.com. Jaime Arguello, from the School of Information and Library Science at the University of North Carolina at Chapel Hill, has been researching 'Predicting Speech Acts in MOOC Forum Posts' and explains how he has used MTurk in Arguello and Shaffer (2015).

FIGURE 7.8 Example of Twitter advanced search results

Source: Author's own

Mini-case 7.5

Amazon's Mechanical Turk

Amazon has created a crowdsourcing internet marketplace for businesses that need tasks completing by humans; these are called human intelligence tasks or HITs. This started in 2005 and was intended to provide a facility for companies to subcontract digital tasks where computers failed, such as transcribing, writing and tagging images (see mturk.com).

Since this time, the Mechanical Turk has been used as a way of gathering widespread opinions and conducting surveys. There is bias attached, as the population is already digitally literate. The fee rate for the task is set by the researcher and people decide whether or not to take on the task. Typically rates range from a few cents to a few dollars and there have been debates from the online community as to the ethics of using people as machines.

> One task that Mechanical Turk is geared towards is sentiment analysis. Instructions are provided online in a 'ready to go' format. See https://requester.mturk.com/create/sentiment/about
>
> NB At the time of writing, Mechanical Turk does not support researchers from countries outside the US.

Another third party option is volunteer science. This is an online semi-gaming environment created by another US university. Researchers can set up surveys, forums and panels and recruit volunteers to participate (see volunteerscience.com).

Stage 4: conducting the data mining

The methodological approach taken is experimental and deductive (where the researcher has a structure of themes and a set hypothesis), using a structure of themes emerging from the literature.

The data extraction depends on the platform selected. By 'platform' we mean social media network (SMN) and the main SMNs which facilitate data extraction are Facebook and Twitter.

Data extraction can take place by either human coding or machine coding. Okazaki et al. (2014) argue that machine coding is more reliable than human coding, due to inconsistent coding practices when people are involved, whereas machine coding can focus on an agreed algorithm and is replicable.

Data mining via Twitter is not without challenges. Twitter imposes limits on the volume of data obtained over specific timescales. Marc Cheong (2013) conducted research into specific organisations (micro-breweries) and here describes how he captured data from Twitter:

> In order to obtain Twitter data from different [organisations], we used a 'best-effort' data collection strategy (Cheong and Lee, 2010) involving the 'Twitter REST API' (Application Programming Interface). The Twitter REST API is a service that obtains raw metadata about a particular handle or user and their messages, allowing researchers to 'harvest' tweets from particular users. We harvested tweets using a collection of 'scripts' written in the Perl programming language by first using the Search API (a subset of the REST API). The output of the scripts contains more than just plain message text as it also consists of metadata (data about data) that explains the context of a given user and its postings.

REST stands for REpresentational State Transfer and can be described as a software format. REST API is like a key which provides access to read Twitter data.

This illustrates some of the technical skills required, using machine mining.

Once the data has been extracted, the next step is data processing. If the data is extracted manually, via machine or using mixed methods, it is likely the data will be added to a spreadsheet for further analysis.

Mini-case 7.6

Truth and trolls! Beware the authenticity trap

One consideration is the concept of self-presentation of identity (see for example, Marwick, 2005), which is an issue across all social media networks (SMNs). Is the researcher reviewing content from real users? There are caveats of which researchers need to be aware.

- Facebook is keen for its users to use their real names and for a time introduced its 'real names policy'. The issue was with people whose real names were creative and Facebook thought they were fake profiles, threatening to close their accounts if they were unable to provide proof of their identity.
- Twitter users are restricted to 15 characters to create their identity, which means it can be difficult to obtain your real name on the SMN.
- Some people behave badly across SMNs. This anti-social behaviour is often characterised by 'trolls' and users who are banned for offending the community. Some of these users create fake profiles which may need to be excluded from the work – unless it is about anti-social behaviour! Read 'Antisocial Behaviour in Online Discussion Communities' by Cheng et al. (2015) which describes this behaviour.

Stage 5: analysis options

Within social media data, whilst there are different techniques for data analysis including thematic, sentiment and brand analysis, these techniques are derived from content analysis and can be used for quantitative and qualitative analysis, as well as mixed methods. For more on content analysis we have found two useful texts: *Content Analysis: An Introduction to Its Methodology* by Klaus Krippendorff and *The Content Analysis Guidebook* by Kimberly A Neuendorf.

One of the advantages of market sensing via social media is that the content is usually limited in terms of the number of characters. Twitter posts are required to have fewer than 140 characters (including punctuation and spaces) and posts on Facebook are usually short, although the limit is around 60,000 characters.

Themes identify the essence of a piece of content and enable researchers to understand ideas and concepts related to the research question. Thematic analysis has been well defined by Braun and Clarke (2006) in their paper which proposes clear guidelines for undertaking this method. There are two decisions to be taken before the thematic analysis starts:

- is the work at a semantic level, where the themes are explicitly identified in the data? or
- is the work at a latent level which identifies the 'underlying ideas' (Braun and Clarke, 2006: 84)?

Regardless of whether the analysis is semantic or latent, the best process for undertaking thematic analysis that we have found is that proposed by Braun and Clarke (2006) which follows six steps: (1) familiarising yourself with your data; (2) generating initial codes; (3) searching for themes; (4) reviewing themes; (5) defining and naming themes; (6) producing the report.

1. Familiarising yourself with your data

   This is about ensuring you understand what your data is. If you have followed this process so far, you will already be familiar with your data, be it brand names or specific hashtags used in a social media network between specific dates. Figure 7.9 shows an example of the use of Twitter advanced search, seeking tweets based on the hashtag coffee (#coffee).

2. Generating initial codes

   When you are familiar with your data, it is time to generate the initial codes. Depending on your objectives, you might start to code at the top level, perhaps based on brand name, product or sentiment.

FIGURE 7.9   Example of Twitter advanced search seeking tweets based on the hashtag coffee (#coffee)

3. Searching for themes

   This phase only starts when all data has been initially coded and a long list emerges. The aim is to reduce the long list of codes and start to apply themes. Braun and Clarke suggest different approaches from the search for themes, including using mind maps and other visual tools, to bring the themes to the fore.

4. Reviewing themes

   Reviewing themes comprises reducing the themes and may involve merging. At this stage additional researchers may be involved to check the codes, test the validity level using an agreed mechanism to check intercoder reliability and to ensure the research can be replicated.

5. Defining and naming themes

   This stage seems repetitive of the previous stage as it involves further refining and defining themes. Braun and Clarke suggest (2006: 92):

   > For each individual theme, you need to conduct and write a detailed analysis. As well as identifying the 'story' that each theme tells, it is important to consider how it fits into the broader overall 'story' that you are telling about your data, in relation to the research question or questions, to ensure there is not too much overlap between themes.

6. Producing the report

   The last phase is also about presenting the data, which we consider after this section.

Stage 6: presenting your data

The style of data presentation may become obvious as the thematic analysis evolves. Thematic analysis can involve using visual tools and for the definitions of social media and social media networks, the software being used (NVivo 10) provided several visual options including a tree graph, as shown here.

The tree graph succinctly compares the sub-themes (nodes) within each theme and highlights the degree of use (the larger the box, the more used the term).

The same data can also be displayed as a horizontal dendrogram which shows the cluster analysis.

Conclusion

Using social media for market sensing is a new domain. Tools, technology and platforms are evolving, facilitating the process and making the data collection process easier for researchers. Whilst this approach could be considered as largely positivistic, seeking to prove evidence of positive or negative content, this depends upon the approach taken to data mining. A machine-led approach warrants such an approach as it is founded on the selection of specific words and phrases, without room for an interpretive approach.

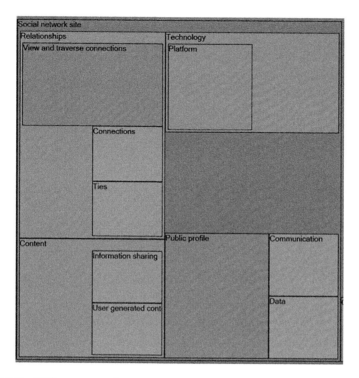

FIGURE 7.10 NVivo tree graph

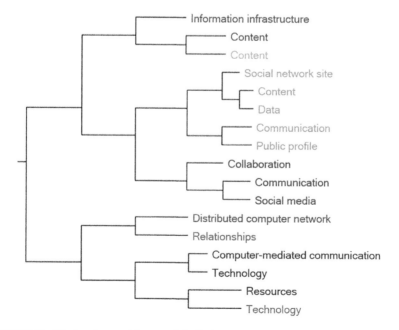

FIGURE 7.11 Nodes clustered by word similarity

However, it is possible that the researcher using social media may choose instead to follow a more interpretive philosophy (as we discussed in the Theory Box at the start of this chapter). Studies involving manual mining may be better suited to the interpretive philosophy.

One major consideration with all market sensing via social media is the need for rigour in collecting the data. With 6,000 tweets a second, if the original data is not prudently collected, it may not be possible to reacquire the same information at a later time.

Social media affords both a rich source of material and unparalleled access to behavioural data. Whilst there have been many discussions about users sharing too much content and some users moving away from various networks, regardless of how the social media platforms evolve and potentially become more segmented, users will continue to share personal data across many networks, providing a prolific and continuing source of research material.

Summary

This chapter has demonstrated how data from social media can be extracted to reveal feelings, behaviour and opinions of customers, in a way which was not previously possible.

This type of research may help marketers in areas of:

- new product development: providing insights into customers' needs and preferences;
- customer services: enabling organisations to better manage customers' opinion giving and opinion passing, and to ensure that major issues are addressed sooner rather than later;
- business development: sharing insights into opportunities for areas of business development;
- brand management: enabling marketers to understand and gather customers' perceptions of brand offers and brand values.

Exercise

This is a classroom exercise which requires students to have access to computers or laptops (or perhaps in a computer lab). It will provide students with an understanding of the data available online and the issues that arise.

This works especially well where students have their own Twitter accounts and can see how their own tweets feature in the results.

The tutor should ascribe a hashtag, for example #coffee or #technology or #travel. The aim is to select a hashtag which is relatively neutral (avoiding politics and religion). This can also form the start of the session where suggested hashtags are proposed by the students.

Once the hashtag has been agreed, those with Twitter accounts should compose a tweet using the hashtag.

Working individually, students should select a method to download Twitter data. This can be achieved using the tools mentioned in stages 2 and 3.

It is likely that this data will need to be exported to or opened in Excel in order to better see and to possibly group the results.

Once the data is downloaded, the students should:

- Identify the type and volume of data – what is included and what is excluded?
- If different data collection tools were used, how did the results vary? Did the students find their own hashtag-based tweets in the results?
- Discuss in pairs how this data could be used.

A group discussion can take place at the end of the session to explore the uses, benefits and challenges of using social media for market sensing.

Bibliography

Abrantes, J. L., Seabra, C., Lages, C. R. and Jayawardhena, C. (2013) 'Drivers of In-Group and Out-of-Group Electronic Word-of-Mouth (eWOM)', *European Journal of Marketing* 47, no. 7, pp. 1067–88. doi: 10.1108/03090561311324219.

Adjei, M. T., Noble, S. M. and Noble, C. H. (2009). 'The Influence of C2C Communications in Online Brand Communities on Customer Purchase Behavior', *Journal of the Academy of Marketing Science* 38, no. 5, pp. 634–53. doi: 10.1007/s11747-009-0178-5.

Amblee, N. and Bui, T. (2011). 'Harnessing the Influence of Social Proof in Online Shopping: The Effect of Electronic Word of Mouth on Sales of Digital Microproducts', *International Journal of Electronic Commerce* 16, no. 2, pp. 91–114. doi: 10.2753/JEC1086-4415160205.

Arguello, J. and Shaffer, K. (2015). 'Predicting Speech Acts in MOOC Forum Posts', in *Ninth International AAAI Conference on Web and Social Media*. Oxford, UK. Available at: http://www.aaai.org/ocs/index.php/ICWSM/ICWSM15/paper/view/10526.

Berthon, P., Lane, N., Pitt, L. and Watson, R. T. (1998). 'The World Wide Web as an Industrial Marketing Communication Tool: Models for the Identification and Assessment of Opportunities', *Journal of Marketing Management* 14, no. 70, pp. 691–704. doi: 10.1362/026725798784867635.

boyd, D. M. and Ellison, N. B. (2007). 'Social Network Sites: Definition, History, and Scholarship', *Journal of Computer-Mediated Communication* 13, no. 10, pp. 210–30. Available at: http://onlinelibrary.wiley.com/doi/10.1111/j.1083-6101.2007.00393.x/full/ (accessed 23 July 2014).

Braun, V. and Clarke, V. (2006). 'Using Thematic Analysis in Psychology', *Qualitative Research in Psychology* 3 (July 2015), pp. 77–101. doi: 10.1191/1478088706qp063oa.

British Airways (2014). Twitter, Twitter page. Available at: https://twitter.com/British_Airways.

Brunner, C. B. and Ullrich, S. (2014). 'How to Deal with a Negative Online Consumer Review: Can Different Response Scenarios from Various Sources Rebuild Consumers' Product Purchase Intentions?', in *47th Academy of Marketing Conference*. Bournemouth, 7–10 July 2014. Academy of Marketing.

Bruns, A. and Stieglitz, S. (2013). 'Towards More Systematic Twitter Analysis: Metrics for Tweeting Activities', *International Journal of Social Research Methodology* 16, no. 2, pp. 91–108. doi: 10.1080/13645579.2012.756095.

Buttle, F. A. (1998). 'Word of Mouth: Understanding and Managing Referral Marketing', *Journal of Strategic Marketing* 6, no. 3, pp. 241–54. doi: 10.1080/096525498346658.

Canhoto, A. I. and Clark, M. (2013). 'Customer Service 140 Characters at a Time: The Users' Perspective', *Journal of Marketing Management* 29, no. 5–6, pp. 522–44. doi: 10.1080/0267257X.2013.777355.

Ceron, A. (2015). 'Internet, News, and Political Trust: The Difference Between Social Media and Online Media Outlets', *Journal of Computer-Mediated Communication*, p. n/a–n/a. doi: 10.1111/jcc4.12129.

Cha, M., Haddai, H., Benevenuto, F. and Gummadi, K. P. (2010). 'Measuring User Influence in Twitter: The Million Follower Fallacy', in *International AAAI Conference on Weblogs and Social Media*. Association for the Advancement of Artificial Intelligence (AAAI), pp. 10–17. doi: 10.1.1.167.192.

Chamlertwat, W. and Bhattarakosol, P. (2012). 'Discovering Consumer Insight from Twitter via Sentiment Analysis'. *Journal of Universal Computer Science* 18, no. 8, pp. 973–92. Available at: http://jucs.org/jucs_18_8/discovering_consumer_insight_from/jucs_18_08_0973_0992_chamlertwat.pdf (accessed 13 September 2015).

Chen, J., Haber, E., Kang, R., Hsieh, G. and Mahmud, J. (2015). 'Making Use of Derived Personality: The Case of Social Media Ad Targeting', in *Proceedings of the Ninth International AAAI Conference on Web and Social Media*. Association for the Advancement of Artificial Intelligence (AAAI), pp. 51–60.

Cheng, J., Danescu-Niculescu-Mizil, C. and Leskovec, J. (2015). 'Antisocial Behavior in Online Discussion Communities', in *International AAAI Conference on Web and Social Media, Ninth International AAAI Conference on Web and Social Media*. Oxford, UK, pp. 61–70.

Cheong, M. C.-Y. (2013). *Inferring Social Behavior and Interaction on Twitter by Combining Metadata about Users and Messages*. Monash University. Available at: http://arrow.monash.edu.au/vital/access/manager/Repository/monash:120048.

Cheong, M. and Ray, S. (2011). 'A Literature Review of Recent Microblogging Developments', Victoria, Australia: Clayton School of Information Technology. Available at: http://www.csse.monash.edu.au/publications/2011/tr-2011-263-full.pdf.

Chu, S.-C. and Kim, Y. (2011). 'Determinants of Consumer Engagement in Electronic Word-of-Mouth (eWoM) in Social Networking Sites'. *International Journal of Advertising* 30, no. 1, p. 47. doi: 10.2501/IJA-30-1-047-075.

Cotelo, J. M., Cruz, F. L., Troyano, J. A. and Ortega, F. J. (2015). 'A Modular Approach for Lexical Normalization applied to Spanish Tweets'. *Expert Systems with Applications*. Elsevier Ltd, 42, no. 10, pp. 4743–54. doi: 10.1016/j.eswa.2015.02.003.

Dichter, E. (1966). 'How Word-of-Mouth Advertising Works'. *Harvard Business Review* (Nov–Dec), pp. 147–66.

Duggan, M., Ellison, N. B., Lampe, C., Lenhart, A. and Madden, M. (2015). 'Social Media Update 2014'. Available at: http://www.pewinternet.org/files/2015/01/PI_SocialMediaUpdate20144.pdf.

Ellison, N. B. and boyd, D. M. (2013). 'Sociality through Social Network Sites', in W. H. Dutton (ed.), *The Oxford Handbook of Internet Studies*. Pre-press. Oxford: Oxford University Press, pp. 151–72. doi: 10.1093/oxfordhb/9780199589074.001.0001.

Fang, E., Palmatier, R. W. and Evans, K. R. (2008). 'Influence of Customer Participation on Creating and Sharing of New Product Value'. *Journal of the Academy of Marketing Science* 36, no. 3, pp. 322–36. doi: 10.1007/s11747-007-0082-9.

Gallaugher, J. and Ransbotham, S. (2010). 'Social Media and Customer Dialog Management at Starbucks'. *MIS Quarterly Executive* 9, no. 4, pp. 197–212. Available at: http://misqe.org/ojs2/index.php/misqe/article/view/301 (accessed 25 October 2014).

Granovetter, M. S. (1973). 'The Strength of Weak Ties', *American Journal of Sociology* 78, no. 6, pp. 1360–80. doi: 10.1037/a0018761.

Groeger, L. and Buttle, F. (2014). 'Word-of-Mouth Marketing Influence on Offline and Online Communications: Evidence from Case Study Research'. *Journal of Marketing Communications* 20, no. 1–2, pp. 21–41. doi: 10.1080/13527266.2013.797736.

Hennig-Thurau, T., Gwinner, K. P., Walsh, G. and Gremler, D. D. (2004). 'Electronic Word-of-Mouth via Consumer-Opinion Platforms: What Motivates Consumers to Articulate Themselves on the Internet?'. *Journal of Interactive Marketing* 18, no. 1, pp. 38–52. doi: 10.1002/dir.10073.

Hong, L., Convertino, G. and Chi, E. H. (2011). 'Language Matters in Twitter : A Large Scale Study Characterizing the Top Languages in Twitter Characterizing Differences across Languages Including URLs and Hashtags', in *Proceedings of the Fifth International AAAI Conference on Weblogs and Social Media*, pp. 518–21.

Huang, Q. and Xu, C. (2014). 'A Data-Driven Framework for Archiving and Exploring Social Media Data'. *Annals of GIS* 20, no. 4, pp. 265–77. doi: 10.1080/19475683.2014.942697.

Kane, G., Labianca, G. and Borgatti, S. P. (2014). 'What's Different about Social Media Networks? A Framework and Research Agenda', *MIS Quarterly* 38, no. 1, pp. 275–304. Available at: http://papers.ssrn.com/sol3/Delivery.cfm?abstractid=2239249 (accessed 12 October 2014).

Kaplan, A. M. and Haenlein, M. (2010). 'Users of the World, Unite! The Challenges and Opportunities of Social Media'. *Business Horizons* 53, no. 1, pp. 59–68. doi: 10.1016/j.bushor.2009.09.003.

Kietzmann, J. H., Silvestre, B. S., McCarthy, I. P. and Pitt, L. F. (2012). 'Special Issue Paper Unpacking the Social Media Phenomenon: Towards a Research Agenda'. *Journal of Public Affairs* 12, no. 2, pp. 109–19. doi: 10.1002/pa.

King, R. A., Racherla, P. and Bush, V. D. (2014). 'What We Know and Don't Know About Online Word-of-Mouth: A Review and Synthesis of the Literature'. *Journal of Interactive Marketing* 28, no. 3, pp. 167–83. Elsevier B.V. doi: 10.1016/j.intmar.2014.02.001.

Kozinets, R. V, de Valck, K., Wojnicki, A. C. and Wilner, S. J. S. (2010). 'Networked Narratives: Understanding Word-of-Mouth'. *Journal of Marketing* 74 (March), pp. 71–89.

Kozinets, R. V. (2002). 'The Field behind the Screen: Using Netnography for Marketing Research in Online Communities'. *Journal of Marketing Research* 39, no. 1, pp. 61–72. Available at: http://journals.ama.org/doi/abs/10.1509/jmkr.39.1.61.18935 (accessed 2 August 2014).

Krippendorff, K. (2004). *Content Analysis: An Introduction to Its Methodology*. Thousand Oaks, CA: Sage.

Laskey, N. and Wilson, A. M. (2003). 'Internet Based Marketing Research: A Serious Alternative to Traditional Research Methods?'. *Marketing Intelligence and Planning* 21, no. 2, pp. 79–84. doi: 10.1108/02634500310465380.

Leeflang, P. (2011). 'Paving the Way for "Distinguished Marketing"'. *International Journal of Research in Marketing* 28, no. 2, pp. 76–88. doi: 10.1016/j.ijresmar.2011.02.004.

Lima, A. C. E. S., de Castro, L. N. and Corchado, J. M. (2015). 'A Polarity Analysis Framework for Twitter Messages'. *Applied Mathematics and Computation* 270, pp. 756–67. Elsevier Ltd. doi: 10.1016/j.amc.2015.08.059.

Maity, S. K., Sarup, J., Sahni, S. and Mukherjee, A. (2015). 'Analysis and Prediction of Question Topic Popularity in Community Q & A Sites: A Case Study of Quora', in *Proceedings of the Ninth International AAAI Conference on Web and Social Media*, pp. 238–47.

Mamic, L. I. and Almaraz, I. A. (2014). 'How the Larger Corporations Engage with Stakeholders through Twitter'. *International Journal of Market Research* 55, no. 6, pp. 851–72. doi: 10.2501/IJMR-2013-070.

Mangold, W. G. and Faulds, D. J. (2009). 'Social Media: The New Hybrid Element of the Promotion Mix'. *Business Horizons* 52, no. 4, pp. 357–65. doi: 10.1016/j. bushor.2009.03.002.

Mangold, W. G. and Smith, K. T. (2012). 'Selling to Millennials with Online Reviews'. *Business Horizons* 55, no. 2, pp. 141–53. Kelley School of Business, Indiana University. doi: 10.1016/j.bushor.2011.11.001.

Marwick, A. (2005) 'I'm More Than Just a Friendster Profile: Identity, Authenticity, and Power in Social Networking Services'. Association for Internet Researchers 6.0, pp. 1–26. Available at: http://ssrn.com/abstract=1884356.

de Matos, C. A. and Rossi, C. A. V. (2008). 'Word-of-Mouth Communications in Marketing: A Meta-Analytic Review of the Antecedents and Moderators'. *Journal of the Academy of Marketing Science* 36, no. 4, pp. 578–96. doi: 10.1007/s11747-008-0121-1.

Morstatter, F., Pfeffer, J., Liu, H. and Carley, K. (2013). 'Is the Sample Good Enough? Comparing Data from Twitter's Streaming API with Twitter's Firehose'. *Proceedings of ICWSM*, pp. 400–8. doi: 10.1007/978-3-319-05579-4_10.

Muñiz, Jr., A. M. and Schau, H. J. (2007). 'Vigilante Marketing and Consumer-Created Communications'. *Journal of Advertising* 36, no. 3, pp. 35–50. doi: 10.2753/JOA0091-3367360303.

Neuendorf, K. A. (2002). *The Content Analysis Guidebook*. Thousand Oaks, CA: Sage.

O'Reilly, T. (2005). What Is Web 2.0? Design Patterns and Business Models for the Next Generation of Software, O'Reilly Blog. Available at: http://oreilly.com/web2/archive/what-is-web-20.html (accessed 18 October 2014).

Okazaki, S., Diaz-Martin, A. M., Rozano, M. and Menendez-Benito, H. (2014). 'How to Mine Brand Tweets Procedural Guidelines and Pretest'. *International Journal of Market Research* 56, no. 4, pp. 467–89.

Pew Research Center (2013). 'How We Analyzed Twitter Social Media Networks with NodeXL'.

Prabowo, R. and Thelwall, M. (2009). 'Sentiment Analysis: A Combined Approach'. *Journal of Informetrics* 3, no. 2, pp. 143–57. doi: 10.1016/j.joi.2009.01.003.

Rowley, J. (2004). 'Just Another Channel? Marketing Communications in e-Business'. *Marketing Intelligence and Planning* 22, no. 1, pp. 24–41. Available at: http://www.emerald insight.com/journals.htm?articleid=854660&show=abstract (accessed 18 October 2014).

Schweidel, D. A. and Moe, W. W. (2014). 'Listening In on Social Media: A Joint Model of Sentiment and Venue Format Choice'. *Journal of Marketing Research* 51 (August), pp. 387–402. doi: 10.1509/jmr.12.0424.

Spiliotopoulos, T. and Oakley, I. (2014). 'Predicting Tie Strength with the Facebook API', in *Proceedings of the 18th Panhellenic Conference on Informatics*. New York, pp. 1–5.

Sriram, B., Fuhry, D., Demir, E., Ferhatosmanoglu, H. and Demirbas, M. (2010). 'Short Text Classification in Twitter to Improve Information Filtering', in *Proceeding of the 33rd International ACM SIGIR Conference on Research and Development in Information Retrieval – SIGIR '10*, p. 841. doi: 10.1145/1835449.1835643.

Stephen, A. T. and Toubia, O. (2010). 'Deriving Value from Social Commerce Networks', *Journal of Marketing Research* 47 (April), pp. 215–28. Available at: http://journals.ama. org/doi/abs/10.1509/jmkr.47.2.215 (accessed 21 April 2014).

Surowiecki, J. (2004). *The Wisdom of Crowds, How Collective Wisdom Shapes Business Economies, Societies and Nations*. New York: Anchor. doi: 10.3174/ajnr.A3417.

Walsh, J. and Godfrey, S. (2000). 'The Internet: A New Era in Customer Service'. *European Management Journal* 18, no. 1, pp. 85–92. doi: 10.1016/S0263-2373(99)00071-7.

Watne, T. A., Cheong, M. and Turner, W. (2014). '#Brand or @User ? How Australian "Mass Brewers" and "Craft Brewers" Communicate with Consumers through Twitter', in *47th Academy of Marketing Conference*. Bournemouth, 7–10 July 2014. Academy of Marketing.

Weinberg, B. D. and Pehlivan, E. (2011). 'Social Spending: Managing the Social Media Mix'. *Business Horizons* 54, no. 3, pp. 275–82. Kelley School of Business, Indiana University. doi: 10.1016/j.bushor.2011.01.008.

Williams, M. and Buttle, F. (2014). 'Managing Negative Word-of-Mouth: An Exploratory Study'. *Journal of Marketing Management* (July), pp. 1–25. doi: 10.1080/0267257X.2014. 933864.

8

USING NARRATIVE AND STORYTELLING IN RESEARCH

Alison Lawson

Purpose

The purpose of this chapter is to introduce the idea of using narrative and storytelling, both in collecting research data and in analysing that data.

Context

Narrative and storytelling are qualitative approaches that seek to examine the depth of people's experiences through allowing them to tell their own stories in their own words. The approach also considers people's stories in the context of the broader narrative of contextual factors that surround the story and its actors. There are many ways of encouraging research participants to tell their stories – this chapter considers appreciative inquiry, critical incident technique and question laddering. The chapter contains examples to help explain and demonstrate how to gather and analyse the data gathered using narrative and storytelling techniques.

Learning outcomes

After reading this chapter, you will:

- be confident to try out the techniques in your own research;
- understand the importance of the broader narrative that frames the stories that people tell of their own experiences and the impact that external and internal factors will have on those people;
- understand how introducing a structure to narrative and storytelling can be beneficial while also having possible implications for limiting understanding of the broader context;

- have an insight into the potential ethical issues raised by using narrative approaches;
- know how to judge the quality of qualitative research using measures appropriate to the type of data collected.

THEORY BOX

Narrative inquiry and the use of storytelling is an interpretivist and subjective ontological approach to research in which the researcher believes society and its actors are not discrete, observable entities that are completely unaffected by each other or by the researcher. All actions and words are open to interpretation. The approach is qualitative, using interviewing methods that elicit stories and build narrative. Analysis may involve structuring the narrative in order to find patterns or themes, thematic analysis based on research questions and/or keyword or critical discourse analysis of the text. The analysis takes into account not only the words used in the participants' responses, but the broader narrative context in which the data collection takes place and in which the original stories took place. The results may be presented in a structured format and may be written up using elements of the narrative to illustrate themes and key points. It may also be possible to write and present the results of narrative inquiry as a narrative account.

Introduction, background and context

Are you sitting comfortably? Then I'll begin.

Our lives are made of stories – some of them big, some small, some complex and convoluted, some simple. Some we may keep to ourselves and some we share with others, usually with a purpose – to inform, entertain, unload or confess.

Stories are not objective truth (the question of whether there is ever such a thing as objective truth is beyond the scope of this chapter!). If five people share an experience and tell their own story about it later, you will hear five different versions of the story. Which one is true? The answer is that each one is true for the person telling it. Our understanding and interpretation of experiences and our ways of communicating about them are particular, personal and true to each individual.

Contextual and personal factors impact on the way we experience events and on the way we tell others about them. All experiences are contextual and individual. Therefore, our accounts of those experiences will differ. They may still have the same facts beneath the surface, but coloured by context, experience and emotion. Consider, for example, individuals' accounts of a wedding or a funeral. How much will the accounts be affected by the context? How much will individuals' experiences and emotions affect not only what they choose to include in the account, but also the way in which they give their account?

Consumer behaviour theory tells us that our thoughts, words and actions are a product of many internal and external factors, making segmentation and broad generalisations about 'people' sometimes very difficult. Some advocate a much more tailored and personal approach to marketing that eschews segmentation. It is through our own experiences and a myriad influences that we construct our sense of self – an idea in our own mind of who we are. Figure 8.1 shows some of the factors that influence who we feel we are.

It is precisely because of the differences between people and of the difficulties of generalisation that it is important to hear and value individuals' stories. The complex nature of business and the daily interaction of all those who work in it and their many, varied customers paints a multi-faceted picture. Numbers alone cannot hope to describe and explain the processes, actions and behaviours involved. In attempting to understand the way people think and feel and act, numbers are not able to give the depth of information needed to inform marketing strategy and tactics. So much of the way we behave as customers is hidden even from ourselves that we need research methods that are able to delve deeper in order to uncover feelings, opinions, attitudes, beliefs and thoughts that may not be admitted through more superficial quantitative methods.

Emotions can be the root drivers of consumer behaviour. Consumers' subjective experience of goods and services can inform their impressions of brands and inform future purchasing and referral decisions. Yet many research methods fail to reach the emotions at the bottom of consumers' experience. It may be more expensive, more time-consuming and more difficult to do but qualitative research can achieve vitally useful consumer insights.

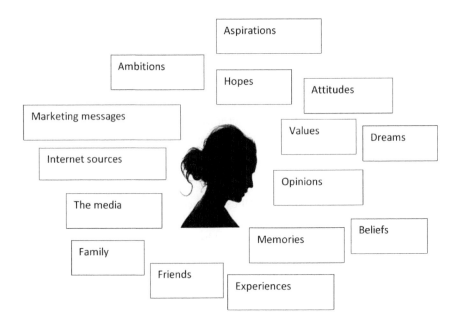

FIGURE 8.1 Who are you? Some of the factors that help to build your sense of self

What is a narrative approach?

Narrative inquiry began, perhaps unsurprisingly, in the discipline of sociology in the 1920s and 1930s, but was superseded by quantitative methods. The method became popular again from the 1960s onwards, perhaps buoyed by movements of freedom of speech and expression that valued how people think and feel. Researchers in a variety of social and human sciences recognised the value in examining language, speech and oral narratives (Butler-Kisber, 2010). In Butler-Kisber's words,

> [it is] no longer . . . possible to think of research as a process that takes place in a controlled, objective and decontextualized space existing outside of time where facts can be examined, hypotheses tested and principles/theories generated as typically is done in the physical sciences' (p. 64).

Chase's (2005) description of the main approaches to narrative inquiry includes sociological, psychological, anthropological and autoethnographic approaches, but does not address the use of narrative in marketing and business research. This may be because the method was not popular in business research at the time of Chase's writing. It is clear, however, that psychological and sociological approaches are likely to have much in common with consumer behaviour research, in which we attempt to understand consumers in as much detail and depth as possible. Use of a narrative approach is now more common in qualitative marketing research.

Narratives may be spoken, written or visual. All tell of a personal experience and give insights in people's own words. This chapter deals with spoken narrative, although the ideas could be applied to written or visual methods too.

The stories may be personal experiences, autobiographical, dreams and wishes, anecdotes, reflection, historical, future gazing, exposing how people think and feel about the world around them.

The method requires an open format of questioning allowing participants to tell their stories. There may be no questions at all – the prompts may instead instruct/allow participants to indulge in storytelling.

- *Tell me* about a time when . . .
- *Describe for me* the first time you . . .
- *Explain* how you felt when . . .
- *Give* an example of . . .

These forms are very open and participants may not be used to this or be expecting this. It would therefore be helpful to tell participants before you start that you want them to tell stories, to go into as much detail as possible and not to worry if it does not seem relevant or interesting.

Let us go back to the example mentioned in the introduction to this chapter and think about the different stories that could be told about a wedding. Box 8.1 shows an activity based around a real experience of mine, with changes to names to protect identity.

Box 8.1 Happy ever after?

The wedding is over and all the guests are celebrating at the wedding reception – a big party with food, drink, music and dancing. Everyone is having a wonderful time. But the father of the groom has a heart attack and is taken to hospital.

- Imagine you are the bride. What factors will have an impact on your account of the event?
- Imagine you are a guest at the wedding, the groom's mother or the hotel manager.
- Imagine how different the stories will be; how emotional some will be; how some may have more detail than others; some may not know how the story ends.

You may like to work with some friends to write down your imagined story based on the simple facts given above, with each of you writing from the perspective of a different person at the wedding. Use as much detail as you can. Think first about your chosen character. What might they have felt? How might they have reacted? Compare your stories afterwards and discuss the differences and similarities.

No matter what the contents of a narrative, it will have a beginning, middle and (probably) an end. Even if participants do not know how the overall story ends, they will say how it ends for them. Labov and Waletsky (1997) suggest a structure that may be used to present stories in a methodical way following the typical way a story unfolds, including an abstract, orientation, complicating actions, evaluation, resolution and coda.

Using the wedding story from Box 8.1, Box 8.2 shows how my own story as a guest at the wedding can be broken down using Labov and Waletsky's structure.

Box 8.2 Example structured narrative

Tell me about a wedding you've been to that was particularly memorable.

Abstract or summary of the story

It was Diana's wedding and her father-in-law had a heart attack.

Orientation (time, place, situation, participants)

We'd all had a great day and were at the hotel for the reception. It was about 8pm and the place was packed. I was sitting talking to friends. I remember we were really hot because we'd been dancing.

Complicating actions (sequence)

Suddenly, the music stopped and the best man was on the stage and he said Steve's Dad had been taken to hospital with a heart attack.

Evaluation (significance and meaning of action, attitude of the narrator)

It was terrible; such a shock. The room went silent. I felt so guilty that I was there having a good time while Diana and her family must have been feeling so awful. I hadn't even noticed that they weren't at the reception. I didn't know what to do and felt pretty helpless.

Resolution (what finally happened)

He said we should carry on with the reception but everyone was so subdued and the band looked really awkward. A few people left straightaway. My family is pretty close to Diana's so we stayed until her sister appeared so we could wish them our best and say goodbye properly. She said Steve's Dad was going to be OK and was in hospital.

Coda (return to the present)

So we went home and felt very sad, but glad that it looked like Steve's Dad would be OK. What a terrible thing to happen on your wedding day.

Introducing a structure to the narrative can help with comparison of one person's story with another's and can help structure the approach to analysis, which we shall come to later in the chapter. This structured approach is not the only way to order or analyse narrative, but may be helpful.

Building stories

Narrative enquiry can also involve constructing a story from speech and documentary evidence rather than encouraging participants to tell stories (Butler-Kisber, 2010).

Some narrative approaches also involve living alongside participants to experience their stories with them – here there are clear links with ethnography.

Wider narrative

Events described in research interviews do not occur in isolation. They are part of a broader narrative (Ezzy, 2002) that helps to explain the individual's experience and their account of that experience. The broader context includes not only the immediate influences on the participant and her/his life experience and attitudes, etc., but also broad societal issues that shape our experience and provide a context for the narrative that is inevitably situated at a particular time in a particular place. This broader interpretation of 'narrative' has links to cultural studies (Ezzy, 2002). Figure 8.2 shows contextual influences on participants that help to shape their stories.

Role of the researcher

In an interview situation in which the participant is encouraged to tell stories and give depth and detail, it becomes difficult for the researcher to remain entirely divorced from the process of storytelling. For example, the researcher may use a conversational approach to help participants to share their stories. This goes further than the questions-and-prompts approach to interviewing in which the researcher attempts to remain separate from the participant, and involves the researcher in a way that could invite bias. As a result of this, the role of the researcher and her/his approach to interviewing must be made clear both to participants and to those who read or engage with the results of the research.

Analysing results of narrative research methods

As interviews progress and participants seem to take stories off in different directions and each interview seems completely different from the last, the researcher

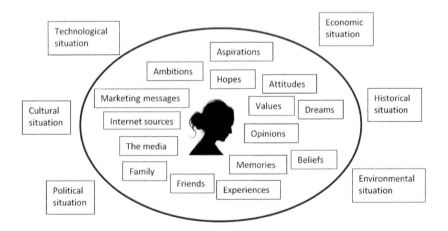

FIGURE 8.2 Contextual factors that affect participants' stories

may worry about how all this data will ever submit to analysis. For those more used to concrete statistical data and worrying about how to use storytelling and narrative, Bell (2014) gives a personal view in her very readable book for first-time researchers.

In selecting your analytical approach you may wish to use an established method that has been used in previous research work (which would improve validity and transparency of process) or you may like to devise your own approach. Some researchers focus on the content of the story, common themes, key issues raised, key words and phrases used, some on the nature or type of story, some on the way it is told. Whichever analysis method you decide to use, set it down clearly and apply it consistently. You must be able to justify your chosen approach.

One problem of analysing narrative is obtaining an objective view. It is tempting for the researcher to interpret narrative in ways that conform to previously held views or opinions or in ways that prove or disprove hypotheses. There are several ways to alleviate this problem. First, the researcher may use a thorough, structured approach to the analysis with a coding frame or headings to break down narrative into its constituent parts. A coding frame may use ideas, themes, keywords and issues arising from the literature on the subject in question or may use ideas, themes, keywords and issues that arise from the primary data. Headings imposing a structure may be based on similar ideas or may be based on the structure of the narrative itself. Another way to lessen the possibility of subjectivity in analysis is to ask for an independent view on the analytical approach. For example, a research supervisor, tutor, fellow researcher or student could be asked to look at an extract of narrative and to suggest keywords, phrases, ideas and themes that they feel arise from that extract. These could then be compared with the researcher's own interpretation. Where there is broad agreement the analysis is likely to be objective (unless, of course, the third party has similar pre-conceptions and biases to those of the researcher). Where there is disagreement some further investigation of objectivity is required through discussion and close scrutiny of the narrative and of the researcher's own approach and subjective views. One should also be mindful that concentrating on individual words and phrases does not remove them from the context of the overall narrative. An understanding of the overall narrative is needed in order to interpret those words and phrases (Punch, 2005).

In using key words and phrases in the data analysis there are clear links with critical discourse analysis (see Chapter 5), in which the researcher examines the specific words and turns of phrase used by participants as well as those that have specifically not been used and the context in which they have been used. For example, in his campaign for the US Presidential candidacy in 2015, Jeb Bush used the logo 'Jeb!'. Critical discourse analysis (CDA) would note that Jeb has used his well-known nickname, based on his initials JEB, and has deliberately not used his surname, in order to distance himself from the Bush political dynasty and stand for his own views. CDA might also comment on the exclamation mark, perhaps used to inject some excitement and enthusiasm into the campaign (Zurcher, 2015).

If using thematic analysis, predetermined themes based on the literature review could be used in analysis, as the narrative will have resulted from open questions based round those themes. When using themes that arise from the narrative itself it may take longer for themes to emerge and sometimes there may be no theme at all – the stories could instead give many individual examples that build to make one overall point about how people experience a particular product, service, brand, organisation, etc.

Hawkins and Saleem (2012) propose three key components that should be noted when analysing narrative data: the context of the storytelling, the role of personal (broader) narratives and the time taken to think about and tell the story. Gaps and pauses in storytelling can be significant.

The rest of this chapter will consider three methods for seeking narratives – use of critical incident technique, laddering and appreciative inquiry to encourage people to tell stories and share feelings, seeking depth, detail, richness, real voices and emotions.

Taking you through the process stage by stage

Traditional interview techniques seeking specific answers to specific questions are not covered in this chapter. Instead, several methods for seeking deeper insights using narrative will be used – appreciative inquiry, critical incident technique and laddering.

Summary of methods

Appreciative inquiry – this allows participants to tell their stories in a positive rather than a problem-based approach to research. The interview process has four stages: (1) discovering what works; (2) dreaming about what could or might work in the future; (3) designing ideas and plans for the future; and (4) delivering the plan that shows what is needed to realise the ideas put forward.

Critical incident technique – this approach to interviewing allows participants to tell a structured story. The interview uses specific questions to examine a particular service encounter or product experience in depth.

Laddering – this approach to interviewing allows the researcher to dig deeper than more superficial interview approaches, to reach the deeper emotions and values associated with products and services.

Appreciative inquiry

Much business and marketing research uses a problem-solving approach. An issue, problem or challenge has been identified and the research sets out to discover more and solve the issue and meet the challenge. This deficit model, which starts from the point of view that 'XYZ is not working in the ABC department', automatically identifies workers or processes in that department as being at fault. The potential disadvantage of the deficit model is that those involved in the project may feel immediately as if they are under the microscope and as if the researcher is looking for someone to blame for the issue or problem under study, which may then affect interviewees' responses. Appreciative inquiry (AI) takes the opposite approach – the method starts the research not from the point of problem solving but from a continuous improvement perspective – what's going well and how can we emulate that elsewhere and use it to improve things? AI celebrates good performance rather than focusing on poor performance and can help motivate people to engage in the research process.

AI was developed by Cooperrider and Srivastva (1987) who felt that the problem-based approach limited the creation of new ideas and of new theory. They suggested that the use of a more positive approach would help to bring about organisational change. The approach consists of four stages (see Figure 8.3) that may be used in a cycle to bring about change.

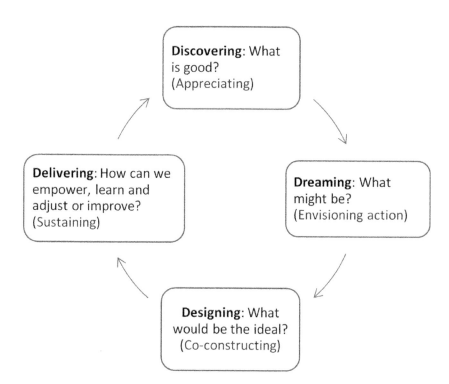

FIGURE 8.3   Cycle of appreciative inquiry

Source: Based on Shuayb et al. (2009)

The approach may be easily adopted and adapted (by using appreciative questions) for use in action research in marketing settings, focusing on what is good and how that may be amplified, emulated elsewhere and lead to improvement in service, products, communications, etc. The approach uses interviews or focus groups to uncover stories and examples of good practice. The important point is always to start with a question about what is working well or what is good right now. Box 8.3 shows a short example of AI in action.

Box 8.3 Appreciative inquiry in action

Mark was a postgraduate student who wanted to write his dissertation about the way the company he worked for selected international business partners. He felt that the process was haphazard and did not lead to sensible decision making. The company was a small, family-owned and family-run business in which everyone knew each other well. Mark felt uncomfortable researching the issue, as he did not want the owner-manager to feel that he was being criticised for poor decision making. I recommended the use of AI. Rather than using the deficit model ('there's something wrong with the way we select business partners'), Mark used AI to interview employees in the UK and at existing international partners about what worked well for them in the partnership experience. Using the AI approach meant that participants did not feel 'picked on' for doing something 'wrong'. Instead they were given the opportunity to talk about what worked well (discovering), what might work even better in the future (dreaming), what the ideal situation would be (designing) and how that could be achieved (delivering). Mark found that participants were very willing to talk. As a result of the research, Mark recommended a strategy for selecting partners based on criteria developed from knowledge of how successful partnerships worked. The results of Mark's research were well received by the owner-manager, who implemented the strategy.

Of course, when asked what is working well participants may also mention things that are not working well, and this information is also useful to the researcher. The point is that the participants give this information in the more positive atmosphere of celebrating success rather than concentrating on failure. Relaxing participants into a positive frame of mind is likely to allow them to tell more detailed stories and to express their feelings about products, services, processes and so on, in a way that would not be possible using other interviewing techniques.

Having read the example in Box 8.3, can you think of ways this approach could be used in your own organisation to make improvements to processes or services? Can you think of a way it can be applied to marketing research in these settings?

- research about service experience at a restaurant or hotel;
- research about integrated marketing communications in an organisation;
- research about the marketing planning process in an organisation.

The advantages of AI are that the process empowers the participants to tell positive stories and that the outcomes identify areas of good practice. For the full AI process to work, all levels of an organisation must be committed to making changes identified through the research – without this, identified improvements will not take place. A disadvantage may be, therefore, that the intended outcome of organisational improvement may not happen in all cases. (However, if using an appreciative approach to interviewing rather than the full AI process, organisational change may not be the intended outcome.) Participants must have a good understanding/experience of the issues at hand – without this the results will not be relevant. Finally, it should be noted that AI is not appropriate for all research topics, such as societal problems or issues where it would not be deemed appropriate to ask what is working well (Shuayb et al., 2009).

Critical incident technique (CIT)

This is a method of structuring participants' stories around a set of predefined questions. CIT is commonly used in research in services, e.g. in research about expectations and perceptions of hospitality and leisure services (see, for example, Bitner et al., 1994). It is particularly useful for studying the experiences of customers and frontline employees, allowing customers to describe significant events that led to satisfaction or dissatisfaction. CIT gathers stories in participants' own words and allows identification of management issues using real examples.

The questions used in a CIT interview are as follows:

1. Think of a time when, as a customer of [name of service] you had a particularly satisfying (or dissatisfying) experience.
2. When did the incident happen?
3. What specific circumstances led up to this situation?
4. What exactly did the employee or member of staff do?
5. What resulted that made you feel the interaction was satisfying (or dissatisfying)?
6. What could or should have been done differently?

Using this structure allows participants to tell their own stories within a structure that will help you to aggregate results about service delivery and service quality. Note that there are no questions about the participants' backgrounds and no questions that specifically address broader contextual issues. It is likely, however, that the broader narrative will become clear in the participants' responses. Box 8.4 gives an example of CIT in action.

Box 8.4 Example story using critical incident technique

1. *Can you think of a time when, as a customer of Costa Coffee, you had a par-*
    ticularly satisfying (or dissatisfying) experience?
    Yes – I remember one time when the coffee I bought tasted terrible and
    they replaced it with a new one.

2. *When did the incident happen?*
    A couple of weeks ago, when my husband and I were driving on the M1 –
    we stopped at a service station.

3. *What specific circumstances led up to this situation?*
    It was a long journey and we both needed a break, so we decided to stop
    for a coffee. We were pleased when it turned out there was a Costa at the
    next services, as we've always been very happy with their coffee. I was look-
    ing forward to my usual latte. So we bought our coffees and got back in
    the car and headed out onto the M1 again. I don't like very hot coffee so I
    had to wait a while for it to cool down before I started to drink it. I took a
    taste and thought it was a bit odd. I waited until it was a bit cooler and took
    another mouthful and it was just terrible. It tasted like the coffee beans had
    been burned. I tried to drink it, but I couldn't. I was really disappointed, as
    I'd been looking forward to that coffee. It sounds a bit silly, but when you've
    had a long day and you're on a long journey, these little things matter. So,
    anyway, we stopped at the next services with a Costa, which was about
    twenty miles down the M1, and I went in with my latte and explained the
    situation. They replaced the bad latte with a new one, which was fantastic.

4. *Exactly what did the employee or member of staff do?*
    Well, at first they looked a bit stunned. I'm not sure that what I did was
    normal! But they were very professional about it. They asked exactly what
    was wrong with the coffee and took a quick look at the receipt, but they
    made a decision very quickly just to give me a fresh one. They were very
    nice about it all and didn't make me feel stupid – unlike my husband, who
    had said I was a loony to expect them to replace the drink!

5. *What resulted that made you feel the interaction was satisfying (or dissatisfying)?*
    I got a brand new drink with no fuss – I felt I'd received excellent customer
    service and went back to the car with a big grin on my face.

6. *What could or should have been done differently?*
    Nothing – the Costa staff were great!

You can see from the story in Box 8.4 that the participant has been allowed to give
detail and depth. The questions have not narrowed her responses, but instead have
steered the story in a particular direction – one that will help the service company
improve their service in future. Now that you have read the story in Box 8.4,
consider the following points.

- Can you apply Labov and Waletsky's structure to this narrative? What are the similarities and differences between their suggested structure and CIT?
- Is there any evidence of a broader narrative to this story? Can you pick out any words or phrases that indicate a broader context?

There are clear advantages to using CIT to encourage participants to tell stories – the method is well documented, easy to use, clearly structured and allows participants to unravel their story one idea at a time. However, there is some evidence that people will talk more about products, services, organisations and brands with which they have high involvement, that women are more likely to disclose information about themselves than men are, and that people disclose more to friends than to strangers (Burns et al., 2000). This presents some interesting issues for the researcher, who is likely to be a stranger and would like all participants to feel able to disclose information in a similar depth. It seems sensible not to use CIT interviews with participants who feel little or no involvement with the product/service/organisation/ brand under study. How would you deal with the other potential issues?

Laddering

The idea of 'laddering' questions is that you start with a top question – the question you really want the answer to, and keep asking further questions until you get to the deeper answers. In this way you start at the top of the ladder and use each question to go one rung down the ladder, taking the interviewee deeper into the story. The technique allows the researcher to go beyond information about why a particular product or service has been purchased (which features were desired) to what the feature offers in terms of function, the benefits of those features for the consumer and finally why that benefit is sought. Laddering was first proposed by Reynolds and Gutman (1988), based on the means–end chain theory, which links perceived product features to individuals' values (Gutman, 1982). When asked which product features are important, consumers will give a superficial answer – the laddering technique digs for the deeper functional and emotional benefits and individual values
Box 8.5 shows how the technique could work when finding out the deeper emotional drivers that lead to purchase decisions about televisions.

Box 8.5 Example of laddering questions

What particular feature is it that you like about this television?
The fact the screen is so large.

What is important about having a large screen?
Well, everyone has a big telly these days, don't they? It makes it much easier to see – I used to have to squint at the telly from the other side of the lounge, but now I can see it much more easily from wherever I am in the room.

(continued)

(continued)

How does the large screen improve your experience?
The picture quality is much better – you can see all the detail that I used to miss on our old telly and that's important to me because I like to watch nature programmes and see all the detail.

How does having the large screen make you feel?
It's more like being in the cinema than in my lounge. Sometimes I feel like I'm actually part of the programme. I like to immerse myself in a programme and let it wash over me – you can do that with a big screen and you can't with a small one.

The story told in this interview is quite brief, but is nevertheless revealing. Consider these questions.

- What are the emotional drivers for the purchase?
- Are there any particular words or phrases that help to show the emotional drivers?
- What is the broader narrative around this participant's story?

Box 8.6 shows another example of laddering questions. In this example, the researcher is investigating why students have decided to go to university. The participant's first answer is the superficial truth and the laddering digs deeper to reveal more about the reasons for the student's decision. In this example, the researcher is using 'why?' and 'how?' to dig deeper.

Box 8.6 Laddering questions – why did you come to university?

Researcher:	*Why did you come to university?*
Participant:	To get a degree.
Researcher:	*Why did you want to get a degree?*
Participant:	Because it will help me get a good job.
Researcher:	*Any other reasons?*
Participant:	Er . . .
Researcher:	[Keeps quiet, allowing the participant to think]
Participant:	Well, the teachers at school encouraged us all . . . And I was interested in doing more education.
Researcher:	*Why do you want to get a good job?*
Participant:	Because it will pay more money . . . And I'll need that to repay my loan [laughs]. But seriously, I want to do the best I can to get a good start in my career.

Researcher:	*How will the degree help you get a good start in your career?*
Participant:	It will show employers the range of skills I have developed, especially in the placement year. I want to apply for graduate training schemes, so I don't have to start at the very bottom and work my way up.
Researcher:	*How will you feel if you don't get a place on a graduate training scheme?*
Participant:	Well, disappointed, I suppose. But if I can get a graduate job in the right area I won't mind. It's just that people talk about these graduate training schemes as if they're the best thing to do, so I sort of thought . . . I mean, I don't really know.
Researcher:	*Let's go back to the other reasons you gave for doing a degree. You said you were interested in 'doing more education'. Why were you interested in that?*
Participant:	I think because I enjoyed school. Well, sixth form anyway. I enjoyed my subjects and was quite good at them. Mr Robins, my Geography teacher, was a great laugh. I got an A in that and was really chuffed. He always said I should go to university. And my Mum, too. She was dead keen on me doing more, I think maybe because she didn't.
Researcher:	*Why do you think Mr Robins said you should go to university?*
Participant:	I don't know. Because I was good at his subject? I think he thought we should all go. It was a kind of accepted thing that you should go to university if you got good A levels. Not everyone went, so I was pretty lucky.
Researcher:	*Why do you think you were lucky?*
Participant:	Because, well, because . . . I happened to be good at my subjects so I got good grades.
Researcher:	*Why was your Mum so keen?*
Participant:	I think maybe because she always wants us to do well – me and my sister, that is. And maybe because she didn't go to university herself. I think she kind of feels she missed out and doesn't want us to miss out like she did.
Researcher:	*Why do you think she feels like that?*
Participant:	Because you can make a better life for yourself if you get a good job. I want to do the best I can so she'll be proud of me.
Researcher:	*Why do you want your Mum to be proud of you?*
Participant:	Because she's done a lot for me, you know. She's my Mum! I know she's chuffed that I've gone to uni and she wants my sister to go, too, even though it will cost a lot of money. I want to show her how successful I can be, to sort of repay her somehow.

Now consider these questions.

- Why did the student go to university?
- Do any themes emerge?
- Look again at Figure 8.2, showing the contextual factors that may affect an individual's story. What is the broader narrative around the student's story?

The advantages of laddering for narrative research are that the researcher can dig to the deeper emotional drivers behind consumer behaviour in a structured way, allowing the participant to tell their story one step at a time. The disadvantages are that the story can become broken into very small chunks and, as the researcher signposts the direction of the story, the participant may not branch out into related areas of interest that would enrich the overall narrative.

Judging the quality of narrative enquiry: potential issues and challenges

It is important to be able to judge the quality of narrative research work, just as it is with any interpretive, qualitative approaches. You may like to consider traditional measures of internal and external validity, reliability and bias, but these are not always appropriate for qualitative work and there are several other factors that you may like to consider. Riessman (1993) suggests persuasiveness (theoretical claims are supported by participants' stories) and coherence are better measures for qualitative work. The list below draws on ideas from Lieblich et al. (1998), Barone and Eisner (1997) and Clandinin and Connolly (2000).

- The role of the researcher – Given the closeness of the researcher to the process of narrative enquiry, it is essential to make it clear exactly what the researcher's role is and how this is communicated to participants.
- Process – Is the research process made clear?
- Originality – Does the research offer new insights?
- Situated in the literature – Do the findings agree with or counter existing literature?
- Coherence – Do the various parts of the research make a coherent whole?
- Language – Does the language used in the research (especially in the participants' stories) truly reflect the context of the work and use the words actually spoken by participants?
- Voice – Are the individual voices (including that of the researcher, if used) made clear?
- Issues – Are issues raised by the research recognised rather than glossed over?
- Ethics – Were ethical issues adequately considered and allowed for?
- Practical application – Are the practical applications of the results made clear for relevant audiences?
- Future research – Are avenues for future work identified?
- Consequences – Are the implications of the results for wider society made clear for relevant audiences?

This seems like a long list, but a thorough approach to this kind of qualitative work will reap benefits.

Use of narrative approaches in the literature

The application of narrative inquiry and the use of storytelling in marketing research is not limited to interviews and focus groups; it ranges from studies of consumers' voices in blog posts to online feedback, reviews, Twitter posts, Facebook posts and may also include storytelling using images on Pinterest and Instagram, video on YouTube (Pace, 2008) and other platforms.

Consumers' voices are crucial to understanding their wants, needs, expectations and perceptions, also their motivations, inner drivers, external influences, emotions and attitudes towards brands, products, services, organisations – all these insights help inform marketing strategy, marketing communications, customer relationship management, loyalty schemes and much more.

Narrative inquiry is not limited to consumer research and may be used with employees, clients and partners – any individual involved with the product, service, brand or organisation has the capacity to tell a story about it. Box 8.7 shows some examples of narrative inquiry in marketing research.

Box 8.7 Narrative and storytelling in marketing research

Helkkula and Pihlström (2010) describe the use of the event-based narrative enquiry technique (EBNIT) in three pieces of research designed to generate ideas for new service development. The technique combines elements of CIT (describing a meaningful event) with narrative inquiry (allowing the participant to tell the story of this event and of other similar events) and use of metaphors as part of projective research. The authors point out that traditional interview and CIT methods are usually based on past events and therefore do not generate many ideas for future improvements in the way that a projective technique would. The use of a metaphor, such as a magic wand, was shown to help participants imagine what might or could happen that would be better in the future. Interviews using a metaphor generated more ideas than those that did not. The projective technique was more likely to yield positive stories than traditional interviews and may have links with AI, in that participants are asked to imagine what might be, rather than to describe what they have already experienced.

Guthrie and Anderson (2010) used unstructured interviews to collect stories from visitors to two UK destinations to explore the relationship between the consumers' experience of the destination and the destination's image. Thematic analysis allowed the researchers to categorise visitors into groups and the narrative illuminated their experiences with richness and detail. The

(continued)

(continued)

narrative showed how visitors make sense of their experiences and pass on that sense (sense giving) through word of mouth. The authors note that the narratives collected could be useful in tailoring destination marketing to suit specific target markets.

Ruane and Wallace (2013) used interviews to gather narrative from Generation Y women about their use of the internet and social media in their relationships with fashion brands. The analysis drew on themes that emerged from the narratives and the resultant text extracts were checked for overall coherence. Two people coded the data independently to improve reliability. The findings showed that social media not only drives consumption of fashion brands but is also a source of information, inspiration and reassurance for consumers. The internet fitted with the participants' busy lifestyles, was used as an information source and to aid decision making, helps Generation Y women to communicate 'who' they are through their fashion choices and offers a different shopping experience from that of physical shopping. The authors note that the use of a narrative approach allowed them to understand how consumers make sense of their own experiences.

Advantages and disadvantages of using a narrative approach

One of the main advantages of gathering stories and understanding their deeper meaning and broader context is similar to the main advantage of all qualitative methods – that is, reaching a deeper, more detailed and more nuanced level of understanding than is possible through quantitative approaches. The specific advantages of using narrative and storytelling while gathering data are (1) that it allows participants to feel more natural as they tell stories of their own experience or of their own devising; and (2) it allows participants to take ownership of their responses – rather than responding to a series of set questions, telling a story allows more freedom of expression. The advantage for the researcher is that the data is often very detailed and rich, giving insights into emotions and relationships that may not be revealed through traditional interview approaches. The advantage of then using the data to form a narrative, given the broader narrative context, is that the resultant analysis of data encompasses a wider perspective, uses real words from real stories and should be engaging for readers.

The disadvantages are similar to those for qualitative research in general – the process may be time-consuming and projects will often use far fewer participants than those using, for example, a survey methodology. This may be perceived by some as reducing the validity of the project but, as we saw in the previous section, judging qualitative research by quantitative quality measures may not be appropriate.

This is not, then, a disadvantage but an opportunity for the researcher to defend and justify the approach using appropriate measures of quality. Another disadvantage is the potential bias in interpretation of narrative data – the structured approaches outlined here will help to guard against this. Using more than one data collection technique or a mixed method approach would also help to alleviate any concerns about bias in interpretation.

ETHICS BOX

One of the potential problems with narrative inquiry is that participants may uncover uncomfortable life experiences and/or may reveal more than they thought they might, leading to possible withdrawal from the study. In my own recent research about consumers' emotional response to books and the possible connection to self-concept, several interviewees said during the interviews that they had never thought about this before and/or had never spoken before about how they feel about books or the life experiences to which they relate. The interviews uncovered thoughts and feelings that helped participants understand themselves in new ways so they left feeling that they had learned something about themselves. Delving deep for stories can be transformative, revealing and potentially upsetting or stressful. Researchers must take care, therefore, to make it clear to participants that they do not have to continue if they feel uncomfortable. There are clear ethical considerations here, as researchers are not trained counsellors and should not put themselves in a position where a participant leaves an interview upset or stressed, having uncovered an unpleasant memory, for example.

Writing up the results of narrative research

When writing up the results of your research, remember that this, too, is a narrative encompassing various stories. Ensure your own narrative is coherent, with a beginning, middle and end and a logical progression from one point to the next. It is the story of your research (see Table 8.1).

Seminar exercises

Exercise one

Design an open interview schedule using the ideas of appreciative inquiry to investigate a business issue or consumer experience of your choice.

TABLE 8.1 The story of your research

Traditional story	Research outcome
Set the scene	Provide background information to set the context of the wider narrative in the introduction and literature review
Introduce dramatic situation	Ensure research questions are clear, new and engaging
Introduce believable characters	Explain and justify the sampling method and selection criteria
Use watertight plotting with no holes	Explain and justify the methodology
Ensure no plot threads are left unresolved	Ensure discussion covers all relevant areas and relates back to research questions and literature
Close story with satisfying ending	Ensure conclusion answers research questions and makes clear any implications for research and practice
Potential sequel	Recommend any future avenues of related research

Write five questions or prompts that encourage participants to indulge in storytelling. Working in pairs, try out your interview questions.

Take brief notes under the headings suggested by Labov and Waletsky (1997) as the participant tells his/her story.

Afterwards, discuss how useful or otherwise you found the narrative structure. Did it fit the narrative given?

Exercise two

Design a set of open interview questions to find out why people come to university, using the laddering technique. Try to get to the deeper motives and drives that move people.

Working in pairs, interview each other and make notes of the motives that are revealed. Beware that this may uncover uncomfortable memories for some people, so if your colleague is unprepared to go deeper, do not push them.

Make a note of the final reasons arrived at for the decision to go to university. It is likely to be much deeper than the answer to the first question you asked.

Discuss in pairs how the method can be used to reveal deep insights and how it can be used in marketing research.

Consider also the broader narrative revealed in the stories.

Exercise three

Use critical incident technique to examine customers' experiences of a shop, brand, outlet or service that is well known to you.

Work in groups of six; three must tell their stories in answer to the other three's questions. One group of three must tell stories of good/satisfying experiences they have had, while the other group must tell stories of bad/unsatisfying experiences they have had.

When you have finished hearing each other's stories discuss them to find the themes that emerge.

References

Barone, T. and Eisner, E. W. (1997). 'Arts-Based Educational Research', in R. M. Jaeger (ed.), *Complementary Methods for Research in Education*. Washington, DC: AERA.

Bell, J. (2014). *Doing Your Research Project: A Guide for First-Time Researchers*, 6th edn. Maidenhead: McGraw-Hill.

Bitner, M. J., Booms, B. H. and Mohr, L. A. (1994). 'Critical Service Encounters: The Employees' Viewpoint'. *Journal of Marketing* 58, pp. 95–106.

Burns, A. C., Williams, L. A. and Maxham, J. T. (2000). 'Narrative Text Biases Attending the Critical Incidents Technique'. *Qualitative Market Research: An International Journal* 3, no. 4, pp. 178–86.

Butler-Kisber, L. (2010). *Qualitative Inquiry: Thematic, Narrative and Arts-Informed Perspectives*, pp. 62–81. London: Sage.

Chase, S. E. (2005). 'Narrative Inquiry: Multiple Lenses, Approaches, Voices', in N. K. Denzin and Y. S. Lincoln (eds), *The Sage Book of Qualitative Research*, 3rd edn. Thousand Oaks, CA: Sage.

Clandinin, J. (2007). *Handbook of Narrative Inquiry: Mapping a Methodology*. London: Sage.

Clandinin, D. J. and Connolly, F. M. (2000). *Narrative Inquiry: Experience and Story in Qualitative Research*. San Francisco: Jossey-Bass.

Cooperrider, D. L. and Srivastva, S. (1987). 'Appreciative Inquiry in Organizational Life', in, R. Woodman and W. Pasmore (eds) *Research in Organizational Change and Development*, Volume 1. Greenwich, CT: JAI Press.

Denzin, N. K. and Lincoln, Y. S. (eds). *The Sage Book of Qualitative Research*, 3rd edn. Thousand Oaks, CA: Sage.

Ezzy, D. (2002) *Qualitative Analysis: Practice and Innovation*, pp. 95–109. Abingdon: Routledge.

Guthrie, C. and Anderson, A. (2010). 'Visitor Narratives: Researching and Illuminating Actual Destination Experience'. *Qualitative Market Research: An International Journal* 13, no. 2, pp. 110–29.

Gutman, J. (1982). 'A Means-End Chain Model based on Consumer Categorization Processes'. *Journal of Marketing* 46, no. 2, pp. 60–72.

Hawkins, M. A. and Saleem, F. Z. (2012). 'The Omnipresent Personal Narrative: Story Formulation and the Interplay among Narratives'. *Journal of Organizational Change Management* 25, no. 2, pp. 204–19.

Helkkula, A. and Pihlström, M. (2010). 'Narratives and Metaphors in Service Development'. *Qualitative Market Research: An International Journal* 13, no. 4, pp. 354–71.

Labov, W. and Waletsky, J. (1997). 'Narrative Analysis: Oral Versions of Personal Experience'. *Journal of Narrative Life History* 7, pp. 3–38.

Lieblich, A., Tuval-Mashiach, R. and Zilber, T. (1998). *Narrative Research: Reading, Analysis and Interpretation*, Thousand Oaks, CA: Sage.

Pace, S. (2008). 'YouTube: An Opportunity for Consumer Narrative Analysis?' *Qualitative Market Research: An International Journal* 11, no. 2, pp. 213–26.

Punch, K. (2005). *Introduction to Social Research: Quantitative and Qualitative Approaches*, 2nd edn. London: Sage.

Reynolds, T. J. and Gutman, J. (1988). 'Laddering Theory, Method, Analysis and Interpretation'. *Journal of Advertising Research* 28, no. 1, pp. 11–31.

Riessman, C. K. (1993). *Narrative Analysis*. Newbury Park, CA: Sage.

Ruane, L. and Wallace, E. (2013). 'Generation Y Females Online: Insights from Brand Narratives'. *Qualitative Market Research: An International Journal* 16, no. 3, pp. 315–35.

Shuayb, M., Sharp, C., Judkins, M. and Hetherington, M. (2009). *Using Appreciative Inquiry in Educational Research: Possibilities and Limitations*. Slough: National Foundation for Educational Research.

Zurcher, A. (2015). 'Just Jeb! Five things Bush's logo tells us about him'. BBC News, 16 June [online], available at http://www.bbc.co.uk/news/world-us-canada-33104412 (accessed 16 June 2015).

Other resources

The Centre for Narrative Research, University of East London http://www.uel.ac.uk/cnr

The David L. Cooperrider Centre for Appreciative Inquiry, Champlain College http://www.champlain.edu/appreciativeinquiry

9

GAMIFICATION

Using game technology for marketing research

David Longbottom and Kuldeep Banwait

Photo © mypokcik. Courtesy of Shutterstock

Purpose

This chapter explores the popular and emerging concept of gamification in a marketing context. Marketers are increasingly concerned to connect and engage with their customers in order to better understand their thoughts, opinions and decision-making processes. By the use of games and game technology deep insights may be gained into marketing creativity and understanding the mindsets of consumers.

Context

Understanding consumer mindsets is vitally important for modern marketing; for example, in order to inform marketing strategy, brand development, promotion and advertising. Traditional research methods such as surveys and focus groups simply do not go deep enough to understand consumer minds and behaviours. By involving people in games and play situations, activities, problem solving and decision-making processes can be observed (often in real time).

Learning outcomes

At the end of this chapter you will be able to confidently design, plan and conduct a research project based around the use of gamification principles to gain deeper insights into the mindsets of consumer participants.

Introduction, background and context

In this chapter we will be considering:

- What is gamification, and how can this be used in a marketing context?
- How can gamification be used in a marketing research/market sensing context?

A recurring theme of this textbook is the issue of adding depth and meaning into marketing research projects. Traditional methods such as focus groups, interviews and surveys may just not go deep enough into understanding the mindsets of modern-day consumers. Gamification seeks to address this depth deficit in research by engaging participants in gaming environments, where activities and behaviour can be carefully observed.

Gamification is defined by Deterding et al. (2011) as 'the use of game design elements (virtual or real) in non-game contexts'. Burke (2014) identifies that many organisations are realising the potential of gamification in order to engage and motivate consumers; gamification in this context being 'the use of game mechanics and experience design to digitally engage and motivate people to achieve their goals'. He warns, however, that many organisations have approached the process in a simplistic way, tending to focus on rewards and prizes (extrinsic motivators), without really understanding the underlying reasons and motivations of why consumers might give up their time to engage in game scenarios (understanding both extrinsic and intrinsic motivators). He believes that the key in his definition is to recognise that gamification should focus on helping the consumer to 'achieve their goals' and not primarily be just another sales incentive (focusing for the benefit of the company). He calls for a more serious approach to understanding the roots and principles of gaming.

Chou (2015) presents similar arguments, warning that, for some, gaming will be just a passing fad. He describes real gamification as a craft, where the marketer designs a means of deriving fun and engaging play elements typically found in games and by thoughtfully applying them to real-world activities. He presents that games may enable us to better understand human elements (as opposed to purely functional and process elements) and that this understanding may be applied to solving marketing and organisational problems.

For the purposes of this text we will take a broad view of what constitutes a game. We will consider the principles and attributes that are found in traditional and modern games, focusing particularly on what makes games engaging and enduring. We will also consider wider activities where marketers engage consumers in dialogue and exchange (perhaps situations not traditionally considered as game play).

An early example of the power of gaming in research: Foldit

Take the example of the game Foldit (see Foldit web page). Foldit is described as a scientific game to engage gamers in solving puzzles, providing a fun game experience but with an added dimension that the results might contribute to solving 'real-world' problems. One example recorded on the website is as follows. In 2008 a scientist at the University of Washington launched a Foldit project using the gaming platform which enabled participants to digitally play with constructing patterns of 'protein structures'. Scientists had come to the view that understanding protein structures was a key to understanding how they might treat or prevent Aids (but in 15 years of scientific research they had struggled with making connections in some specific types of protein structures). Within 10 days, it is claimed that a gamer 'solved the puzzle' and that this knowledge presented researchers with a breakthrough in their thinking.

Attention deficit disorder: are you paying attention?

In modern-day marketing, overcoming consumer inertia and attention deficit has become a priority for marketers. Just how do you get customers to engage with your brand? They are not watching your adverts and they are savvy of any direct approaches. Getting people to engage in a market research project multiplies this difficulty ten-fold. Gamification seeks to overcome these issues by:

- gaining awareness and interest;
- achieving engagement;
- providing a platform for creativity and interaction;
- creating an enjoyable and rewarding experience;
- adding real value to the participant.

Consider the two mini-cases presented: one is about Coca-Cola and the 'Happiness Campaign'; the other is about a popular European-based car manufacturer launching a new model.

Mini-case 9.1

Coca-Cola's 'Happiness Campaign'

Photo © Elliott Brown via Flickr. Courtesy of Creative Commons

Photo © Mike Mozart via Flickr. Courtesy of Creative Commons

From 2011 to 2015 Coca-Cola has been using a promotional campaign based around the theme of creating 'happiness'. In order to attract attention and gain customer engagement, Coke has conducted many events throughout the world. These include:

Photo © chong chongchongchong via Flickr. Courtesy of Creative Commons

Photo © Elliott Brown via Flickr. Courtesy of Creative Commons

Photo © warrenski via Flickr. Courtesy of Creative Commons

(continued)

(continued)

- The Happiness Vending Machine: a vending machine is installed in a public place (examples include university/college campuses, shopping malls). The machine, however, is not all that it appears and begins to dispense anything from free Cokes to pizza, fresh flowers and even giant-sized sandwiches (for sharing).
- The Happiness Truck: the truck stops at prime locations in towns and cities and again attracts interest with a free dispenser button at the rear of the truck.

In addition to gaining an immediate impact (large crowds gathering at the event), word of mouth quickly spread on social media, giving Coke a massive global reach. Coke followed up the campaign enticing social media followers to suggest 'where will happiness strike next' and 'what happiness will strike next'? Thus Coke facilitated a global discussion of happiness. In some countries suggestions were made that 'do no harm' and 'causes for good' should be future campaigns. Coke has facilitated global events which seek to bring together disparate groups.

Check out the many examples of the Coke happiness campaign posted on YouTube.

Mini-case 9.2

'Finders keepers': new car launch in Europe

A major European car manufacturer decided to create interest prior to the launch of a major new model. The company, having a perceived reputation for well-built, safety-conscious cars, had a worry that their models were seen as the choice of the 'mature' consumer. They were keen to establish a new model which might appeal to the sportier and style-conscious consumer and the younger generations.

It announced in advertisements and social media that it would be parking three unmarked vehicles in three European locations with a strapline of 'finders keepers'. In game theory this is a classic take on the traditional children's game of 'hide and seek' which ticks all the elements of strong game design (which we discuss in later sections of this chapter).

The company presented some 'clues' as to location and also the appearance of the car. It invited discussion and interaction with interested 'gamers'. Within hours the company had over 2 million hits, sparking a debate on possible sites but also receiving many suggestions and images as to what customers expected from the car and how this might appear.

The first two cars were found within a few hours and company representatives were on the scene to present the keys and capture the events for broadcast. The final car proved more difficult and was eventually discovered (after a week of further social media engagement) in a railway station car park, more difficult to spot as it had been partly disguised by giving it a 'need to be washed down' appearance.

The company gained much attention and feedback from the consumer target group it was seeking to engage in the future.

Photo © Mattes via Wikepedia. Courtesy of Creative Commons

Theoretical foundations

There are many theoretical texts on the science of gaming and game theory. For the purposes of this chapter we are seeking to focus on the creative and practical dimensions of good game design, and how the principles and practices often found in games can be used in a marketing and marketing research context.

The best texts we can recommend are Chou (2015), *Actionable Gamification: Beyond Points, Badges and Leaderboards*, and Burke (2014), *Gamify: How Gamification Motivates People to Do Extraordinary Things*. Chou also has a companion website and the author has made several keynote presentations captured on YouTube and a Tedx talk. Chou presents us with a comprehensive model (which we shall discuss in the process sections of this chapter) which make up the main elements essential for designing and developing an effective gaming experience.

Burke (2014) presents his case for a more serious approach to gamification based on personal work experiences with clients over many years (he is a partner in Gartner Inc., an international US-based business consultancy company). He believes that many companies want to develop games and social media platforms but that they are failing to get the basics of good game design mechanics right. In this scenario there may be real dangers of diminishing the brand status in the mind of the consumer if gaming efforts are seen as flimsy and insincere. We will present the key principles for sound game design in the later sections on process.

The idea of gamification has grown rapidly on the agenda for marketers in recent times with the very powerful growth of social media platforms and networks. However, the idea of game play is not a new phenomenon for the marketer. Indeed, many successful marketing campaigns have in the past been built on tantalising and playing with the consumer. Tactics used by marketers include moves such as shock advertising, funny advertising, controversial advertising, withholding supplies, retro marketing and nostalgia marketing. To some extent these are stock-in-trade for many marketers – part of the marketing manager's DNA. Professor Stephen Brown considers some of these tactics in greater detail and provides some classic examples in his seminal paper (published in the *Harvard Business Review*) 'Torment Your Customers (They'll Love It)' (Brown, 2001).

For more recent empirical research we find Harwood and Garry (2015), in a study of gamification and brand experience, find significant interest from most serious brands, citing examples of application from Nike, Coca-Cola, Apple, Samsung, McDonalds and many others (some of these examples and others we will explore within this chapter). They attribute massive growth in this move toward engagement in social media as it provides a ready platform for game designers to engage with customers. They conclude that effective gamification can be achieved by combining two fundamental disciplines:

- building brand communities by facilitating and enabling communications (consumer to consumer, consumer to brand) which may contribute to identifying value-creating opportunities;
- constructing loyalty programmes which enable users to gain points and rewards.

In this context consumers are viewed as 'content creators' and 'task performers' motivated and captivated into participating (Liu et al., 2011). Game designers will also strive to achieve a pleasurable participant experience which may in turn evoke positive feelings and emotions towards the brand (Zicherman and Linder, 2010). Gamification embraces the modern concept of marketing as 'service-dominant' (Vargo and Lush 2010) with customers as active participants engaged in co-creative activity. Table 9.1 illustrates the shifting context as marketers move from a goods-dominant perspective to a service-dominant perspective.

Gamification typically uses points systems, leaderboards and badges to measure a participant's progress and status. However, research suggests that where extrinsic rewards (such as points, leaderboards and badges) are the primary focus there may be a possibility that negative responses may be evoked, for example:

- doubts over the long-term value of schemes primarily based on extrinsic rewards (Dowling and Uncles 1997; Shugan 2005);
- creates in the customer a calculative rather than relational culture (Johnson et al., 2001);

TABLE 9.1 The shifting context in marketing: from goods-dominant to service-dominant logic

Goods dominant	Service dominant
Products	Experiences
Features and attributes	Customer solutions
Price	Value propositions
Supply chain management	Network engagement
Promotion	Interactive dialogue
Market to	Market with
Functional orientation	Relational orientation
Process orientation	Emotional orientation
Creation for	Creation with (co-creation)

Source: Adapted from Vargo and Lusch (2010)

- benefits may be perceived as utilitarian (Chandon et al., 2000);
- may provide only relatively weak indicators of future behaviour intentions and loyalty (Dowling and Uncles 1997; Magi 2003);
- may make forming meaningful relations with consumers more difficult (Wirtz et al., 2007);
- internal marketing techniques such as 'employee of the month' are mostly bound to fail in mature societies and organisation cultures as they are often perceived as being simplistic and demeaning (Chou 2015).

In the following sections we will identify and examine the critical factors needed in successful game design, by distilling down the principles, factors and models found from these studies.

Gamification principles and critical success factors

Harwood and Garry (2015) investigate the approach to gamification and the effect on customer engagement and the customer engagement experience. Using a case study example, the Samsung Nation, the study explores actions and behaviours of consumers, uncovering some critical success factors and also some potential flaws and inhibitors. A conceptual framework for gamification brand experiences is presented by the authors (illustrated in Figure 9.1). The framework identifies critical factors derived from a literature review in three core areas for effective gamification: brand communities, loyalty programmes and game play.

Brand communities

In building brand communities marketers are seeking to add value to customers. Programmes will typically focus on consumer-to-brand engagement, and also consumer-to-consumer interaction (Muñiz and Oguin, 2001; McAlexander et al., 2002). In this scenario the organisation is seen as the facilitator providing opportunities for participants to engage in experiential encounters (Payne et al., 2008). The focus tends to be on achieving participant intrinsic motivation (Ouwersloot et al., 2008), and the participants engage to become content creators (Cova and Pace (2006). Through these processes the marketer is seeking to gain valuable research insights (from studying key content and interactions), and also to realise the potential for gaining stronger links with customers, and the possibility of increased brand loyalty.

Loyalty programmes

Harwood and Garry (2015) suggest that many loyalty programmes have tended to focus too much on extrinsic rewards; for example, loyalty cards and the like. Research by Dowling and Uncles (1997) and Shugan (2005) questions the long-term value of such schemes in achieving loyalty. In scenarios dependent on rewards, customers in the long term may become calculative and fickle. This suggests that whilst extrinsic rewards may have a role in game design, marketers should seek longer-term opportunities for building relationships with consumers. Using such programmes in combination with building brand communities, and game play, may present a broader and more interactive platform in which deeper relationships are possible (for example, through better interactions with customers, marketers may discover what real value means from the customer perspective).

Game play

Through game play marketers are seeking to appeal to both intrinsic and extrinsic motivators. The organisation becomes the facilitator of interactions (between organisation and customer, and customer and customer). The challenge for the marketer is to design game play that attracts interest and motivates participation over a long term. Game play offers the potential to achieve contact with the customer at a different level of engagement and under different conditions (Chou, 2015). For example, the emphasis is on fun, enjoyment, achievement. These may be stronger intrinsic motivators than those traditionally associated with brand communities and loyalty programmes. The ability to connect with customers at a deeper emotional level may be critical for modern-day brands (Zaltman and Zaltman, 2008; Roberts, 2014).

Words of warning on entering gaming

In entering the arena of greater customer engagement the marketer is opening up (and potentially exposing) elements of what Kapferer (2012) describes as the 'real brand'. Consumers are now well informed and savvy, and will check out claims and hold brands to account for their actions. Brands have to deliver real added value and have to be authentic, sincere and transparent. Roberts (2014) has suggested that the branding landscape is changing, with brands moving from

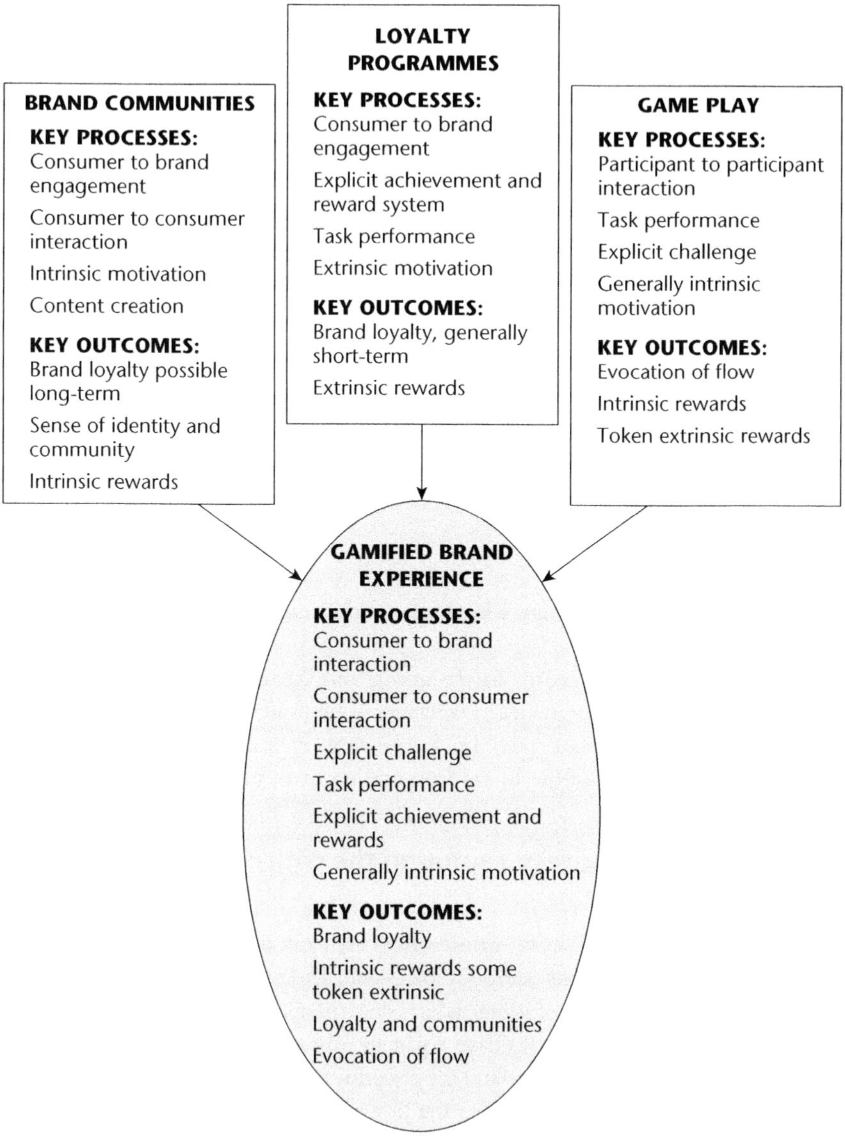

LOYALTY PROGRAMMES

KEY PROCESSES:
Consumer to brand engagement

Explicit achievement and reward system

Task performance

Extrinsic motivation

KEY OUTCOMES:
Brand loyalty, generally short-term

Extrinsic rewards

BRAND COMMUNITIES

KEY PROCESSES:
Consumer to brand engagement

Consumer to consumer interaction

Intrinsic motivation

Content creation

KEY OUTCOMES:
Brand loyalty possible long-term

Sense of identity and community

Intrinsic rewards

GAME PLAY

KEY PROCESSES:
Participant to participant interaction

Task performance

Explicit challenge

Generally intrinsic motivation

KEY OUTCOMES:
Evocation of flow

Intrinsic rewards

Token extrinsic rewards

GAMIFIED BRAND EXPERIENCE

KEY PROCESSES:
Consumer to brand interaction

Consumer to consumer interaction

Explicit challenge

Task performance

Explicit achievement and rewards

Generally intrinsic motivation

KEY OUTCOMES:
Brand loyalty

Intrinsic rewards some token extrinsic

Loyalty and communities

Evocation of flow

FIGURE 9.1   Conceptual framework for gamified brand experiences

Source: Adapted from Harwood and Garry (2015)

a focus on functional aspects to relational and emotional dimensions ('lovemarks'; see Figure 9.2).

In this scenario, brands will need to have a clear set of underpinning values which can be presented and defended in a wider public space, and which will stand up to scrutiny and resonate with their target consumers. Gamification must be part

BRANDS	LOVEMARKS
Information	Relationship
Recognised by consumers	Loved by people
Generic	Personal
Present a narrative	Creates a love story
The promise of quality	The touch of sensuality
Symbolic	Iconic
Defined	Infused
Statement	Story
Defined attributes	Wrapped in mystery
Values	Spirit
Professional	Passionately creative
Advertising agency	Ideas company

FIGURE 9.2   From cold brands to warm lovemarks: the changing landscape of brands

Source: Adapted from Roberts (2014)

of an overall marketing strategy which reflects the company and the core values it seeks to present.

There is a cost implication in designing and creating content, but also in responding and site maintenance. Damage can be done by failing to respond in an immediate environment (response is too slow or unhelpful) or by failing to support the core values of the brand (responding in an inappropriate way).

The gamification process: capturing the critical elements of gaming

Chou (2015) suggests that many gamification strategies fail to achieve their objectives because they focus only narrowly on points, badges and leaderboards, (PBLs) and fail to address the intrinsic values which draw people to long-term engagement. Whilst acknowledging that PBLs have a part to play in game design, he argues that games must go deeper and understand the core drivers of why people want to engage voluntarily in games. To demonstrate the power of games he presents examples of classic games which have endured for many years and engaged millions, mostly for no extrinsic reward: chess, backgammon, Scrabble, Monopoly and many others. Modern digital examples include titles such as *Call of Duty*, *Football Manager*, *FIFA* and many others. He claims that from his own studies over many years he has found that participants may invest a considerable amount of time each day in game play (in some cases where they may be classified as addicted). On a university campus, for example, he finds evidence that some students devote more time per working week to digital game play than would be required to complete their university degree. He challenges marketers to better understand these phenomena in order to better direct behaviour into activities and pursuits for individual and societal gain.

TABLE 9.2 Points badges and leaderboards (PBLS)

Points

Participants earn points in the form of a reward for achieving a level within the game. These points can often be cashed in for prizes or perhaps discounts for future purchases. Supermarket loyalty cards have been successful in engaging customers to save for discounts but it remains doubtful as to the impact on achieving brand loyalty.

Badges

Participants gain recognition, or a badge indicating and publicly acknowledging their achievement. Badges must have some real value and meaning for the participants and the community, otherwise they may be seen as tokenistic and shallow.

Leaderboards

Participants are typically competing against others to achieve gaming objectives. Results are published so that each participant can monitor progress of their own performance against a league table of performers.

PBLs tend to focus on extrinsic motivational factors (for example, receiving an external reward for doing something) and we need also to consider intrinsic factors (for example, why do people engage simply for their own personal reasons?).

In his book *Actionable Gamification: Beyond Points Badges and Leaderboards* (2015), Chou sets out to examine the characteristics which make for successful games, and how these may be translated into business, marketing and life contexts. He has created what he calls the 'Octalysis framework'; 'a complete framework to analyse and build strategies around the various systems that make games engaging' (Chou, 2015: 23). The framework focuses on eight core drives (derived from the eight-sided shape of an octagon), which are summarised below in Table 9.3. The eight core drives which motivate people are similar to work presented by Zaltman and Zaltman (2008), who identify seven categories of deep emotions which they say direct our long-term behaviours (balance, transformation, journey, connection, container, resource, control).

TABLE 9.3 The eight core drives of the Octalysis framework

Meaning	Where people are motivated because they believe they are engaged in something bigger than themselves.
Accomplishment	Where people are driven by a sense of growth and need to accomplish a desired goal.
Empowerment and creativity	This is effectively the 'play' element. We are engaged because it is fun, appeals to our sense of creativity, and we are empowered to enter into a playing environment.

(continued)

TABLE 9.3 *(continued)*

Ownership	Represents our desire to own something, and consequently to improve or protect it or gain more from it.
Social influence	This core drive relates to our desire to engage with others in social activity, companionship and relatedness, and a sense of belonging.
Scarcity	Here we are motivated by a desire to have something where we may perceive that there is a difficulty in obtaining it or a risk of losing out.
Unpredictability	Here we are motivated by the challenge of uncertainty and elements of chance and risk.
Loss avoidance	Here we are motivated by the fear of losing something or having undesirable events transpire.

Source: Adapted from Chou (2015)

Contemporary case examples

In Table 9.4, we examine the eight core drives by giving some examples based on contemporary marketing campaigns.

TABLE 9.4 Contemporary case examples

Meaning

Wikipedia

Consider the example of Wikipedia. Many people (unpaid volunteers) devote their time, energy and expertise to maintain online content. They are giving up their time voluntarily and unpaid in order to protect a service (in this case an online not-for-profit encyclopaedia) that they value. Similar motivations may drive people to engage in online forums or undertake volunteering activity.

Apple

For over 25 years Apple has built an engaged and loyal customer base on the back of a successful strategy of 'Think Different'. Apple appeals to those who seek creativity, defy convention, achieve things. (The original 1984 commercial, a take on the classic George Orwell book *1984*, referred to such people as 'the crazy ones', 'misfits', 'rebels' and 'troublemakers').

Coca-Cola

In the period 2011 to 2015 Coca-Cola has been running a 'Happiness Campaign', where specially rigged trucks and vending machines turn up at public gatherings and dispense everything from free cokes to pizza, games and all sorts of other prizes (usually with a view to bringing people together, or sharing a moment in time). News of the campaigns spread quickly on social media with Coke inviting followers to suggest 'where happiness will strike next'. Millions engaged to suggest locations and also future content. Campaigns have been used to provide happiness in locations troubled by poverty and conflict, and some have developed into more serious initiatives to facilitate bringing people together to try and resolve local issues.

Ecosia

Ecosia is an online search engine, set up in 2009 and based in Berlin, which aims to make charitable donations from advertising revenues. The company pledges 80% of surplus from advertising revenues to support environmental initiatives. As at January 2015 the company reported to have contributed over 1.5 million US dollars to charitable causes. Users can see a rolling calculator with live updates of total donations.

Accomplishment

University fees

Students these days are faced with very high costs for education; for tuition fees, accommodation and living costs. Despite this, demand for places at good institutions continues to grow. The prospects of achieving a good degree and opening up employment opportunities remains for many a top priority for which they are willing to make sacrifices.

(continued)

TABLE 9.4 *(continued)*

eBay

Launched in 1995, eBay became the first online company to offer products for sale using a bidding/auction format. Buyers might achieve bargains by skilfully outbidding other consumers. Sellers were offered a worldwide platform to sell their goods, and were also targeted to achieve star ratings for service. These star ratings are keenly sought after by businesses, big and small, seeking to enhance their corporate reputation.

Nike

For over 25 years Nike has challenged sporting people to 'just do it'. The brand promotes sporting excellence (rather than focusing marketing effort on product specifications and functions). Recent devices launched by Nike, Apple and other brands enable the measuring of steps, heart rate and calories to enable individuals to monitor their lifestyles.

Amazon

Amazon has developed very sophisticated big data analysis which monitors shopping habits. Customers are often notified of 'similar products you may be interested in'. In creating this relationship with customers it may be seen as a useful resource, but also presents the customer with interesting opportunities to engage and challenge. One example is the practice of 'trolley dumping'. Here, consumers select goods that they may be interested in purchasing, and proceed to checkout. However, at checkout they appear to lose interest and exit the site not having competed the purchase (effectively trolley dumping). Amazon, being alert to our shopping behaviour, spots the abandoned trolley and may remind us that our goods are still available. Some customers have found that in order to clear the dumped trolley Amazon have offered further discounts or incentives to complete the purchase. The savvy customer may well achieve a bargain but also, perhaps, the satisfaction of outwitting the experts.

Bargain hunting

Most people cannot resist a bargain. We are in an era of savvy shoppers who will seek out opportunities to achieve bargains, even if in reality they can afford to pay normal prices. Witness the growth of shopping in charity shops (which appeals to a sense of social responsibility but also the sense of achievement of picking up a discarded designer outfit at a fraction of the original cost). Other examples may include growth in the UK (for example) of grocers Aldi and Lidl. For years seen as a cheaper option than the big four (Tesco, Sainsbury's, Asda and Morrisons), Aldi and Lidl have successfully gained market share from the affluent middle classes.

Empowerment and creativity

Lego

Traditional games such as Lego have captured imagination and creativity from a very early age. The brick-building brand has engaged many generations, and has in recent times created digital platforms to extend the reach of the brand.

Build-a-Bear

Founded in 1997, this US toy company has grown in to a worldwide retailer of soft toys. Rather than simply sell teddy bears the Build-a-Bear Workshop outlets engage children and their parents in selecting and building their own bear or soft toy in a 'workshop environment' where 'best friends are made'. The process engages the participants in creativity (creating their own personal bear), forms a longer relational bond with the company (birth certificates, events and birthday cards are celebrated for the new 'family member'), and embraces the spirit of co-creation.

In 2015 the toymaker Mattel announced that it was developing technology

(continued)

TABLE 9.4 *(continued)*

for a digital 3D printer that would allow a child (presumably in a guided workshop environment) to design a toy from a selection of materials and proceed to print the toy in full 3D.

Pandora

The Danish jewellery company founded in 1982 has grown to be a worldwide brand (the third largest jewellery retailer in the world, according to its website in 2015). A major feature of its offer has been the ability to customise collections; for example, in wristbands and necklaces. Individual items are often used by customers to celebrate key moments in their lives. Whilst not a 'new' idea in retailing jewellery Pandora has been successful in capturing the imagination and creative skills of consumers with new and innovative products.

Instagram

Instagram is a social media network which allows participants to create and share pictures and images. Co-founder Kevin Systrom claims that it has over 400 million regular users, making it the most popular social media platform in 2015.

Ownership

Collections

Previous examples have been given (Build-a-Bear and Pandora) where these brands encourage empowerment and creativity, involving the customer creating something new and unique to them and encouraging 'collection' of additions over time. This may appeal to their sense of ownership, something to be treasured with a value that is greater than the unit cost.

Emotional brands

Some brands tap into our emotional responses, eliciting deep emotions which we value, perhaps through tapping into heritage or nostalgia. Examples might include Gibson (guitars), Harley Davidson (motor cycles) or Hovis (bread). In recent times car manufacturers have used iconic models from the past re-launched in modern updates; Fiat (Fiat 500), BMW (Mini) and VW (Beetle). Some car manufacturers encourage 'owners' clubs' which seek to bring like-minded customers together and share their ownership of cherished possessions.

Internal marketing

John Lewis is an often-cited example of a successful UK multi-channel retailer that uses a shared ownership business model. Staff are 'partners' in the business and take a share of profits. In this way John Lewis believes it achieves better commitment and loyalty from its staff.

Social influence

Connecting people

O_2 has repeatedly used 'connecting people' as a main strapline and theme for promotional activity. The growth of contracted networks facilitates a desire for social interactions. The growth of online social media networks (Facebook, Twitter, Instagram and others) reflect this social need to connect.

(continued)

TABLE 9.4 *(continued)*

Carling

The beer brand Carling promotes the brand by profiling consumers as a group of 'mates', fun-loving and good-natured but always willing to stand up for each other as a 'band of brothers'. Budweiser also used this approach in its popular 'Whassup?' advertising campaign. The sports betting company Ladbrokes uses a similar method profiling 'gangs' of predominantly 'lads' out for a 'Saturday afternoon' enjoying the 'game' of football and betting.

Scarcity

Limited editions

Limited editions and restricted supplies have long been a stock-in-trade for the manipulative marketer. Being told that you might not be able to own something you desire seems to have an effect on us that increases the desirability many times over. Brands such as Apple have been accused of such tactics, announcing months in advance a 'new product launch' without being overly specific about what the new product is or does (only that it is 'going to be big'), and that they may not be able to fill demand in the short term. This sets 'Apple-isters' into a frenzy of desire and pre-ordering. Similar events have occurred in the Christmas tactic of the must-have toy or gadget (remember such campaigns as the Cabbage Patch dolls).

Unpredictability

Lottery games

Many countries have 'National Lotteries' where consumers have the chance (albeit small) of winning a substantial prize of money for a relatively small stake. Profits are usually donated to 'good causes' (which perhaps also appeals to the 'Meaning' value in consumers).

In the UK a leading bank, the Halifax, introduced a lottery game attached to some of its popular savings accounts. At a time when interest rates on savings were very low, the incentive of a cash windfall might persuade customers to prefer this brand.

The People's Postcode Lottery targets streets and communities to join up. In The Netherlands the Lottery cleverly targeted streets and communities to 'join together' and increase their chances of a payout. It also hinted that you would not wish to 'miss out' if all of your neighbours were celebrating a win.

Loss avoidance

Car buying

New cars are now mostly promoted and sold on a monthly contract basis. Consumers sign up to a monthly payment for an agreed term, after which they have the option of purchasing the car (for a guaranteed future value) or simply handing back the car to the retailer. This reduces the initial cost of acquisition and also the risk of the consumer suffering 'depreciation', a significant concern to many when car buying. This tactic is also thought to have been influential in encouraging buyers into newer technology vehicles; for example, the growth of hybrid cars.

Investment

Many leading investment companies offering plans linked to stock market shares have introduced 'market smoothing' practices. This seeks to offset some of the volatility in markets, protecting consumers when prices fall unexpectedly.

(continued)

TABLE 9.4 *(continued)*

Betting

Many online betting companies now promote the idea of 'cashing out'. This allows the customer to withdraw from the bet before or during an event if the perceived risk of further loss (or protection of a gain) is too much. Online betting companies have also been very active in transforming a simple betting transaction into a gaming experience; witness the growth of 'bet in play', which provides the punter with many options during an unfolding event.

Warranties

Companies offering returns and warranties (often that go beyond a consumer's statutory rights) help build confidence and loyalty in a brand. Amazon has a strong reputation for putting right any errors or customer complaints in a no-fuss manner. Kia, the automotive company, offers extended seven-year warranties giving buyers reassurance on the quality of major components.

Student assessment

In computer gaming we are familiar with achieving 'levels'. This makes the gamer strive to make progress (initially easy, then getting harder) to move to the next level. A similar method was introduced at a UK university in the assessment of student assignment work.

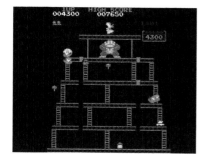

To reduce the risk of poor final grades a series of levels were introduced, the student being allowed to submit at stages throughout the course (rather than just at the end). Progress through the levels meant that in preparing for the final submission the student was already confident and aware that the majority of the grade marks had been achieved (typically 60%). The scheme significantly reduced the risk and stress factors students faced (and overall results and grades improved).

PROCESS BOX: THE MAIN STAGES AND ACTIVITIES FOR THE RESEARCH PROCESS

Stage	Activities (and key issues)
1	**Engaging your participants** Though gamification is not necessarily linked only to internet and social media activity, clearly these facilities are available and attractive to the game designer, giving quick and comprehensive reach to consumers. The choice of platform may be: • website only: easy to manage but may have a negative influence on consumer perception (feeling of being 'managed' rather than 'free'; • all networks: offers most consumer choice but difficult to manage (probably not practical for most);

(continued)

(continued)

- selected networks: probably the best compromise is to use
  your own website plus a few selected popular platforms
  (Twitter, Facebook, Instagram).

  Research by Hanlon (2015) suggests that most of the popular
  social media platforms offer a broadly similar range of options,
  and there is very little empirical work to guide companies on
  criteria for selection.

  A point to keep in mind is that in research of this nature there
  is a natural built-in form of bias in sample selection; not all
  consumers engage in social media activity.

2 **Gaining interest and content design**
   The task here is to get the consumer involved and participate
   actively (and encourage others). We discussed in the previous
   sections how the Octalysis Framework proposed by Chou
   (2015) identifies key elements of successful games. It may
   not always be possible to include all of the elements but the
   framework provides a useful measure of content design.

3 **Maintaining engagement and spread**
   Good design will appeal to intrinsic motivators (typically strong
   in meaning, accomplishment, creativity, social influence) as well
   as extrinsic motivators (typically in points, badges, leaderboards
   and rewards).

   Resources must be available to support the gaming experience;
   consumers will expect instant responses to issues and will
   quickly migrate if company responses are slow or lacking in
   commitment.

4 **Participation and 'net-nography'**
   The gaming researcher may be just an observer of
   activities, seeking to interpret the content of game play
   and the interactions of gamers. Most game designs will
   require interventions by the designer, so in practice the
   researcher becomes involved with the community as an
   active participant. Some researchers have called this type of
   approach in research 'net-nography' (see Kozinets, 2015),
   where the researcher becomes immersed in the activities of
   people in a community (in this example, one being played
   out online and in social media).

5   **Closing down**
           The researcher should plan for closure. What are the desired
           endings that will leave the gamer and the researcher satisfied
           that the objectives have been achieved? This could be a time
           limiter or achievement of a desired goal. Leaving a game
           to simply dwindle or run out of steam may have negative
           implications.

6   **Presenting your data**
           As in all formats of qualitative research this presents challenges
           as the researcher is faced with the challenge of interpreting the
           events and activities. Some quantitative measures are available
           (number of participants, levels achieved, etc.). Qualitative
           analysis could be in the case by case or thematic (discussed in
           Chapter 4). Visuals (Chapter 4) are likely to be important as
           is discourse analysis (Chapter 5). Animated extracts of game
           play are a particularly creative way of presenting, and involve
           the use of both audio and video techniques combined with
           interpretation and discourse analysis.

Summary

This chapter has examined gamification in the context of marketing and marketing research. The growth of social media and digital networks has opened up opportunities for marketers to engage with customers. We have examined the principles and critical factors that are the vital ingredients in designing a successful gaming experience, finding that these combine the activities found in building brand communities, loyalty programmes and in engaging game play. We have presented that gamification needs to focus on both the extrinsic and intrinsic elements which motivate participants and we have provided contemporary case examples which demonstrate how the Octalysis framework devised by Chou (2015) might be applied in practice (covering the motivators: meaning, accomplishment, empowerment and creativity, ownership, social influence, scarcity, unpredictability and loss avoidance).

In the Process Box we have considered the steps that need to be taken in the research process, identifying activities in six key stages.

Gamification presents researchers with vast opportunities to be creative and join up with customers in discovery and real co-creation. Gamification challenges researchers to come up with creative research ideas and designs to achieve engagement of participants at a deeper and more meaningful level which traditional market research methods may simply not achieve. It should also allow us to enjoy the experience.

Exercises

Choose some popular brands that you are familiar with. Search the internet for any examples of engagement in gamification.

- What are they doing?
- What are the key elements?
- Is there any evidence of customer engagement?

Using the eight motivators of the Octalysis framework, evaluate the strengths and weaknesses of the gamification examples you have discovered.

If you are seeking to use your examples for academic work you might also wish to seek out any independent analysis or reporting to better judge if the outcomes have been successful, and search for any lessons learned.

Some interesting gamification mini-case studies

Mini-case 9.3

Merrell Trailscape

In 2015 hiking boot brand Merrell created a digital virtual reality game Trailscape – an immersive journey that had people feeling like they were walking around a crumbling ledge and over treacherous wooden bridges high in the mountains.

The experience, Merrell says, was the first commercial use of 'walk around' virtual reality and was created with partners from Oscar-winning film specialists with experience of working on the motion film *Gravity* and the popular digital *Game of Thrones*.

The project comes as the 30-year-old company, owned by Wolverine Worldwide, aims to redefine its brand voice under the leadership of Gene McCarthy, who became president of the company in August 2013.

'We don't own this brand, consumers do. We just manage it for them,' said Mr McCarthy, who joined Merrell from Under Armour in 2012 after stints at Nike and Reebok. 'What I'm trying to do is go from being a shoe company to being a brand and start a dialogue with consumers on their terms.'

Merrell's Trailscape experience coincided with the launch of Merrell's new Capra hiking boot, which was inspired by a type of goat that lives in the Dolomite mountains in Italy. The activation allows users to virtually walk through the mountainous region, and the experience is supported with physical elements like ropes that mark a bridge, a rock wall and fans that simulate wind.

It aimed to inspire adventure and encourage people to explore the outdoors. 'We feel our purpose is to be a catalyst and outlet to get to the outdoors,' said Mr McCarthy.

The company decided to invest in digital technology in an effort to reach a broader consumer base and revive the brand as its core customers, who are mostly over 40, start to age.

'I wanted to refresh the brand and give it a loud voice, but I wanted to do it in a way that was appealing to a broader audience that is more youthful,' said Mr McCarthy.

Jamie Mandor, head of global brand marketing, says the technology is the best way to communicate with Merrell's target market; outdoor enthusiasts who love adventure. 'It's changing the way we speak and communicate with our customers.'

Involving customers in such game play provides a platform for social media; customers talk about the brand and their experiences. Market sensing researchers can watch and listen to the unfolding messages and ideas that are generated in this creative and entertaining environment.

Consider the following questions:

- What is Merrell trying to achieve by creating a virtual reality experience?
- How does this tie into the theme of customer as co-creator?
- How does this tie in the theme of brands to lovemarks?

Adapted from Nudd (2015) and Rodriguez (2015)

Mini-case 9.4

How Coca-Cola is gamifying vending machines in Japan

Photo © Wikimedia. Courtesy of Creative Commons

(continued)

(continued)

Coca-Cola wanted its customers in Japan to get to know their favourite vending machines. As part of Coke's Happiness Campaign, Coca-Cola used gamification to get people to check in and interact with its vending machines.

Coco-Cola affixed QR (Quick Response) codes to its vending machines across Japan. By the end of March 2012 it had 820,000 machines with codes affixed and what Coca-Cola considered to be a unique identity.

As part of what Coca-Cola calls the 'Happiness Quest', users were motivated to scan the QR code on their favourite vending machine and create its virtual identity. This entailed naming the machine and choosing its avatar from a library of 20 designs. Users could scan multiple machines and create each machine's unique identity as a sort of catalogue of check-ins and a personal address book of virtual friends. Each user was asked to designate a single machine to be 'my machine' which would communicate with the user on a more personal level. This communication included campaign news, weather information and other relevant news.

The real game began once users started checking in to machines on a regular basis. Each check-in awards the user points that can be spent to customise their machine. These virtual items included shoes, character skins and backgrounds.

Checking in under certain conditions would also earn the user badges. For example, a check-in on Christmas gets the user the 'Merry Christmas' badge and 20 check-ins during lunchtime awards the lunchtime badge. There were also random prizes allotted for particular check-in times.

The aim was to further strengthen Coca-Cola's brand loyalty. The check-in game strives to get users interacting with its physical machines multiple times a day. The in-game rewards keep users coming back and form the check-in habit.

Consider the following questions:

- What is Coca-Cola trying to achieve by gamifying vending machines?
- How does this tie into the theme of brand loyalty?
- How might this take Coca-Cola's physical presence to a different level?

Adapted from Halcomb (2011)

Mini-case 9.5

Disney's 'Circle of Life' – 360-degree video for *The Lion King*

Disney Theatrical Productions created a 360-degree immersive video of 'The Circle of Life' recorded at New York's Minskoff Theatre.

Photo © ValeStock. Courtesy of Shutterstock

The film crew used a simple mix of six GoPro cameras to shoot the action. The film lets viewers feel as if they are moving around within the performance. In parts, the viewer seems to be actually in the scene.

Disney Theatrical Productions was hesitant going into the project, but the end result subdued any doubts. The company is fiercely protective of its brand and quality, especially with something so successful as *The Lion King*, which has been running for over 18 years.

> We did go forward with the knowledge that it was an experiment, and that if we went through the filming and editing process and we didn't love what we saw, or it somehow didn't enhance or improve upon or expand upon the original vision of *The Lion King*, then we weren't going to release it.

The results encouraged consumers to try out the experience. It resulted in significant discussion as consumers engaged in social media. They reported seeing characters in a new light, and being able to see events unfolding from the perspectives of the different characters. The results have given Disney food for thought about building characters and set design. To enhance the viewing experience still further, some additional content (for example, the activities of different characters outside the main plot) might be added in digital format.

Virtual-reality headsets are trying to crack the mainstream film and gaming markets. They offer the opportunity to give users a completely different and more involved experience.

Consider the following questions:

- What is Disney trying to achieve by creating a 360-degree video?
- How does this tie into the theme of immersive experiences and storytelling?
- How might this shape the future of theatre productions?

Adapted from Moynihan (2015) and Cox (2015)

References

Brown, S. (2001) 'Torment Your Customers (They'll Love It)'. *Harvard Business Review* (October), pp. 83–8.

Burke, B. (2014). *Gamify: How Gamification Motivates People to Do Extraordinary Things.* Brookline, MA: Bibliomotion.

Chandon, P., Wansink, B. and Laurent, G. (2000). 'A Benefit Congruency Framework of Sales Promotion Effectiveness'. *Journal of Marketing* 64, no. 4, pp. 65–81.

Chou, Y. (2015). *Actionable Gamification: Beyond Points Badges and Leaderboards.* Available at Yu-Kai Chou.com.

Cova, B. and Pace, S. (2006). 'Brand Community of Convenience Products: New Forms of Customer Empowerment – the Case my Nutella the Community'. *European Journal of Marketing* 40, nos 9/10, pp. 1087–1105.

Cox, Graham (2015). 'Broadway's *The Lion King* to Roar in Virtual Reality'. *Variety*, 17 November.

Deterding, S., Dixon, R., Khaled, R. and Nacke, L. (2011). 'Gamification: Towards a Definition'. Paper available online from the *Proceedings of the 16th International Academic MindTrek Conference.*

Dowling, G. and Uncles, M. (1997). 'Do Customer Loyalty Programs Really Work?' *Sloan Management Review* 38, no. 4, pp. 71–82.

Halcomb, Scott (2011). 'How Coca-Cola Is Gamifying Vending Machines in Japan'. *TechinAsia*, 10 November.

Hanlon, A. (2015). 'A Framework for Social Media Network Selection to Add Value to Business to Consumer Companies'. *Academy of Marketing Conference,* working paper, July 2015, Limerick.

Harwood, T. and Garry, T. (2015). 'An Investigation into Gamification as a Customer Engagement Experience Environment'. *Journal of Services Marketing* 29, no. 6/7, pp. 533–46.

Johnson, M., Gustafsson, A., Andreasson, T., Levik L. and Cha, J. (2001). 'The Evolution and Future of National Customer Satisfaction Index Models'. *Journal of Economic Psychology* 22, no. 2, pp. 217–45.

Kapferer, J. N. (2012). *The New Strategic Brand Management*, 5th edn. London: Kogan Page.

Kozinets, R. V. (2015). *Netnography: Redefined*, 2nd edn. London: Sage.

Liu, Y., Alexandrova, T. and Nakajima, T. (2011). 'Gamifying Intelligent Environments'. *MUI '11: Proceedings of the 2011 International Workshop on Ubiquitous Meta User Interfaces*, New York: ACM, pp. 7–12.

Magi, A. (2003). 'Share of Wallet in Retailing: The Effects of Customer Satisfaction, Loyalty Cards and Shopper Characteristics'. *Journal of Retailing* 79, no. 2, pp. 97–106.

McAlexander, J., Schouten, J. and Koenig, H. (2002). 'Building Brand Community'. *Journal of Marketing* 66, pp. 38–54.

Moynihan, Tim (2015). 'The Lion King Musical in VR Is an Incredible Experience'. Available at wired.com, 18 November.

Muñiz, A. M. Jr. and O'Guinn, T. C. (2001). 'Brand Community'. *Journal of Consumer Research* 27, no. 4, pp. 412–31.

Nudd, Tim (2015). 'Merrell Thrills and Frightens People With a Crazy Oculus Rift Mountainside Hike'. *Adweek*, 6 February.

Ouwersloot, H. and Oderkerken-Schröder, G. (2008). 'Who's Who in Brand Communities and Why?' *European Journal of Marketing* 42, nos 5/6, pp. 571–85.

Payne, A., Storbacka, K. and Frow, P. (2008). 'Managing the Co-Creation of Value'. *Journal of the Academy of Marketing Science* 36, no.1, pp. 83–96.

Roberts, K. (2014). *The Future Beyond Brands; Lovemarks.* New York: Power House Books.

Rodriguez, Ashley (2015). 'Outdoor-Apparel Brand Merrell Uses Virtual Reality to Refresh Brand'. *Advertising Age*, 6 February.

Shugan, S. (2005). 'Brand Loyalty Programs: Are they Shams?' *Marketing Science* 24, no. 2, pp. 185–93.

Vargo, S. L., and Lusch, R. F. (2010). 'A Service Dominant Logic for Marketing', in P. Maclaren, M. Saren, B. Stern and M. Tadajewski (eds), *The Sage Handbook of Marketing Theory*. London: Sage.

Wallace, E., Buil, E. and de Chernatony, L. (2014). 'Consumer Engagement with Self-Expressive Brands: Brand Love and WOM Outcomes'. *Journal of Product and Brand Management* 23, no.1, pp. 33–42.

Wirtz, J., Mattila, A. and Lwin, M. (2007). 'How Effective are Loyalty Reward Programs in Driving Share of Wallet?' *Journal of Service Research* 9, no. 4, pp. 327–34.

Zaltman, G., and Zaltman, L. (2008). *Marketing Metaphoria: What Deep Metaphors Reveal about the Minds of Consumers*. Boston, MA: Harvard Business Press.

Zicherman, G. and Linder, J. (2010). *Game-Based Marketing*. New York: Wiley.

Bibliography

Buttle, F., (2012). *Customer Relationship Management*. Oxford: Butterworth Heinemann.

De Chernatony, L., McDonald, M. and Wallace, E., (2011). *Creating Powerful Brands*, 4th edn. Oxford: Butterworth Heinemann.

Kapferer, J. N. (2012). *The New Strategic Brand Management*, 5th edn. London: Kogan Page.

Piercy, N. F. (2009). *Market-Led Strategic Change*, 4th edn. Oxford: Butterworth Heinemann.

10

UNDERSTANDING THE CUSTOMER JOURNEY THROUGH THE PRISM OF SERVICE DESIGN METHODOLOGY

Polina Baranova

Purpose

This chapter explores how use of service design methodology can contribute to in-depth understanding of the customer journey and to the design of service improvement interventions aimed at enhancing customer experience.

Context

The notion of customer journey is becoming increasingly important for both private and public sector organisations. Understanding customer experience and interactions that take place during service delivery is critical to the service design, delivery and improvements where the quality of customer experience take a strategic priority.

Learning outcomes

At the end of this chapter you will be able to confidently use the service design methodology in order to understand customer experience, develop a service blueprint, design in-service improvements to enhance service user experience or redesign and re-engineer existing services in order to respond to changes in organisational environment.

THEORY BOX

Philosophy: interpretive

- ontology: no single objective reality;
- epistemology: use of consistent, rational and logical approaches in research (to map and understand consumer processes).

Approach: inductive

There is no pre-determined hypothesis; theory development emerges from the research.

Strategy: in-depth examination of the customer-service interactions at every stage of the service delivery process, including flowcharting, observation, and interview.

Design: application of service design project methodology in five stages: mapping of the customer journey; detailing each stage of the journey; identification of fail points and areas of excessive wait; prioritisation; and finally, development of service improvement plan, implementation monitoring and evaluation. During these stages a range of research methods is deployed, including in-depth interviewing, focus groups, 'mystery' shopping, observations, video diaries, experiments and others.

Analysis:

- stage-by-stage examination of the service process: in-depth analysis of each stage of the service delivery process;
- service delivery process examined holistically: analysis of the service flow, fail points and areas of excessive wait in the service delivery process;
- customer journey/experience explored holistically: analysis and evaluation of the overall quality of customer experience.

Presentation:

- service blueprint: a detailed graphic representation of the service delivery process;
- customer profiling: development of personas using images and annotations;
- service improvement plan: a management tool to develop, implement, monitor and evaluate service improvements.

Introduction, background and context

The notion of market sensing includes a wide range of considerations about the major market players affecting the performance of organisations. Customers, by far, attract considerable attention when it comes to marketing research. Customer research is rather diverse; the most popular directions include research into customer behaviour, customer decision-making and consumer psychology. Often customer-focused studies explore how customers behave, make decisions, perceive, respond and engage with organisations to access their products and/or services. There is a great amount of well-established techniques and methodologies in customer research: market segmentation, market positioning, emotional scaling and others discussed in the earlier chapters. Very few of these techniques consider the customer experience holistically or with a great deal of precision in considerations of every stage of the customer journey. Amongst many approaches to market sensing, service design methodology offers a unique perspective on the customer journey and equips individuals and teams with tools and techniques to enhance service performance (based on the understanding of process and process mapping).

Service design methodology is firmly rooted in the field of services management and services marketing (Schostack, 1984; Kingman-Brundage, 1989; Palmer, 2014; Bitner et al., 2008; Lovelock et al., 2008). Despite its service-based origins, this methodology has been well received in a variety of organisational settings across primary, secondary and tertiary sectors. This is not surprising as services have become an important part of organisation growth strategies and companies that considered themselves as 'purely manufacturing' are increasingly exploring growth strategies through service provision, i.e. 'servitisation' (Vandermerwe and Rada, 1988; Vandermerwe, 1993; Van Looy et al., 2013). Services are increasingly becoming an important source of wealth creation in economies around the globe (see Mini-case 10.1 which illustrates this trend).

Recently, service design methodology has seen an increase in interest from the public sector, particularly from health sector and higher education sector institutions, where increasing pressures from government and regulators results in a demand to design and deliver services to ensure a high quality of customer experience. For instance, in UK higher education, the quality of student experience is firmly placed on the strategic agenda for the majority of higher education institutions as a result of increasing marketisation of higher education (Browne Report, 2010; Brown and Scott, 2009). Introduction of the industry-wide student survey mechanisms, the National Student Survey (NSS) and the Postgraduate Taught Experience Survey (PTES), highlights a clear drive and urgency towards raising the quality of student experience in university settings.

This chapter provides an overview of the service design methodology with a particular emphasis on one key technique – services blueprinting (Schostack, 1984; Kingman-Brundage, 1989; Baum, 1990; Bitner et al., 2008). There is a step-by-step guide to the blueprinting technique, supported by examples of its application. Service improvement approaches, which form an important part of service design methodology, are discussed and a range of examples provided to differentiate between service enhancement, redesign and re-engineering. The chapter concludes with the case study 'DERBI Project', demonstrating application of the service design project methodology at one of the JISC-funded flagship projects in the context of UK higher education.

Mini-case 10.1

Rise of the service-based economies

In the UK, according to the Office of National Statistics (ONS), the services sector has grown in importance over the past half century, accounting for 79% of the UK economy in 2013 compared with 46% in 1948 (ONS, 2014). The analysts explain this trend by the growth in services output, which is outpacing that of other parts of the economy. The services sector grew by 3.0% per annum in real terms between 1990 and 2013 compared with GDP growth of 2.2% per annum.

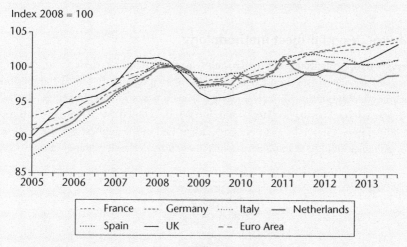

Index 2008 = 100

France ···· Germany ······ Italy —— Netherlands
······ Spain —— UK – – Euro Area

FIGURE 10.1   Total services output in the largest European economies (2008 = 100)

Source: Eurostat in ONS, 2014

The largest EU economies also benefit from the rise in service outputs despite still recovering from the recent economic recession in 2008–09. The services sector across the seven largest European economies is currently out-performing pre-downturn growth rates by 3.9% (ONS, 2014).

Services provide a substantial contribution to the global economy. In 2012, the services sector accounted for 65.9% of global gross domestic product (GDP). In developing economies, the services sector constituted approximately 51.4% of GDP. In developed economies, the services sector contributed 74.9% to the GDP and in transition economies such contribution came to 58.4% in 2012 (UNCTAD, 2014). Whilst the services sector contributions to the GDP of developing and

(continued)

(continued)

transition economies has seen a slight decline of 0.3% and 0.7% respectively during 2010–12, in developed economies it is still on the rise. The contributions of the services sector to the GDP of these countries is still growing at a modest 0.1 percent during the same period. The services sector provided 39% of global employment in 2011 (UNCTAD, 2011). According to the World Bank, as countries move upward in the development path, the share of services in GDP and employment expands. With acceleration of the economic recovery (World Bank, 2014) the share of service sector contribution to world GDP is expected to grow.

Service design project methodology

Service design methodology is advocating an understanding, design and improvement of services in the context of the 'customer journey'. It calls for application of a key technique in the service design domain – service blueprinting – initially introduced by Schostack (1984) and further developed by Kingman-Brundage (1989). There are five key project stages identified in the application of the service design methodology to explore and improve customer experience (Figure 10.2).

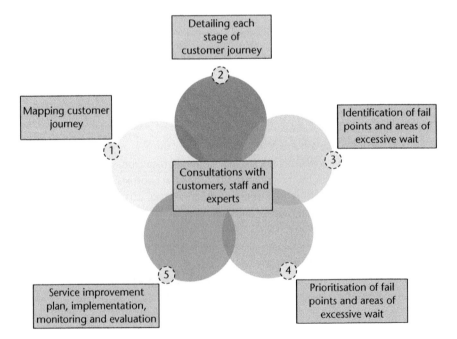

FIGURE 10.2 Service design project methodology

Source: Based on Baranova et al. (2010)

The stages identified are:

- mapping of the customer journey;
- detailing each stage of the journey;
- identification of fail points and areas of excessive wait (AEW);
- prioritisation;
- development of service improvement plan, implementation, monitoring and evaluation.

These stages will be discussed in more detail in the third section of this chapter. For now, we introduce the services blueprinting technique as a critical component of the service design methodology.

According to Schostack (1984), service blueprinting was developed as a process control technique for services as it offered several advantages:

- it was more precise than verbal definitions;
- it could provide a useful starting point for solving problems with efficiency and effectiveness of the service process;
- it was able to identify failure points in service operations.

Schostack's adaptation of this technique originally involved mapping the customer process stages through the service delivery process and aligning it with the organisational structure. Further adaptations of the blueprinting technique (Kingman-Brundage, 1989) involved considerations for frontstage (onstage) and backstage activities as well as later additions of physical (tangible) and intangible evidence and possible consideration for target and actual timing of each stage in the customer journey (Palmer, 2014; Bitner et al., 2008; Lovelock et al., 2008).

Essentially developed as a graphical tool, a service blueprint is a detailed map of a service process. It shares similarities with other process modelling approaches: visual representation of the key activities in the service process; possibility of representation of the high-level conceptual processes or detailed sub-processes and sub-systems to reflect service delivery; it could also be linked to the more internally focused process modelling tools and languages (Bitner et al., 2008: 71).

Main components of a service blueprint

Throughout the service blueprinting literature (Zeithaml et al, 2008, Bitner et al, 2008), five typical components of a service blueprint can be identified:

- customer actions (stages of the service process): timing and relationships between the stages are depicted graphically;
- frontstage participants and contact employee actions;
- evidence (tangible and intangible);

- backstage participants and principal actions;
- support systems.

Customer actions include all the steps that customers take as a part of a service delivery process. These are plotted in a sequential order from left to right at the top of the blueprint. When developing a blueprint it is advisable to start at 'big picture level' and then drill down to obtain a higher level of detail. The blueprint is further divided into two zones – frontstage and backstage – separated by the line of visibility. Everything that appears above the line of visibility is what the customer is exposed to and comes in direct contact with. In the literature, these are also referred to as touch points (Palmer, 2014; Lovelock et al., 2008).

Below the line of visibility, so-called backstage elements of the blueprint are drafted. These include participants and their actions which need to be performed in order to support the frontstage activities. It is important to note that the conventional understanding of the backstage operations as being secondary to the frontstage activities is challenged by the service blueprinting approach. According to the service blueprinting methodology, both are considered to be equally important for the success of the service process, both need to be properly resourced and managed, and both need to be made aware of the importance of the other for the delivery of quality services (Lovelock et al., 2008).

The fifth critical component of blueprinting is 'support systems'. These are crucial for the delivery of every stage of the service process and are drafted below the line of visibility. Support systems (for instance, payroll, procurement, CRM and other mainstream support systems of business operations) are displayed at the bottom of the blueprint and in some instances connected by vertical lines with other areas of the blueprint to show the inter-functional connections and support that are essential to delivering the service to the customer.

Mini-case 10.2

Blueprint of a GP surgery visit

Figure 10.3 shows a blueprint of a typical service encounter at a doctor's surgery. It is produced by one of our student groups studying service design methodology as part of their undergraduate studies. This version of a service blueprint is particularly successful due to visual representation of a service encounter. Such an approach helps to visualise the actions, actors and servicescape of a surgery visit as well as to provide useful guidelines for staff to ensure 'smooth' delivery of a service and prevention of service failure.

Fail points (F) and areas of excessive wait (W) displayed in circles carry high risk and take priority as they are 'felt' by the customers. Fail points without a circle carry a lesser risk and they are often identified below the visibility line.

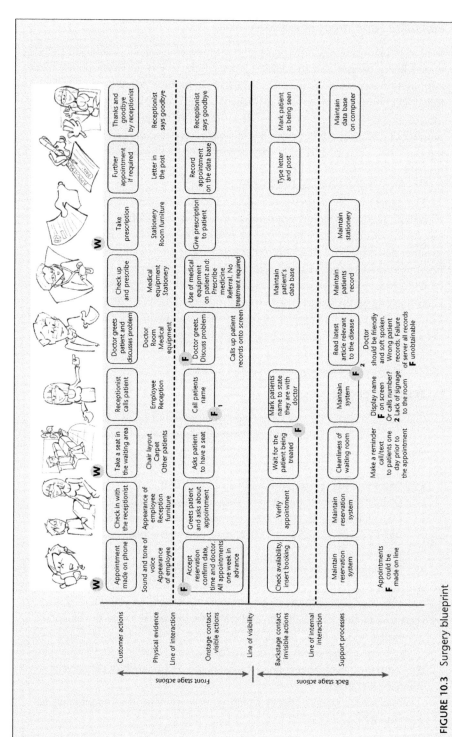

FIGURE 10.3 Surgery blueprint

Fail points and areas of excessive wait

Service blueprinting not only provides the foundation for the analysis of the service delivery process and its visual representation, it also identifies points where customers may potentially perceive failure in the service delivery process. The so called 'fail points' are the critical incidents on which customers base their perception of quality (Palmer, 2014). The identification of fail points could start from a number of directions: direct customer feedback regarding the problems faced during the service experience, secondary data available from customer surveys over a number of time periods, or operational data with regards to process failures, underperformance, bottlenecks and other items.

The blueprint also displays the areas of excessive wait. These could either contribute to the fail points or stand on their own as signifying the areas where customers commonly have to wait. The task of the service redesign team then lies in either designing areas of wait out of the process, if it is feasible, or minimising the negative impact of the wait on customer perception of service quality. The latter could include redesign of the servicescape (Booms and Bitner, 1981) where waiting occurs; setting up the standards for carrying out each activity in the areas of excessive wait including times for completion of a task and maximum wait times between the tasks; and training staff to manage queuing and to perform service recovery.

Study exercise

Consider a service that you have recently experienced (a visit to a dentist or doctor's surgery, a hairdressing appointment, a visit to a cinema, a visit to a library, etc.).

- Develop a step-by-step process map of your visit.
- Map all the participants at each stage of the service encounter.
- Map all tangible and intangible elements of the service encounter;
- What backstage operations could have been taken place at each stage of the process?
- Develop a blueprint of the service experienced.

From your point of view as a customer, what steps of your journey were you most and least satisfied with and why? Please mark them on the blueprint developed.

Are there any fail points and/or areas of excessive wait? In your view, would the company be able to recognise the fail points and/or areas of excessive wait you have identified?

What service improvements would you recommend the organisation to implement?

Service improvement

Service design methodology is more than just a drafting of complex drawings of the service encounters. The critical element of the approach is in the development and implementation of the service improvements developed on the basis of the in-depth understanding of the fail points within the service delivery, customer preferences and service operations' capabilities. Service improvement approaches include service enhancement, service redesign and service re-engineering.

Service enhancement is the least radical of the three approaches identified. It is concerned with the service enhancement initiatives which could include a wide range of services improvement techniques referred to as 'poka-yoke' techniques or fail-safe methods (Chase and Steward, 1994). They differentiate between the server and customer poka-yokes (1994: 37), broadly defining server poka-yokes around the 'three Ts' (task, treatment and tangibles) and customer poka-yokes around the stages of the service delivery (preparation, encounter and resolution).

The 'three Ts' refer primarily to the design of service delivery where the majority of errors occur around the task itself – the service is incorrectly performed due to poor design, i.e. tasks performed in a wrong order, being too slow or incorrect. Treatment errors are usually referred to as the mistakes made in human-to-human and/or human-to-technology interface within the service process. Tangible errors are those in the physical elements of the service, such as poor design of the room, incorrect or unclear written documents or instructions, unreliable equipment, etc. Service poka-yokes include activities, features and systems to allow for minimising the risk of the occurrence of the above errors in the service delivery. Examples of service enhancement initiatives include:

- improving signage to ensure better customer flow;
- improved communication with customers;
- changes to the layout of facilities used by staff and customers;
- increasing capacity of IT resources to cater for fluctuations in demand.

The service redesign approach to service improvements involves changes in the service delivery process, for example:

- changes in the sequence of stages for service delivery;
- illuminating unnecessary stage(s);
- designing new stage(s) in the existing process to accommodate for different customer types.

Such redesign efforts need to include consultations with staff, customers and the experts inside and outside an organisation to ensure mitigation of reputational, processual and dependability risks (these are discussed later in the chapter).

The service re-engineering approach often requires complete overhaul of the service delivery process. This is often needed when services become obsolete or fail to deliver, or where recent major changes in the business model of a company initiate changes in the service delivery processes. Service re-engineering is associated with radical change initiatives in organisations. It is characterised by short-term but impactful interventions that radically transform organisational systems and processes. Service re-engineering needs to be carefully managed, like any radical change efforts, as it often encounters resistance from staff and can have a negative 'halo' effect on operations and strategy.

Advantages of service blueprinting

- Conventional process mapping techniques are often very formal and do not allow for the detailed analysis of the customer encounter within the service process. In order to understand customer experience, there is a need to analyse every stage of the customer journey and within each stage: this includes every detail, from the quality of the written language, for instance in the correspondence with a bank or GP surgery, or the layout of the room or web interface where a service is delivered, to the frequency of text messaging to inform customers about new product and service offerings. Service blueprinting allows for capturing this level of detail to develop a comprehensive picture of the customer journey.
- Blueprinting involves plotting the participants at each stage; this allows for greater understanding of the role of each participant in the process and prompts conversations with the purpose of clarifying roles and responsibilities of the individuals and teams involved. This should be treated as an opportunity to surface possible duplication of tasks and activities, waste and mismanagement of resources, and inconsistency of services. For all participants involved, the mapping out of the blueprint provides the opportunity to learn from each other, to communicate between different individuals and teams who have responsibility for the service delivery, and to find solutions to enhance service delivery and, ultimately, customer satisfaction.
- According to Bitner et al. (2008), service blueprinting upholds the focus of services redesign and improvement efforts on human-to-human and human-to-technology interfaces at the institution level, rather than at the software engineering level, 'allowing service designers to drill down into the firm without losing the connection to the customer action and the processes' (2008: 71–2).
- When applied in organisations with numerous departments involved in service delivery (for instance, universities, hospitals, airports), service blueprinting can be a silo-breaking tool. It encourages collaboration across various departments and understanding the customer journey holistically – presenting a bigger picture of the customer journey. The overarching focus of the service blueprinting is to understand what is like to be a customer of the organisation and what needs to be done to ensure creation of the customer experience which is valued by the customers. In doing so, different teams need to be open and to be prepared to challenge existing processes and practices in order to put customers at the heart of the design of its services.

Limitations

Despite its strong customer orientation and broad overview of the service delivery processes, services blueprinting fails to provide an in-depth analysis of the process components at each stage of the customer journey. During a service encounter, a customer could be exposed to a number of backstage processes; for instance, payment processing, order placing, updating personal details and booking the next appointment. Each of these processes 'feed in' to overall customer experience at a dental practice. A service blueprint of a visit to a dental practice would account for them, but would not consider these sub-processes in detail. A further process mapping exercise is required when closely analysing sub-processes involved in the delivery of the customer experience. Such exercises are necessary to account for any interoperability of various departments in complex organisations.

A service blueprint attempts to capture a dynamic process of frontstage and backstage interaction in the service delivery process in its static form. In such attempts there is always a danger of inability to account for dynamics, contingencies and ever-changing customer preferences and expectations. Capturing dynamic processes requires an understanding that a service blueprint should be continuously modified and updated.

Taking you through the process stage by stage

This section details the key stages involved in a research project based on service design project methodology, as illustrated in Figure 10.1 earlier in this chapter. It is based on application of the service blueprinting technique and other methods to gain deeper, holistic, understanding of customer experience in organisations.

A summary of the key stages and activities identified in the service design project methodology (Baranova et al., 2010) is presented in the Process Box below.

PROCESS BOX: MAIN STAGES AND ACTIVITIES OF THE SERVICE DESIGN METHODOLOGY

Stage	Activities	Through stages (see over)
1	Mapping customer journey through a service process • Identify services for mapping. • Develop a process map of a service including main stages of a service delivery process.	
2	Detailing each stage of customer journey • Working with each stage of the service map, detail frontstage and backstage elements of the service blueprint. • Include considerations for actions, actors, servicescape, supporting systems and processes.	

(continued)

(continued)

3   Identification of fail points and areas of excessive wait

- Develop and deploy a range of techniques to research customer experience, including considerations for fail points and AEWs broadly and in relation to key service user profiles.
- Develop 'personas', i.e. profiles of the key service users.
- Research specifics of customer journey, including analysis of fail points and AEWs, of the personas developed.

4   Prioritisation of fail points and areas of excessive wait

Prioritisation could be done by:

- level of reputational risk (severity of problems from customer perspective);
- level of processual risk (severity of problems from process efficiency and effectiveness perspective);
- level of dependability risk (severity of impact on other systems and processes).

5   Service improvement plan, implementation, monitoring and evaluation

- Consider the service improvement approach.
- Develop the service improvement plan.
- Implement service improvements.
- Monitor and evaluate service improvements.
- Feed forward about the progress of the initiatives to inform management at operational and strategic levels.
- Go back to step 1 to re-start to ensure continuous efforts towards customer-centric service design and service provision.

Consultations with customers, staff, internal and external experts

Stage 1: mapping customer journey through a service process

The starting point of the process is the identification of services for mapping. Depending on the purpose of the project you might select services for mapping that attract the most complaints from your customers and other key stakeholders (for instance, suppliers, business partners, industry regulators); or services that need to be enhanced to outperform your competitors; or services that are out-of-date and in need of a fresh approach to fit better with any recent changes in your business model. Whatever the purpose of your project, ensure that your mapping serves a greater purpose rather than achieving just operational efficiencies. The greater purpose lies in understanding customer experience through service encounter. Hence, the research to support your project should go beyond consultations with the departments involved in service delivery and company management. It should, above all, provide insights into what it is like to be a customer of the organisation and to have experienced the services offered.

When a service is identified for mapping, the key stages of service delivery need to be captured. Customer journey mapping involves graphically representing a series of touch points that customers encounter during a service. At this stage, the mapping process considers the stages and flow of the touch points that form the customer experience. It is important to reflect what takes place in the day-to-day delivery of the service, not what service stages were designed originally or what is wished to have taken place. Over time an original service design could have changed as some stages become obsolete and/or replaced with technology. Be mindful that often managerial ambition of what the service experience should be does not reflect what takes place in operations on a daily basis. Thus, at this stage the aim should be to capture the actual representation of the key touch points of the customer journey. A range of research techniques could be deployed to achieve this, ranging from direct observations of the customer experience, 'mystery' shopping, interviewing and focus groups to asking customers to develop video diaries or written accounts of the service encounter.

Stage 2: detailing each stage of the customer journey

After mapping of the key stages of the customer journey (Stage 1), each stage of the process is analysed in depth, providing as much detail as possible with regard to frontstage and backstage operations. The following elements of a service blueprint provide further insights:

- Customer actions (stages of the service encounter): timing and relationships between the stages are depicted graphically. These could include target and actual timing for each stage. The comparison between the actual and target time could form a useful dialogue with regards to the minimum service standards and whether or not it is effectively delivered through timing promise, i.e. waiting time targets. Frontstage participants and contact employee actions are to be carefully depicted in the blueprint to allow for transparency and accountability of all the parties involved in service delivery.
- Evidence (tangible and intangible): these usually include elements of servicescape (Booms and Bitner, 1981), i.e. physical environment of the service delivery such as layout of the building, signage, equipment, décor and other intangible elements (for instance, lightning, temperature, noise level, music).
- Backstage participants and principal actions: similar information as for the frontstage participants but in backstage situation. In different organisational settings these might be participants from a range of functions and divisions: for instance, in administration it could be placing an order; in a procurement department it could be processing an order and arranging delivery; in a business unit it could be the responsibility for servicing customers in a particular market or geographical region.

- Support systems: these are crucial for the delivery of every stage of the service process and are drafted below the line of visibility. As previously discussed, these systems can be critical to customer experience as they provide essential support for managing resources in organisations to deliver services. Examples might be a CRM system to manage information and interface with customers; a quality assurance system to ensure and manage quality of products and services; a budgeting and finance system to manage financial resources. Bottlenecks in these systems can result in major delays and potential dissatisfaction with the service experience.

Stage 3: identification of fail points and areas of excessive wait

A blueprint is a living document and is used to continuously refine the systems and processes it describes. Identification of the fail points and areas of excessive wait (AEW) drawn from the end-user feedback enables the analyst to drill down into these aspects of the service delivery and to make recommendations for service improvements.

Development of the key service user profiles, i.e. 'personas', is highly suitable at this stage. It not only aids in-depth understanding of the key customer profiles as service users, but also allows for greater insights into their journey as a customer. Further, it provides fine-grained data on fail points and AEWs from the point of view of these personas, whose interpretation of a service encounter could be rather different. For example, there might be more delays in accommodating demands of customers with special needs when compared to other customers. In the case of universities, international students often encounter university process differently from home on-campus students. These might result in delays at different stages of a service encounter due to issues around visas, assessment of comparability of previous studies with UK educational standards or the logistics of arrival and settling in the UK. Thus, understanding how different personas experience a service and identify fail points and AEWs allows for more comprehensive mapping of the customer journey.

Stage 4: prioritisation of fail points and areas of excessive wait

Out of a number of the fail points and AEWs identified, there is a need to select a few which would provide a greater focus for the service improvement efforts. Analysis should differentiate between low, medium and high risk areas, with primary attention then given to the high risk areas. It is important to note that inevitably there could be links between fail points of various levels of risks and AEWs. These links and dependencies need to be thoroughly explored and analysed before initiating the service improvements as they could create further problems when operationalising the services improvement plan.

The prioritisation of fail points and AEW is based on the assessment of the severity of the impact in relation to the following types of risk:

- Reputational risk: these are fail points and AEWs identified by the customers. In stage 4, the data on fail points and AEWs is gathered about the customer experience generically and in relation to key service user profilers. This information is carefully synthesised from the empirical data generated during the project: accounts of mystery shoppers, interviews with customers, video recordings, focus groups, customer survey data, observations of service encounter and others.

- Processual risk: this type of risk is associated with the negative impact of fail points and AEWs on the efficiency and effectiveness of the service process. It typically results from the delays in service delivery, poor service recovery practices and numerous reasons that lead either to service inefficiencies (longer waiting times in hospitals; bottlenecks in service delivery; insufficient resource allocation, such as staff, facilities, equipment, etc.) or failure to deliver the main objective of the service delivery (for instance, serving food of a Michelin star quality or ensuring successful recovery from an operation).

- Dependability risk: as part of the mapping process, there is a necessity to explore operational links with other processes within an organisation and beyond. What impact does performance of the service you study have on other processes within the organisation? What impact does it have on the processes of other organisations you work with: suppliers, business partners, competitors and wider networks? These dependencies need to be explored as part of this project and incorporated in consideration for service design improvements. Benefits of involving key stakeholders in dialogue about service quality and customer experience across multiple organisations can be substantial and lead to sustainability of competitive advantage as a result of collaborative service improvement strategies.

Stage 5: service improvement plan, implementation, monitoring and evaluation

Once fail points and AEWs are identified, careful analysis of the reasons for failure takes place. Analytical techniques such as brainstorming, cause-effect diagrams or Pareto analysis are used to diagnose the critical contributors to service failures. They reveal opportunities for 'failure proofing' (Lovelock et al., 2008) of a range of activities within the service encounter. Such opportunities create foundations for service improvement efforts whatever they might be: services enhancement, services redesign or services re-engineering.

As these approaches are discussed earlier in this chapter, we turn our attention to the later activities characterising this stage. These are concerned with implementation, monitoring and evaluation of the progress towards service improvements. Successful implementation of the service improvements starts with the development of the service improvement plan where service improvement interventions are identified and responsibility and timing are assigned. Ideally, the plan needs to be developed jointly with the key participants of the project. Its draft needs to be timely communicated in timely fashion to the rest of the organisation and beyond. Feedback needs to be invited from the key stakeholders and analysed. It should be taken into account when finalising the plan. When the final version of the plan is agreed, the scheduled interventions are ready to go ahead.

Monitoring and evaluation of the service improvement interventions is important to ensure progress and sustainment of organisational efforts towards service improvement. Monitoring should take place frequently and at regular intervals (depending on the nature of intervention, but preferably once every month) to ensure that service improvement initiatives are in track with the plan. Evaluation is a more complex activity: this involves evaluation of the progress against the target, reviewing customer and other key stakeholders' feedback; benchmarking service performance against competitors and best-in-class performance; and assessing the fit between achieved service performance and strategic priorities of an organisation.

Consultations and engagement with staff, customers and experts

Projects that deploy service design methodology require cross-organisational efforts to engage a wide range of participants at different stages of the service design initiatives. It is critical to engage customers, staff and experts to be a part of a service blueprinting process and development of service improvement interventions. Each of the following groups provide valuable insights to the project: customers about their service experience, problems encountered and possible solutions; staff about their perception of service quality, operational specifics of the service delivery and problems, suggestion for service improvements; experts advise on industry standards, best-in-class performance and future trends.

Often in organisations, when discussing service delivery specifics with blueprinting participants, areas of disagreement and political tensions will be encountered (Bitner et al., 2008: 80). These areas signify the potential areas of interest for further discussion and analysis; however, initially, they could be noted but not directly tackled in the first instance as blueprinting efforts could be derailed into internal politics.

It is important that throughout blueprinting efforts customers remain in focus. It is often too easy to assume that what staff and experts know about the customer experience is a true representation of reality. Extensive research allows for greater objectivity and reduces the risk of data misinterpretation. Blueprinting participants should not be too engrossed with the steps in the process, operational issues and 'blame' talk. They need to be constantly reminded of the customer being at the centre of service design and service improvements initiatives and the quality of customer experience in organisations.

Research tools and techniques

Throughout all stages of the service design project methodology, there is a wide range of research methods to be deployed (see Figure 10.4). Combination of a variety of qualitative and quantitative data from primary and secondary sources could provide valuable insights into the customer experience.

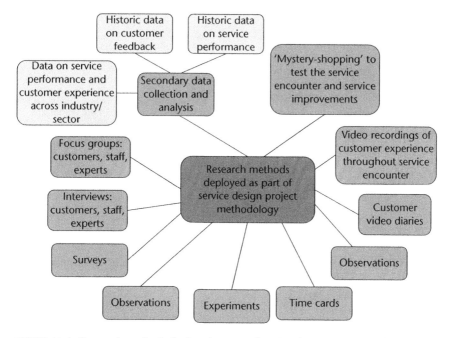

FIGURE 10.4   Research methods deployed as part of service design project methodology

A number of these research methods and their application have been discussed in the earlier chapters of this book. In the context of the service design methodology, their application is aimed at obtaining, analysing and synthesising data to develop greater understanding of a customer journey. Use of data for and as a result of the service design techniques presented in this chapter (namely service blueprint, customer personas, service improvement plan and improvement interventions) allows researchers and practitioners to work with rich materials to understand the complex nature of the notion of 'customer experience' and to inform organisational practices to ensure its strategic importance for competitive success.

Study exercise

Design three research projects to study customer experience of the following services:

- online grocery shopping;
- a cinema visit;
- an airline flight (as part of a holiday trip).

(continued)

(continued)

For each of the research project, consider the following aspects:

- What are the range of research methods you'd like to deploy? What are their appropriateness and limitations?
- How are you planning to deploy each of the methods identified? What are the challenges and how are you planning to overcome them?
- What are the ethical considerations for each of the research methods identified?
- How are you planning to analyse data collected?
- How are you planning to use the results of your data analysis to understand customer experience?
- How can you use the data collected to suggest service improvements?

Finally, compare and contrast research strategies across all three projects. Critically discuss specifics of these strategies for a research project in academic and professional contexts.

Mini-case 10.3

The DERBI Project

In August 2009, the University of Derby was awarded funding for its bid submitted to the Student Lifecycle Relationship Management (SLRM) funding stream as part of the Business and Community Engagement Programme for the Joint Information Systems Committee (JISC). The proposed project, the Development and Enhancement Review of Business Interfaces (DERBI), was aimed at improving the quality of student experience from pre-entry to readiness to engage in learning and teaching. Enrolment, as the point at which an individual's status changes from applicant to student, is considered to be a significant point for which a review of service design and student relationship management would have to be carried out during the project.

The scope of the DERBI Project was focused on further understanding of the students' journey and the experiences of first-year undergraduate (UG) students through the different stages of the enrolment process and on suggesting process improvements based on the analysis of the data generated throughout the project. The key priorities for the project were to identify and implement improvements in order to increase the efficiency and effectiveness of administration for enrolment itself and the processes which lead to and from enrolment, and to explore ways to strengthen the university–student relationship by adding value to the interactions. In the official JISC feedback on the outcomes of the project, it states that the DERBI Project is 'considered to be a flagship service design project (possibly even a flagship JISC project per se)' (JISC, 2010).

The methodological underpinning and the empirical research carried out during the DERBI Project was grounded in broader understanding of the student experience than just that associated with teaching and learning (Lewis, 1984; Sastry and Bakhradina, 2007). At the heart of the project approach was a perspective of student experience where teaching and learning experience is enabled and enhanced (Grönroos, 2007) by a portfolio of administrative and support services and the resulting impact on student experience at the university. Student experience is considered in the context of 'student journey' through the university service processes from pre-entry stage to alumnus/a, and not merely in terms of learning experience or the contacts with tutors.

The project was successfully positioned within the Student Experience Team responsible for the development and implementation of the university-wide Student Experience Strategy and working alongside the Student Support and Information Services Department. The project had a formal project governance structure working effectively with the specialists from various departments within the university and representing key stakeholders at faculty, school and programme levels, operational level and a range of administrative and support functions across a number of university sites. An academic consultant was contracted to the project to carry out training workshops in service design and to advise and oversee the research of the student journey, services design technique application and the development of service enhancement plan.

Throughout the project a wide range of research methods was deployed to gather a variety of information for the development of the blueprint and services enhancement approaches. A crucial combination of various primary and secondary sources, qualitative and quantitative data and their interpretation provided valuable insights into the customer perception and expectations with regards to service quality and satisfaction. The Student Enrolment survey as well as NSS results formed the crucial part of the secondary information available to the projects. As for primary sources, a wide range of research techniques was used: mystery shoppers; video recording of the student experience and feedback; focus groups with students, administrative and academic staff of the University; and time cards analysis to identify queuing times at the different stages of the enrolment process.

The majority of the primary research, focused on student participation and satisfaction with the enrolment process, was carried out during the September enrolment period with further enquiries made during the January enrolment. Consultations with staff to develop and verify the enrolment process blueprint, and on the basis of it to develop and implement service improvement initiatives, were carried out throughout the life of the project over the ten-month period.

Look closely at Figures 10.5 and 10.6 for examples of service blueprints developed as part of the DERBI Project.

(continued)

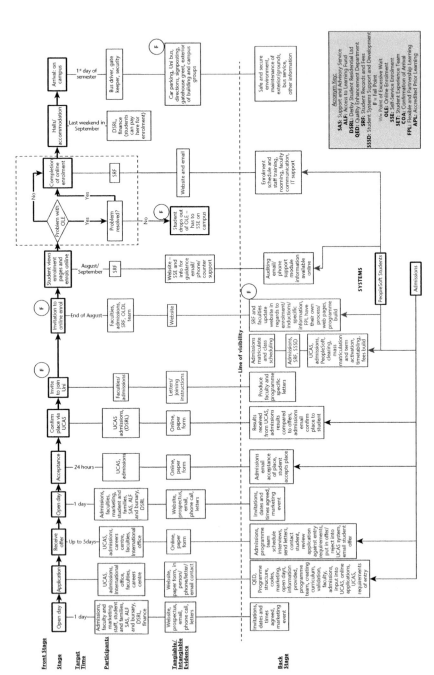

FIGURE 10.5 Blueprint of student transition from application to enrolment – DERBI Project

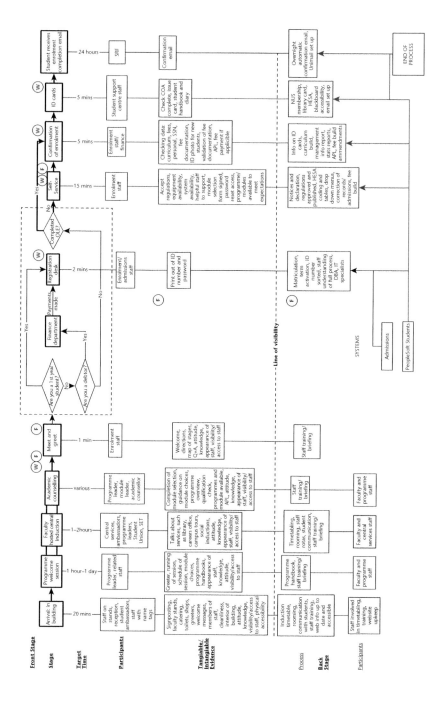

FIGURE 10.6 Blueprint of student enrolment process – DERBI Project

(continued)

DERBI Project outcomes

- **Quality of information**
  Communication was reviewed in the project in order to ensure that information was provided effectively using appropriate media and at the right time. The percentage of students satisfied with the information sent to them increased across the board. In 2009, 36% of returning students rated the whole enrolment experience as 'better than last year'. In 2010 this figure increased to 68%. Three versions of *A Guide to Enrolment*, designed by current students and containing information which they would have liked to have as freshers, were introduced. The guide details the steps needed and included maps of the different campuses showing the locations of the various stages of enrolment.
- **Increased student take up of online enrolment (OLE)**
  OLE screens were improved to reduce jargon and improve accessibility for students. An additional 1,440 students enrolled online in 2010 compared to the previous year, resulting in an OLE total of 8,874.
- **Staffing**
  Staff training proved successful in increasing knowledge and quality of customer service. Visibility of staff was also improved with the introduction of blue T shirts for staff supporting enrolment.
- **Improved signage**
  Approximately 83% of students felt there were enough signs to direct them to their enrolment locations in 2010, 'on campus', 'inside the buildings' and 'at enrolment' compared with 63% in 2009.
- **Reduced number of passwords issued**
  Password issue was a major fail point in 2009. Communication about passwords was improved, including using SMS for new students and extending returning student awareness of password expiry. There has been a 38% drop in demand for the issue of new passwords in 2010.
- **Reduction in queuing**
  The mean wait times for all stages of enrolment was reduced to half the time in 2009, for both self-service and confirmation. At time of sampling, no queues occurred for ID card collection in 2010. Students took less than 20 minutes to complete self-service and normally less than 5 minutes for confirmation.
- **Bite-size induction**
  In 2009 student feedback showed that welcome week schedules did not adequately fill time for new students and that gaps in scheduled time were a cause of anxiety as students tried to fill time in an unfamiliar environment. In response bite-size induction was introduced in the Atrium. This consisted of a stand with information materials, puzzle books, opportunities to ask questions, and register for campus tours.

Unexpected benefits of the project were that staff stress levels were reduced during enrolment week for fulltime students. Furthermore, the structure of the project, combining students, professional staff and academic colleagues, has been very successful in terms of gaining university-wide support and buy-in into the project.

Services blueprinting and service enhancement techniques have proved to be valuable in improving the student experience at the University of Derby. The technique genuinely places students at the heart of the review and redesign of services. This approach relies on research in order to ensure evidence-informed, student-focused decision making. Students must be involved at the design stage of services in order to ensure the experience offered is fit for the future. Student expectations of service delivery are increasing and universities must be prepared to consider relationship management holistically, encompassing learning and teaching as well as professional services and administration.

Cross-sector application

The cross-sector workshops and engagement in the project has improved expertise in the application of service design methodology in the context of higher education. University of Derby experts have undertaken some consultancy work with other higher education institutions wishing to apply this technique to improve their service provision. JISC commissioned the project team to produce a service design guide which has now been published for the sector and the team have presented at various conferences, including AUA and SROC 2011. Copies of the design guide and further information about the project can be found at www.derby.ac.uk/experience/JISC-enrolment-project.

Summary

This chapter has provided an overview of service design methodology and its application in a context of a project aiming to develop holistic understanding of a customer journey. This methodology is particularly valuable for projects in complex organisations where service processes have numerous touch-points with customers and have a high degree of dependability on other internal and external systems and processes.

Service blueprinting is one of the key techniques of the service design methodology. It allows for in-depth analysis of each stage of service delivery, providing detailed insights into front- and backstage elements of the servicescape (Booms and Bitner, 1981). Development of personas reveal customer behavioural patterns and offer important intelligence about the customers as the key focus of service design and service improvement efforts. Researchers would find this methodology of value in projects that study the customer journey holistically and account for interoperability, complexity and temporality of organisational processes. For practitioners, service design project methodology has a proven success record in fostering a customer-centric approach to service design and service improvements in various organisational and sectorial contexts.

Additionally, this type of research may help in areas of:

- competitive strategy: projects aiming to achieve differentiation through services;
- marketing strategy: enhancing understanding of a customer journey with an aim to communicate more effectively with the market and affect customer perception of service quality;
- operational strategy: evaluating service efficiency and effectiveness followed by development, implementation, monitoring and evaluation of the service improvement initiatives;
- brand evaluation: providing insights into customer perception of service quality through service experience and brand values.
- advertising and promotion: working with PR specialists to develop effective communication strategy to create media representation of a customer journey and communicate this to the market;
- internal marketing: providing representation of how customers perceive service quality through service experience and brand, identify any potential gaps, develop recommendations to address potential problems and communicate to staff.

Exercise

This exercise is designed to be carried out over two 2-hour seminar sessions. Prior to the exercise launch, you would need to secure permission from your local (school/college/university) library to host the service design project.

Seminar 1

Students are asked to form design teams (with a maximum of three students in a group). Each group will have to develop their own approach to developing a blueprint of a service encounter at a school/college/university library. As a group they will need to identify potential fail points and AEWs. They will also need to suggest a service improvement approach and improvement interventions. They will need to present their work to the rest of the class during Seminar 2. The duration of presentation is 10 minutes per group. Student can use any medium to present their work.

Students and tutors visit the library. Design teams are asked to collect the data to develop a blueprint. Tutors act as consultants on service design methodology and research methods. Teams can access tutor support up to three times during their library visit. This exercise encourages students to work as a team and to develop individual and group strategies for collecting and analysing data. The groups will have to consider what information they need, how to collect it, how to use it to achieve the objective of the exercise and how to present it in class.

Students might be encouraged to meet outside class hours to collect data and to develop their materials further.

Seminar 2

Design teams are asked to present their projects and materials developed. Each presentation is evaluated by tutors and peers. You might wish to video-record group presentations to give developmental feedback to students in relation to their presentation skills.

After all presentations are carried out, tutors initiate class discussion about value and applicability of the service blueprinting technique. What did teams find easy/ difficult to apply? Would they recommend using the technique to other students? What tips could they provide for other students? What research methods did they undertake? What worked? If they had more time for this project, what research methods would they deploy and why? Overall, what have students learned as a result of this exercise?

Consider, if it is appropriate, to communicate the service improvement recommendations to library staff and ask for feedback. There might be an opportunity for a member of staff to give feedback directly to students. If not, communicate the feedback received and discuss it further with the students.

Bibliography

Baranova P., Morrison S. and Mutton, J. (2010). *Service Design in Higher and Further Education: A Briefing Paper*, JISC CETIS. Available at http://tinyurl.com/3xmsh9v, accessed 18 September 2015.

Baum, S. H., (1990). 'Making Your Service Blueprint Pay Off!'. *Journal of Services Marketing* 4 no. 3 (Summer), pp. 45–52.

Bitner M. J ., Ostrom, A. L. and Morgan, F. N. (2008). 'Service Blueprinting: A Practical Technique for Service Innovation'. *Californian Management Review* 3, no. 3 (Spring), pp. 66–93.

Booms, B. H. and Bitner, M. J. (1981). 'Marketing Strategies and Organization Structures for Service Firms', in J. H. Donnelly and W. R. George (eds), *Marketing of Services*. Chicago: American Marketing Association, pp. 51–67.

Brown, R. and Scott, P. (2009). *The Role of the Market in Higher Education*. Higher Education Policy Institute Report, March. Oxford: HEPI.

Browne Report (2010). *Securing a Sustainable Future for Higher Education: An Independent Review of Higher Education Funding and Student Finance*, available at www.independent. gov.uk/browne-report, accessed 12 February 2011.

Chase, R. B. and Stewart, D. M. (1994). 'Make Your Service Fail-Safe'. *Sloan Management Review*, Spring, pp. 35–44.

George, M. L. (2003). *Lean Six Sigma for Service: How to Use Lean Speed and Six Sigma Quality to Improve Services and Transactions*. Columbus, OH: McGraw-Hill.

Grönroos, C. (2007). *Services Management and Marketing: Customer Management in Service*, 3rd edn. Chichester: Wiley.

Henning-Thurau, T., Langer, M. F. and Hansen, U. (2001). 'Modelling and Managing Student Loyalty: An Approach based on the Concept of Relationship Quality'. *Journal of Service Research* 3, no. 4, pp. 331–44.

JISC (Joint Information Systems Committee) (2010). *DERBI Project: Evaluation of Project Performance and Impact*. JISC Internal Report on DERBI project's performance and deliverables. Unpublished.

Kingman-Brundage J. (1989). 'The ABCs of Service System Blueprinting', in M. J. Bitner and L. A. Cosby (eds), *Designing a Winning Service Strategy*. Chicago: AMA, pp. 3–30.

Lewis, I. (1984). *The Student Experience of Higher Education*. London: Croom Helm.

Lovelock, C., Wirtz, J. and Chew, P. (2008). *Essentials of Services Marketing*. Singapore: Pearson Education South Asia.

Morgan, J. (2011). 'A Starring Role Beckons'. *Times Higher Education*, 14 April.

ONS (Office of National Statistics) (2014). *An International Perspective on the UK – Gross Domestic Product*. Document released 24 April.

Palmer A. (2014). *Principles of Services Marketing*, 7th edn. Maidenhead: McGraw-Hill Education.

Sastry, T. and Bekhradnia, B. (2007). *The Academic Experience of Students in English Universities*. London: Higher Education Policy Institute.

Schostack, G. L. (1984). 'Designing Services that Deliver'. *Harvard Business Review*, January–February, pp. 133–9.

Slack N., Chambers, S., Johnson, R. and Betts, A. (2006). *Operations and Process Management: Principles and Practice for Strategic Impact*. London: Prentice Hall.

Stickdorn, M. and Schneider, J. (eds) (2010). *This is Service Design Thinking*. Amsterdam: S Publishers.

UNCTAD (United Nations Conference on Trade and Development) (2011). *UNCTAD Handbook of Statistics 2011*. Geneva: United Nations.

UNCTAD (United Nations Conference on Trade and Development) (2014). *UNCTAD Handbook of Statistics 2014*. Geneva: United Nations.

Vandermerwe, S. (1993). 'Jumping into the Customer's Activity Cycle: A New Role for Customer Services in 1990s'. *Columbia Journal of World Business* 28, no. 2, pp. 46–65.

Vandermerwe, S. and Rada, J. (1988). 'Servitization of Business: Adding Value by Adding Services'. *European Management Journal* 6, no. 4, pp. 314–24.

Van Looy, B., Gemmel, P. and Van Dierdonck, R. (2013). *Service Management: An Integrated Approach*, 3rd edn. Harlow: Pearson Education.

World Bank (2014). *World Development Indicators 2014*. Washington, DC: International Bank for Reconstruction and Development/The World Bank.

Zeithaml, V., Bitner, M. J. and Gremler, D. (2008). *Services Marketing*. Columbus, OH: McGraw Hill Education.

PART III

Research presentation and research ethics

11

COMMUNICATING YOUR RESEARCH

Alison Lawson and Maria Potempski

Introduction

This chapter is written from the point of view of experienced writers who are academics, practitioners and researchers by profession. The advice and guidance here is based on our own experience dealing with the written word in a range of media and for a range of audiences. We hope it will help you to write up your research in ways that communicate your findings clearly and that suit your readers' needs.

As academics we mark a lot of students' work. Here's a tip to get you started – imagine your lecturer marking, say, 20 assignments. Or 50. Or 150. We have a lot of assignments to get through, so we really appreciate it when they are well structured, well written and well presented. The content is, of course, very important, but the way that you communicate that content is crucial to success. Poor presentation, poor structure and poor writing can stifle excellent content. It's like serving a Michelin star meal on a paper plate with plastic knives and forks. You just wouldn't do it. So if you have finished your research project and it's good enough to eat, make sure you serve it on a beautiful platter with the best silver. Hmmm. Maybe we took that metaphor a bit far . . .

Reading a research paper should be as engaging as reading a good novel – it should have a clear beginning, middle and end, it should have a strong plot (objectives, literature and methodology), believable characters (research participants) and draw the reader in through provoking an emotional/intellectual reaction. Some research papers are dreadfully dull to read even though the research is interesting. We often write in ways we believe we are expected to write in order to sound 'academic' when really we should write in ways that are accessible and understandable for the audiences reading our writing. This is not a call to 'dumb down' academic and research writing, but to make it engaging, readable and quickly understandable for readers.

This chapter gives you some advice on how to go about communicating your research (mainly in writing, but also in other ways), starting with what to do before you begin then moving on to how to draft your work, how to ask for, give and deal with feedback and some tips on how to write for different purposes. Also included here are some helpful checklists, a note of common gripes and some exercises to practise what you will learn.

Before you start

You'll have heard it a hundred times before, but the thinking and planning before you start writing really are a very important part of the process of clear communication. Some time spent here will make the writing much easier to do and more engaging and enjoyable to read.

Think . . .

- What exactly do you want to say?
- Who exactly is the audience?
- If you have a brief to follow, do you understand its key points fully?

Considering these points is important because the answers will help you to shape the narrative.

What exactly do you want to say?

- What are the key points you want to cover?
- In what order should the points be made so they make sense to the reader?
- Is there an overarching message or theme? If yes, is it clear how the key points contribute to constructing that message?

Who exactly is the audience?

- Who is your audience? Are they academics or professionals? Experts or interested non-specialists?
- What does your audience need to know?
- What will interest them or be most relevant to them? Remember that some of your work may be fascinating for you, but may not need to be communicated to others.
- How much detail will your audience want/need?
- What will they already know? Don't waste time explaining basic points in detail if the audience is likely already to be familiar with them – keep these points short and provide a reference to support them.
- What language and tone would be suitable for your audience? Should it be academic or professional or something else?

- What vocabulary do you need to use? Are there any unusual terms that will need explanation?
- What structure will be most helpful so your audience understands your work?
- If your audience wants more information, can you direct them to it?

Following a brief

If you have a brief make sure you understand it and then stick to it. Query any part of the brief that you don't understand. If there is no brief then you may like to construct your own. A basic brief for writing up research could be as follows.

> Present and analyse the data/findings in the context of the wider literature in a manner that is fully understandable by the relevant audience and drawing the appropriate conclusions.

It may also be useful to consider the word count for the document as part of the brief. Whether or not you have a brief it will be useful to plan the structure of your work before starting.

Planning the structure

It will help you to write the work and will help your audience to understand it if there is a clear structure that is easy to follow. Plan headings to divide your work into sections that tell a story in a logical sequence. Many research documents follow a similar structure, for example:

Introduction

Literature review

Methodology

Results/data/findings

Analysis/discussion

Conclusions and recommendations

Appendices

References

Within each section, especially the literature review and the analysis/discussion, you are likely to need subheadings to help signpost the content for the reader. Think of it this way – for every new idea you will need a new heading. This helps the reader to understand and digest your work one idea at a time.

Write down the headings and check they follow a logical sequence. Haphazard sequencing will confuse your audience – the ideas have to be in a sensible order. Consider whether the audience needs to know or understand one idea before progressing to another. How do the ideas build up into a narrative?

If you are working to a word count, plan roughly how many words to use in each section, depending on its importance in the overall structure. You may not stick rigidly to these initial estimates, but they will help you to avoid exceeding any set word limit and help you to concentrate in the right areas. When allocating word counts to headings, err on the short side or allow some words unallocated as contingency. Alternatively, be prepared to go back and cut words if you need to.

Once you have planned the structure, consider the weight of each heading and ensure they are presented consistently. This will help the reader to understand the relative importance of each section, for example:

Chapter heading	18pt bold
First-level subheading	14pt bold
Second-level subheading	12pt bold
Body text	10pt Roman

If using numbered headings (which make it immediately obvious that subheadings 'belong' to a particular heading) check that they are sequential and that they match the weighting of the heading level. For example:

1   Chapter heading
1.1   First-level subheading
1.1.1   Second-level subheading

Don't make the design of your document any more complicated than it needs to be. Audiences (and tutors) will not be impressed by style over substance. Keep it simple, elegant, consistent and easy to follow. If you are using figures/diagrams, tables, boxes or other non-text features, ensure they are clearly identified in the text and that they each have an explanatory heading or caption. Design issues may be specified in the brief; where they are not specified you must make your own decisions about the simplest, clearest way of presenting the document. Readers do not want to spend time working out what to read first on a page – make it easy for them. That said, one of our postgraduate students once presented a dissertation about segmentation in the women's magazines market designed to mimic the style of a magazine, which worked well. If you plan to do something out of the ordinary like this, discuss it with your tutor first.

Getting support

Before you begin, make sure you are aware of all the support you will need and of what is available to you. If you are studying at university there are likely to be a number of support services you can access, such as subject guides in the library, reading lists, help with academic writing, English language classes, support for those with special learning needs and so on. Examine any document that accompanied the assignment, such as the brief, any marking scheme, module handbook, reading lists, notes and tips from the teaching team or support staff, etc. Importantly, don't forget your tutor as a source of support. Be honest with yourself – what help do you really need? What do you struggle with? What has feedback on previous work said that you could do better? Your tutor should be able to support you throughout the writing process and will be able to point you to other sources of support that may be useful.

Now you are ready to start drafting your document.

Drafting

Under each of the headings in your structure make a note of the points you need to cover and of the ideas, concepts or theories you need to explain. This will help to ensure you don't forget to mention something important, which is more likely if you just start writing the text. As with the overall heading structure, check these points are in a logical sequence. Make sure you plan to cover all that is necessary and nothing that is not truly relevant. Having done all the reading for a literature review, say, it's very tempting to feel you must say something about every article and book you have read or to mention every single concept, theory or model you have considered, but that's not the case. Imagine sorting your information using the grid shown in Figure 11.1. Some of what you have read

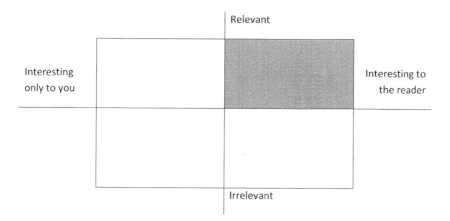

FIGURE 11.1   Using a grid to decide what to include – make sure it's relevant and interesting to the reader

I remember feeling a real pang of anguish when marking an undergraduate dissertation and having to write 'well-written but largely irrelevant' on the literature review.

may have been fascinating, but may be of limited relevance because, for example, the work is rather old or is not on exactly the right topic. Include all the points that are truly relevant and interesting so that they help to advance your argument and avoid mentioning points that are neither relevant nor interesting just because you read the material.

Before you start to write, make sure you have all the information you will need to hand. Stopping to find information once you have started writing will spoil your focus and interrupt the flow of your narrative. Similarly, make sure you are in a comfortable place for writing with no distractions. If you find it difficult to concentrate for long periods, try using a clock or a timer to write for an hour then take a break. Alternatively, set yourself achievable goals (see Box 11.1), such as write one section and then take a break.

Box 11.1 Setting achievable goals

When I was writing my PhD the task was simply too big to contemplate in its entirety. I'd planned the structure and headings and had a list of points under each heading. So I'd sit down and write just one section in each writing session. Knowing that I had to write 500 words on X, Y and Z in section 6.4.2 was much more manageable and gave me a sense of achievement every time I finished a section.

Writing up the literature review

Your review should tell a complete story with a beginning, middle and end.

Introduction

Restate the objective(s) of the review, set the work in context and provide a brief outline of what will follow. This helps the audience to understand the shape of the work, so they know what to expect. For example, you could start with a few sentences along the lines of:

> This review considers a range of literature to determine [whatever your objective is for the literature review]. A number of themes emerged from the literature, including:
>
> - list whatever you've found in a bullet list;
> - to make it quick for the reader to grasp;
> - then use these bullet points as headings;
> - in the literature review.
>
> The rest of this chapter will consider each of these themes and examine how they relate to the research question. [Or, if there are too many themes for you to examine, say that the chapter will consider two or three of these in depth and explain why you have chosen those themes.]

Main body

Split this into relevant sections using the headings discussed earlier. Don't use the heading 'main body' (you'd be surprised how many people do). Headings should encapsulate the content that follows. They are signposts for the reader.

Your literature review must describe, discuss and critically evaluate the evidence you have found. For example, you may have found that several authors of different textbooks or journal articles all recommend that it's important to have a celebrity to launch a new product. You report this in your literature review by saying:

> Smith (2009) and Jones (2007) both recommend that an organisation should enlist the support of a celebrity. They believe this is a good idea because . . . [explain how and why they have come to this conclusion].

Then make your own comment on the evidence, for example:

> This idea clearly has some merits, for example [list the good things, with examples], but there are also some disadvantages, such as [list the disadvantages, with examples].

The examples you use could be from other literature, for example:

> Company ABC used a sports celebrity to launch its range of healthy drinks and found this was very successful. Writing in *Marketing Week*, ABC's Marketing Manager said, 'Thank goodness we had a celebrity on board – without him our product would have failed' (reference, date).

You may also want to comment on the research evidence you have found, for example to say that a particular piece of research is quite old now, or it was based on people in America so it might not be relevant, or that the research was done with a very small number of people so it might not be generalisable or applicable to your study. This way, you use a fact from the literature to illustrate a point then make your own points in addition.

Essentially, you have to construct an argument showing what the literature says, making links between different sources and making your own comment as you go along.

You must always support what you say with a reference. If you say that a particular company is the most successful in its sector, the reader will want to know the evidence on which you have based that statement.

Summary

Write a summary at the end that draws out key points and themes that have arisen and connects these back to the research objective(s)/question(s). You can then connect the literature review to the primary data/findings by saying the discussion/analysis chapter will pick up on these points and themes. This kind of connection helps your work to hang together as a whole, rather than appearing as a series of separate pieces of writing. For example:

> In summary, the literature suggests that the most important factors are [whatever you have found]. These have been discussed, and the disadvantages and advantages of each have been considered. The questions/key points that arise from the review are:
>
> - list the questions/key points in a bullet list;
> - to show how the results of the literature review;
> - have led to specific lines of enquiry;
> - for your primary research.
>
> These questions will now be examined in the primary research.

Using references

When writing up the literature review, make sure you have all your notes and important sources to hand. If you refer to a source, make a quotation or use a source to support a point you have made, include that source in your reference list straightaway. Don't wait until you have completed the review to write up the references list – you are bound to miss some out, include some that you didn't use and create inconsistencies with names and dates. Some software packages such as End Note, Reference Manager and Manderlay are available to help with this task if you find it difficult to do manually. You are likely to be required to follow a particular style for references, such as Harvard (name, date), Vancouver (numbered) or Oxford (usually for the arts). Follow a style guide – there are many available – to ensure correctness and consistency.

Paragraphing and ideas

Your work should tell a story with a logical progression of ideas. Don't worry if you find yourself writing on a topic that you know you covered three or four paragraphs previously. This is the beauty of drafting – you can re-read your work and move paragraphs about so they fit together sensibly. This is very easy to do with word processing software, so there is no excuse for getting it wrong. When combining paragraphs that have been written far apart ensure that you are not repeating yourself. Combining means combining ideas, rather than just tacking one paragraph onto the end of another. You may need to re-draft as one complete paragraph, deleting repetitive text.

Some people are unsure about how to construct paragraphs. If in doubt, use the PEEL model (see Box 11.2), which will help you to write paragraphs that make sense and help to build an argument.

Box 11.2 PEEL paragraphs

P   Make a **point**.

E   **Explain/expand** on that point with more information and examples.

E   Provide **evidence** for the point with reference to relevant sources.

L   **Link** the point to the next point and/or to the research question(s)/ objective(s).

The PEEL model helps to construct self-contained paragraphs that deal with one idea at a time and forces you to think about how the text connects to the rest of the work. When writing long documents you may find it useful to apply the model on a section-by-section basis rather than on each paragraph, as you may need several paragraphs for the explain/expand and evidence elements.

Language

Academic language should be scholarly, showing an understanding and appreciation for the subject and its vocabulary, but does not have to be complex, convoluted or impenetrable. You may be conveying complex ideas and issues and these will not be made easier to understand by using deliberately complex language or jargon. We recommend that you use plain English and short sentences. Long sentences run the risk of losing track of the overall sense and will make the reader run out of breath. Keep it short and simple (KISS). This model is often used in copywriting and is just as applicable to academic writing. This will make your writing more enjoyable to read and much easier to understand. Consider the following poem, with which you are probably familiar:

Scintillate, scintillate globe vivific
Fain would I fathom thy nature specific
Loftily poised in the ether capacious
Strongly resembling a gem carbonaceous.

This is a deliberately convoluted rendition of 'Twinkle, twinkle little star'! Remember, it is not the language but the ideas that will impress your readers – make sure you use language that they will recognise and understand rather than language that may confuse, irritate or alienate them. Box 11.3 shows some examples of complex words and phrases that have simpler alternatives.

Box 11.3 Simple alternatives for complex language

Complex	Simple alternative
Exemplification	Example
The majority of	Most
Lacuna	Gap
Regarding	About
Advantageous	Helpful
Commensurate	Equal
Commence	Start
Remuneration	Payment or reward
Leverage	Use

Can you think of any more?

Active or passive voice and objectivity

A lot of research and other academic writing uses the passive voice. Consider the audience and how it would be best to communicate with them. Sometimes the passive voice can lead to clumsy language. There may be a specific requirement, depending on who will read the work – much academic writing uses the passive voice, but we suggest that trying the active voice is not a bad thing and may help readers to understand. For example, '50 interviews were conducted with clients at the hairdressing salon' could become 'we conducted 50 interviews with clients at the hairdressing salon'. As readers know the work has been written by real people (your name will be on the work) why not use 'we' and 'I' if it is appropriate to the audience and context? As always, check

TABLE 11.1 Writing objectively

You want to say	Try this instead
Everyone knows that . . .	It is commonly accepted that . . .
It's obvious that . . .	It may reasonably be assumed that . . .
	One might sensibly conclude that . . .
	It seems clear from the evidence that . . .
	The evidence seems to suggest that . . .
It's obvious that celebrity endorsements help to sell products.	It may be fair to assume that celebrity endorsements help to sell products and the literature supports this.
I think this research is too old to be useful.	Note that this research was conducted some time ago, and is now quite dated.
TV advertising is too expensive for most companies.	Smith (2006) reports that the cost of TV advertising is beyond the reach of many companies.

the brief in case it specifies use of the passive. If you decide to use the active voice and you feel this is unusual, discuss with your tutor or whoever will read/review your work so you don't have it returned with 'passive voice, please' written on it.

Your writing must be objective (unless you are specifically required to give your own personal view) and some people find this difficult. Even if something seems very obvious to you or if you think it's something everyone knows, you can't say that it's obvious without proving it with some evidence. If you personally agree with a particular author's stance, don't say that he/she is clearly right about XYZ and that you agree with it – this shows not only that you have not given a balanced view on the author's work, but that you have aligned yourself with a particular viewpoint, meaning that the rest of your work may be biased. Table 11.1 shows some ideas about appropriate phrases that may be useful when writing objectively.

Language worries

Many people worry about their use of language; for example, you may know you have problems with spelling, punctuation or grammar. You are not alone! Even the most experienced writers can have problems.

I have to look up 'prejudiced' every time I use it to make sure I've got it right. And even though I've looked it up many times, I still can't remember it. The same goes for 'gauge' (I always want to put the 'u' before the 'a') and 'mnemonic'. So I always work with a dictionary. That's OK. Look words up if you are not sure of their spelling.

Word processing software will pick up a lot of spelling errors, but not all of them. Software is not intelligent and will not know when you have used the wrong word spelled correctly, e.g. 'that' instead of 'than'. Box 11.4 shows some of the most common mistakes people make.

Box 11.4 Common mistakes

- Spelling – don't rely on the spellchecker.
- Punctuation – full points, commas, apostrophes, speech marks and semi-colons are main culprits. getting this right avoids those long stream-of-consciousness paragraphs that appear to be one long unpunctuated sentence or a series of phrases separated by commas.
- Grammar – check your work makes grammatical sense, e.g. subject–verb agreement.
- Sense – ask a critical friend to read your work if you are worried that it doesn't make sense. using shorter sentences and simpler language usually helps to sort out any sense problems.
- Using the wrong words, e.g. 'defiantly' instead of 'definitely', 'there' instead of 'their'.
- Wrong use of i.e. (which means 'that is to say') and e.g. (which means 'for example') can ruin the sense.
- Ending sentences with prepositions – please avoid.
- Saying 'different to' rather than 'different from' – get it right.
- Incorrect use of 'however' – check how to use this correctly.

Many of us also struggle with punctuation, especially apostrophes, commas, semi-colons, colons, commas and speech marks. Our advice is to keep sentences short and simple so you don't need colons and semi-colons (use a full stop and start a new sentence instead), and learn the correct way to use punctuation. If you find it difficult to remember, look it up. It's OK to admit you have to look up how to use an apostrophe, rather than guess and get it wrong. Table 11.2 explains how to use common punctuation correctly. For more detail, refer to a grammar text.

If you find academic writing difficult and/or if you are writing in a second language, find and use the support services available, including your tutor. Here are a few more tips:

- Don't be tempted to use free translation software online as this is more likely to transliterate (translate each word individually) rather than translate (translate the meaning).
- Don't rely on the spellchecker – this simply checks individual words, rather than checking meaning, sense, grammar or punctuation.
- Don't be tempted to use lots of long quotes – use your own words.
- Try to convey the overall sense and work on the fine detail when you read through your work later.

TABLE 11.2 Punctuation rules

Symbol	Name	What is it for?	Examples
'	Apostrophe	Use to show a missing letter or possession. If used to show possession by more than one person, the apostrophe goes after the plural 's'.	It's = it is Its = belonging to it Don't = do not Let's = let us You're = you are The dog's bone = bone belonging to the dog The cats' bowls = bowls belonging to more than one cat
:	Colon	Use to show that what follows is either a list or a statement that clarifies or gives examples of what has been said before the colon	I bought some fruit: apples, pears and bananas. Kotler's theory is simple: it states that . . .
;	Semi-colon	This replaces a conjunction such as 'but' or 'and'. Use to show that the phrase that follows expands on or is related to what has been said before the semi-colon.	Some find writing difficult; others don't. Advertising can be a costly business; some say it is too costly.
–	Parenthetical dash	Use to show that what follows is information that could be put in brackets, i.e. it is not essential. Often performs a similar function to a semi-colon.	I bought some fruit – apples are my favourite. He went into the shop – he always went shopping on a Tuesday – and bought some candles.
,	Comma	Use to separate items in a list or to create a short pause, like taking a breath. The comma separates phrases and should not be used instead of a full stop.	I bought apples, pears, bananas and grapes. People run out of breath if they have to read very long sentences without a break, so use a comma.
"…" '…'	Speech marks or inverted commas	Use to show quotations. Don't use these to show emphasis, as the reader may interpret it as a quotation.	When asked which brand she preferred she said, 'I prefer this one because it's cheaper.' Smith (2015) describes this idea as 'ridiculous'.

Critical analysis

How do you analyse critically? The clue is in the question – be critical. Don't accept all that you read as verbatim truth or fact. Criticise it from an academic perspective. For example, you may have read an article that makes some excellent points, but perhaps the research was conducted a long time ago, the sample size was

I have lost count of how many times I have written 'Be more critical', 'Critical analysis needed' or 'You tend to describe rather than analyse critically' on student assignments.

very small or the research was conducted in a specific context that is different from your own research context. It's OK to point these things out. It does not invalidate the article or your own work – it does quite the reverse. It shows that you have read, understood and engaged with the research. Established models and theories are there for you to dissect. Do they really apply to your work in your context or is some adaptation needed? Are they truly perfect or do they omit a useful detail? Consider the model shown in Figure 11.2, which shows how to make a cup of tea.

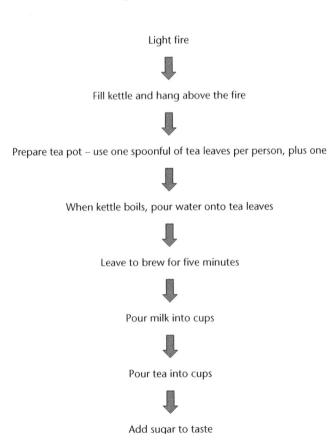

Light fire

Fill kettle and hang above the fire

Prepare tea pot – use one spoonful of tea leaves per person, plus one

When kettle boils, pour water onto tea leaves

Leave to brew for five minutes

Pour milk into cups

Pour tea into cups

Add sugar to taste

FIGURE 11.2 Lawson's (1995) model for making tea

To analyse the model critically, consider these points. Then read an example of critical analysis in Box 11.5.

- What is good about it?
- What is not good about it?
- Does it apply to a range of situations?
- Does it apply just as well now as when it was originally devised?
- Will it still apply in the future?
- Have any other academics/authors commented on it? What did they say?
- What is your own scholarly conclusion, based on this analysis?

Box 11.5 Critical analysis of Lawson's model

Lawson's model of how to make tea (Lawson, 1995) is rather dated now, but still has an elegant simplicity that makes it easy to follow and use. The model is regarded as dated as most people now use electric kettles, rather than an open fire. That said, Smith (2001) points out that Lawson's model works well for outdoor tea-making, such as on camping holidays. The model is, in some ways, more applicable to the UK than to many other countries – for example, making tea in India would involve heating the milk, while tea in some countries is served with no milk at all. Opinion is further divided on the model, as some authors (Jones, 2002) hold that the pot should be warmed first and others (Potempski, 2009) that tea bags should be used. It seems from this mix of views that there are many ways of making tea and there is perhaps no single correct way of doing it.

Critical analysis does not describe; it compares, contrasts, applies, evaluates and provides justified academic critique.

Using non-text elements in your work

Using diagrams and illustrations (known as figures), tables and quotations in your work helps to break up the text and provide interest to the reader, but they also serve their own very important functions. Figures can convey complex ideas that would otherwise take a large number of words to explain. Tables present data quickly and efficiently, making it easier to digest than prose littered with numbers or short phrases. Quotations can highlight key ideas and important points in the words of authoritative others, strengthening your argument. When used well, non–text elements can improve your work. Here are some tips about how to use them well.

Figures

- Mention them in the text so the reader knows why they are there.
- Number them sequentially – this makes it easier to refer to them in the text and helps the reader to identify them, especially if there is more than one figure on a page.
- Give each figure a caption that explains very briefly what is shown.
- Present figure captions in a consistent way.
- If the figure is taken from elsewhere, give the source in brackets at the end of the caption. If the figure is your own creation use (source: author).
- If your figure needs labels ensure they are legible.

Tables

- Mention them in the text so the reader knows why they are there.
- Number them sequentially – this makes it easier to refer to them in the text and helps the reader to identify them, especially if there is more than one table on a page.
- Give each table a heading that explains very briefly what is shown.
- Present table headings in a consistent way.
- If the table is taken from elsewhere, give the source in brackets at the end of the heading. If the table is your own creation use (source: author).
- Ensure column and row headings are clear.
- Use to show text as well as numbers.
- If your table is just one column of information, this should be displayed as a list rather than as a table.

When writing about what is shown in figures and tables, don't repeat what they show – interpret, expand on, evaluate and analyse what is shown, rather than describing it.

Quotations

- Use sparingly.
- Ensure the quote says something important that strengthens your argument – not just a repetition of your argument.
- Always include the source with a page number.
- If the quote is less than a line long, include it as part of the text 'like this'.
- If the quote is longer, it is better to display it separately like this.

    Long quotes set apart from the main text make them clearer straightaway. There's no need to use italics for the displayed quote (unless this is specified in the brief) as the fact it is displayed draws enough attention already. Put the source at the end, underneath the quote.

Quotations usually use single inverted commas rather than double speech marks (check the brief to see if a style is stipulated). If there is a quote within a quote, use speech marks to show the difference. 'Use single inverted commas and speech marks for "a quote within a quote" if needed.'

Punctuation round quotes can be tricky. As a rule of thumb, if the punctuation mark belongs to the text being quoted, put it inside the inverted commas, for example:

> 'I got 50% off!' he exclaimed.

> He said he was 'very disappointed'.

> She reported that 'The work is very nearly finished.'

Feedback

It is useful to ask for feedback on your work, preferably before you finalise it for submission. Feedback is not the end of the writing process – it's an important step in improving your work. Many of us find it difficult to ask for feedback and even more challenging to deal with feedback when we receive it. Perhaps we find it difficult to ask for feedback because we don't know who to ask or how to ask or we are worried about what the response will be. Many of us don't like criticism. What we really want to hear, when we have spent a lot of time and effort on a piece of work is 'That's fantastic! There's absolutely nothing you need to change. It's the best piece of work I've read in a long time.' Unfortunately, this very rarely happens and it's much more common that feedback will be full of comments, suggestions and ideas that will help us to improve our work. This can be disheartening at first, because we really want the 'This is brilliant!' response. We know deep down that our work isn't perfect; that we are probably too close to the work to view it objectively. We just don't want to hear it! Worse, we don't like the idea of the extra work represented by the comments and we feel as if we are being criticised personally rather than our work being criticised. Often, giving the feedback can feel just as awkward and you might not know how to do it without hurting the writer's feelings. This section gives some tips on how to ask for feedback, who to ask, how to give feedback and how to deal with receiving feedback.

Who to ask for feedback

Your tutor/supervisor is an obvious choice. If you are working on an assignment, check how much feedback your tutor/supervisor will give. He/she is likely to be happy to review an outline and to comment once on a draft, rather than commenting on several drafts. All universities and all tutors are different, so check what is expected and reasonable to ensure you are not disappointed and that your tutor/supervisor is not put in a difficult position. Others you could ask include your peers, friends and family who could act as 'critical friends'.

My Dad read every one of my MBA assignments and every chapter of my PhD, giving me very useful feedback on sense, sequencing and use of language. While he was not a specialist in my area, he was an academic and could provide a perspective similar to that of those who would read and assess my work. My tutors supplied specialist feedback on content.

How to ask for feedback

Don't ask 'Would you mind giving me some feedback on my work?' This request is too vague. Try something more specific, such as 'Could you give me some feedback on how to improve my critical analysis, please?' or 'Could you let me know if you think there are any gaps or if I've repeated myself?' or 'Could you tell me if my work makes logical sense?' Asking more specific questions gives the person giving the feedback a more specific job to do. You could also say whether you want overall, general comments or something more detailed.

How to give feedback

Giving feedback is a serious and responsible task. Spend time reading the work properly – don't skimp and cut corners. Be honest with your opinion and gentle in how you communicate it. If you have been asked just for 'feedback', ask the writer what he/she would like you to comment on in particular. There are several kinds of feedback: praise, criticism, questions, helpful suggestions/ideas and overall comments.

You can give praise in a number of ways: for example, by agreeing with a point; saying something has been done well; a good reference has been used; a point has been well argued; there is good use of figures, tables, quotes, etc.; there's a good structure with clear headings; a good opening or closing line; a clear argument, concise summary, etc. There is always something good you can say about a piece of work. And you should always find something positive to say – returning someone's work with nothing but criticism can be very upsetting for the writer.

Critical comments can point out that something needs further explanation, doesn't make sense or doesn't fit well in a particular section. You can note poor grammar or spelling, highlight points that should be supported by references and flag up poor logical sequencing of ideas. Comments may also be phrased as questions for the writer to consider, such as 'Can you comment on this instead of describing it?' or 'How does this fit in with your argument?' or 'Can you explain this acronym in full?' or 'I don't understand this – can you clarify it?' or

'Is this a quotation?' Specific comments and questions such as these will show the writer how to improve his/her work.

You may like to give some helpful suggestions that encourage the writer to expand further on a certain point, ask for examples or more detail, point the writer to a specific reference or theory that would be useful or ask the writer to consider whether it would be better to display material as a figure, table or list.

Writers will find it useful if you give an overall concluding comment that encapsulates your view of the work and draws out the key good point(s) and the key point(s) that need improvement.

Dealing with feedback

Remember that feedback has been offered in order to help improve your work. It is not a criticism of you or of your ability. Look upon it as a series of helpful comments, queries and suggestions. Someone has spent time and effort to read and comment on your work as an objective outsider or critical friend – receive it with thanks. Query any comments you don't understand. If there are comments that you disagree with, think why this may be – perhaps you need to explain your point more clearly or justify it more carefully. Remember, if a point has been raised as part of feedback it may also be raised as part of assessment unless resolved now.

If there are a lot of comments and the rewrites seem daunting, tackle one at a time and remember that every problem has a solution. Our advice would be to make all the quick, easy or small corrections first so the number of comments quickly reduces. It always helps to feel that you are making progress! Of course, this will leave you with only the larger, more difficult or more time-consuming corrections to make, but at least you will have a realistic idea of the amount of work involved. Sometimes the rewrites may take longer than writing the first draft – just remember that this will improve your work and make it the best it can be. Take your time and don't rush this stage – give it the time it deserves. When you are planning your project right at the beginning, remember to allow time for this stage and for all the final checks shown in Box 11.6.

Box 11.6 Final draft and final checks

- Read through for sense, spelling, punctuation and grammar. Sometimes it helps to read your work aloud – this will reveal over-long sentences, poor grammar and unnecessarily convoluted or complex language.
- Is it clear who the audience for the work is?

(continued)

(continued)

- Is it clear what the overall point of the work is?
- Does the executive summary/abstract consider the whole project?
- Does the work flow logically from one idea to the next?
- Are there adequate links between sections or chapters?
- Are points made clearly linked to the overall purpose of the work?
- Is there a clear beginning, middle and end?
- Have points raised in the introduction been thoroughly addressed in the discussion and conclusion?
- Check references cited are shown in the references list and vice versa.
- Check references are cited and listed correctly in the appropriate style.
- Are all figures and tables numbered sequentially, with an appropriate mention in the text and with appropriate figure captions and table headings?
- Are any appendices mentioned in the work? Are they numbered sequentially and referred to in the text? Are they included at the back?
- Have you followed any set style or design guidelines?
- Have you taken on board the comments of reviewers or critical friends?

Writing up qualitative data

As when writing up the literature review, make sure your write-up of the research data has a beginning, middle and end. Remind the reader of the research question(s)/objective(s), set the work in context by referring back to the literature review and outline the structure of the discussion/analysis so the reader knows what to expect. Themes, issues and/or key points will have arisen during your analysis – use these to help structure your discussion.

Analysis of qualitative data is open to bias, not least because none of the data will be truly objective – people's words, voices, images or whatever other form your data takes will be particular to each individual. It will be their perception of the truth. It is important that your analysis and discussion is objective. Don't allow your own opinions and subjective views to affect what you say about the data. Instead, let the data tell its own story.

- What does the data say? There may be one main story to tell or there may be a multi-faceted story. Remember to use the PEEL model to tell the story and use a logical sequence for the ideas and headings that will help signpost the story for the reader.
- How does the data's story tally (or not) with the story told by the literature? Comment on and be critical of any similarities or differences.
- Comment on participants' use of language – why have they used these particular words, phrases and expressions?

FIGURE 11.3   Using a word cloud to show qualitative data

Source: © Thea Goldin Smith. Courtesy of Wikimedia Commons

- Consider semiotics – what is the meaning of the words? What lies beneath the words? What is the context of those words?
- While observing specific words and their meaning, beware of losing sight of the bigger picture. What is the wider narrative around those words?

Don't be afraid to use visual means to display the data – well-chosen quotations or images can illuminate the points you make and strengthen your argument. Tables can also be used to good effect to give an instant impression of the 'look' of the data.

Word clouds (sometimes called Wordles) can be generated by free software online. The size of the words indicates their frequency, providing a very basic form of analysis that still requires your interpretation. These images can give a quick general impression of the relative importance of the words and phrases used by participants (see Figure 11.3 for an example).

If you have used software such as Leximancer for analysis of qualitative data, the images produced can be used in the discussion to highlight key points.

Finish your discussion with a summary that draws together the main points, ties the primary data to the literature and makes it clear that the objective(s) have been met.

Writing for different purposes

Writing abstracts and summaries

It could be argued that an abstract, summary or executive summary is the most important element of your thesis. First impressions are really important and this is the first encounter of your polished, hard work that your audience will see. In fact this is sometimes the only element of your work some people will read. Therefore it makes sense that you put extra effort in getting your messages across in this section to capture their attention and interest. This can often be a tall order if you have just run out of energy crafting your research into words. So here are a few tips to help you interest your reader and gain the attention your report deserves.

- Write your abstract or summary last! It's surprising how many people attempt to do this first and then suffer the consequences of having to re-write in light of their research findings.
- Don't be tempted to copy and paste paragraphs from the body of your report. This section deserves careful wording to guide the reader through the topic and process you have taken.
- What needs to be included? In short, everything – its purpose is to provide a summary of your whole report but in a short, digestible format.
- Break that information down into the subject of the project, your objectives for the study, the approach you took, major points of your critical analysis, decisions and results. You can also summarise your conclusion and recommendation.
- All the information you include in the abstract or summary must appear in the report – don't put any new material in here.
- This is not the place for charts or diagrams.
- Generally you should not need to cite any references in your summary – if you feel you need to then you might be getting into far too much detail.
- Last of all, keep your summary to one page – so be concise, selecting the most important elements of your work.

Writing for different media

In addition to an academic version of your work, you may be asked to communicate your findings to other audiences via the media. If you are in the business of communications today it is inevitable that you will encounter a growing range of media, each utilising different channels from print to broadcast, social networks to blogs, podcasts to videos on YouTube. Differing audiences too. From academic papers to professional interest, trade publications to consumer, brand building – the list goes on. How can we possibly write appropriate, engaging, informative copy for such diversity?

Fortunately some rules apply to all and will enable you to get started.

- Whatever message you hope to communicate you need to be very clear in your own mind what it is that you wish to say and what outcome you wish to influence. Simple? Often not the case and requires some effort to work through. Make sure you are clear about your objectives for writing the piece and what action you wish your readers to take.
- Understanding your audience. What do they read, watch, and listen to? Who influences them? Without that understanding it's impossible to select media to deliver your message – and you have no idea of the language and style that will be appropriate to write a compelling story.

- What makes the news? What is worthy of publication? Firstly it needs to be relevant to your reader, and topical – old news is no news. What are your reader's expectations? Is your content something that your audience should know about? If something is unusual it attracts interest, so search for some points of difference – is it the biggest, smallest or strangest? We all love those stories!

- Find the right emotional hook. If we tell a story effectively it will arouse the reader and draw them into the scenario we have created. This is a very powerful tool which can influence perception.

- Learn to edit. Keeping messages concise is so important. Consider your reader's attention span. They may be reading your story as they travel to work on the train, or are they more likely to be reading your copy in a Sunday publication . . . typically still being read on Wednesday. If it's a radio piece, is it drive time? Attention span can be very short so clarity, key messages and developing an emotional bond will make your story much more memorable.

- An understanding of the media channel is important too. What works as a press release will not necessarily work as a blog. If you are writing for a particular publication, then get a copy and read it. Find out what is specific to that particular publication and determine how your piece would 'fit' with that format and style. That goes for broadcast too – make sure you listen or watch your intended channel before starting to draft copy.

The online dimension could be a whole new chapter – but regardless of the social media channel or web copy you intend to develop there are some ground rules that you need to be aware of that will make your content more appropriate and engaging.

- The focus for social media is very much that of the individual. It is even more personal than talking to your target audience. This is having a one-to-one conversation with an individual.

- If we write for social media there is a hope and expectation that our content will be shared if it is topical, informative and has value to readers. That also means there is a change in style and the language you use. Take care not to patronise, exclude or offend any readers.

- Acknowledging other authors' work can have very positive effects. Re-tweeting or posting brings benefits to your own work, so the spirit of cooperation amongst peers is a powerful force.

- There are no deadlines. This is a 24/7 operation so be prepared to respond to enquiries, positive and negative comments.

Writing presentations

Presenting can be one of the most daunting things we have to do. If you are well prepared, understand your subject and are confident in the way in which you have structured your presentation then your stress levels will start to improve immediately and you can channel all that wonderful energy into your passionate delivery.

As with many beautifully designed things, simplicity is often our best friend. If you are using PowerPoint or other audio-visual aids, too much text can get in the way of making your points. The audience can be confused. Should they listen to you? Maybe they should be writing down the information? Their attention is split and you lose them. Some tips to help you structure your presentation includes the simple but effective 'What, Why, How?' approach (see Box 11.7).

Box 11.7 How to structure your presentation

- What? Open with your key message.
- Be aware of your audience – what language and style are they going to be comfortable with?
- What is going to be in it for them? Make sure you get the benefits across at the beginning of your presentation.
- Now your audience understands the 'what' the natural question is 'why?' Develop your story to show the importance of what you are presenting. By now you should have an audience who is engaged as they understand the 'flow' of your presentation
- Then move on to explaining 'how'. This can be a number of suggestions or recommendations providing food for thought. Remember to keep your slides concise.
- It is often useful to show examples, or use case studies to develop and support your recommendation; we all relate better to concepts that are applied. It shows how things will work in practice.
- Clear, simple visuals to support your argument can be powerful elements in your presentation.
- Bring your presentation to a conclusion. What do you want your audience to do? Be clear about the course of action you want them to take.

Remember to check your first draft and make sure you do an edit. Look for:

- Spelling mistakes; believe me they will be in the headline.
- Keep your sentences short.
- Use bullet points.
- Use appropriate language for the audience.
- Keep typefaces simple and consistent throughout.

- Use powerful visuals.
- Be confident of your presentation content, check video links all work, etc.
- Above all, rehearse!

As a PR practitioner of many years a mistake in the headline has caught me and other colleagues out a few times!

Writing posters

Infographics have become increasingly popular and serve to direct viewers to a website as well as impart facts and figures easily and succinctly. Posters, too, offer the opportunity to condense big data into bite-size, memorable information. So where do you begin in crafting copy that will pack that memorable punch?

As someone who has always enjoyed visual work it is very tempting to start on that angle first. But beware. For your infographic or poster to have any real impact, and therefore value, it is important to make sure the content and copy are correct first.

What makes infographics and posters interesting is 'great content' – and that can be boiled down into what is new, relevant and informative for your target audience. In addition to providing something that is useful, try to establish an emotional connection with your audience. Make them smile, shed a tear or prompt a thought. That will help to make your message memorable. Some tips:

- Make headlines and copy short and punchy.
- Pose a question or use an emotional/intellectual hook.
- Use key words (Google Search can help you with that).
- Use big numbers in headlines.
- Create subheadings – rather than a lot of text.

- Make sure your data is correct and from trustworthy sources. Inaccurate information will tarnish your reputation.
- End your infographic or poster with a strong statement – or a call to action. What do you want your viewer to do as a result of having engaged with your work?

Summary

This chapter has considered how to communicate your research to your audience, mainly as a written piece of work. We have covered how to think, plan and structure your work before you start and have emphasised the importance of considering your audience carefully. We have given some advice about how to draft your work, including tips on writing style and presentation as well as critical analysis and the nitty-gritty of punctuation. We have given our advice about asking for, giving and receiving feedback. It is not until you have responded to the feedback that you can draft the final version of your work and check that it is complete. Finally, we have considered how to write for different purposes and different media. Box 11.8 gives some quick pointers about how to recognise good writing.

Box 11.8 How to recognise good writing

- There is a clear beginning, middle and end.
- The structure is made clear with useful headings.
- The text follows a clear and logical sequence.
- The introduction sets out the context, background and purpose, includes a hook to tempt the reader to read further and outlines the structure of the rest of the document.
- The language is easy to understand, with jargon kept to a minimum and no waffle – just clear points well made.
- The text makes key points clear in the discussion and they are all relevant to the matter under study.
- Figures and tables add value to the work, illuminating the data and making complex ideas easier to understand.
- The conclusion is clearly based on what has gone before, resolves any issues raised in the discussion, demonstrates how the objectives have been met and draws out the academic and/or practical implications of the work.
- References are consistently and correctly used.

We hope the guidance, suggestions and tips we have given about how to improve your work will prove useful to you. Good luck with your writing!

Seminar activities

Task 1 Writing a summary

Choose a recent assignment, a chapter in a book (any book – a text book, novel, travel guide, whatever) or a newspaper article and write a 400-word summary of it, following the steps below.

1. Define your audience and what they would want/need to know. What sort of language and tone would be appropriate? How much do they know already? What might need further explanation?
2. Decide which key points you want to mention.
3. Plan the structure for the work – make sure it has a clear beginning, middle and end.
4. Draft the work using a logical sequence of ideas.
5. Swap with a friend. Read, review and feedback as a critical friend.
6. Re-draft in response to the comments.
7. Do final checks and apply formatting as necessary.
8. Reflect on this process. How did it feel to review and critique someone else's work? How did it feel to receive criticism of your own work? How successful do you feel your summary was? How could you improve it?

Further tasks

- Repeat Task 1 but for a different audience.
- Repeat Task 1 but write the work for publication as a blog.
- Repeat Task 1 but for communication in a presentation.
- Write a tweet (140 characters including spaces and punctuation) to communicate the essence of the summary.

Task 2 Critical analysis

Choose a model or theory with which you are familiar. This could be, for example, the marketing mix, PEST, SWOT, Porter's generic strategies, the Boston matrix, VALS or any other concept you have used in your studies. Write a short critical analysis of the model/theory using the steps shown below as your starting point. Remember to do some thinking first, plan what you want to say and then write a piece that has a proper beginning, middle and end. You may need to do some quick research to answer some of the points properly. Your audience for the work is fellow academics. Write no more than 500 words.

- What is good about it?
- What is not good about it?

- Does it apply to a range of situations?
- Does it apply just as well now as when it was originally devised?
- Will it still apply in the future?
- Have any other academics/authors commented on it? What did they say?
- What is your own scholarly conclusion, based on this analysis?

Bibliography

Bailey, S. (2014.) *Academic Writing: A Handbook for International Students*. London: Routledge. (Also available as an e-book.)

Cutts, M. (2013). *The Oxford Guide to Plain English*, 4th edn. Oxford: Oxford University Press.

Horn, R. (2012). *Researching and Writing Dissertations: A Complete Guide for Business and Management Students*. London: Chartered Institute of Personnel and Development.

Pollock, T. G. and Bono, J. E. (2013). 'Being Scheherezade: The Importance of Storytelling in Academic Writing'. *Academy of Management Journal* 56, no. 3, pp. 629–34.

Roberts, C. M. (2004). *The Dissertation Journey: A Practical and Comprehensive Guide to Planning, Writing, and Defending Your Dissertation*. Thousand Oaks, CA: Corwin Press.

Swetnam, D. (2004). *Writing your Dissertation: How to Plan, Prepare, and Present Successful Work*, 3rd edn. Oxford: How to Books. (Also available as an e-book.)

Ward, L. J. and Woods, G. (2007). *English Grammar for Dummies*. Chichester: Wiley.

Authors' note

All references cited in examples are entirely fictional.

12

RESEARCH ETHICS

Simon Dupernex

Introduction and context

When we think of ethics we tend to think of rules for distinguishing between right and wrong, such as 'Do unto others as you would have them do unto you', a code of professional conduct, or a religious creed like the Ten Commandments.

Ethics can be defined as 'a social, religious, or civil code of behaviour considered correct, especially that of a particular group, profession, or individual' or 'the moral fitness of a decision, course of action' (Collins, 2015).

There are a number of highly publicised breaches of ethics which have dominated the news since the beginning of the millennium:

- Enron failed in December 2001, at that time the largest corporate bankruptcy ever, and the chief executive, Kenneth L. Lay, was convicted of fraud (*Forbes*, 2013). The Enron bankruptcy had wider implications and also led to the demise of the world top-five audit giant Arthur Andersen, which was found guilty of shredding Enron-related documents (BBC, 2002).
- WorldCom, the second largest telecoms company in America, failed in 2002. Its CEO, Bernie Ebbers, was convicted in 2005 on nine counts of conspiracy, securities fraud, and making false regulatory filings (*Time*, 2015).
- In 2009 UK Members of Parliament were involved in a scandal over the actual and alleged misuse of permitted claims for expenses and allowances,

FIGURE 12.1 Stock markets

Source: Photo © Wikipedia, Courtesy of Creative Commons

which was disclosed by the UK *Daily Telegraph* newspaper following disclosures under a contested Freedom of Information Act 2000 enquiry (*Daily Telegraph*, 2009).

- In 2013, Edward Snowden, a former CIA employee, copied classified documents from the United States National Security Agency (NSA), and released the contents of a number of these to the *Washington Post* and *Guardian* newspapers (*Guardian*, 2013a) (*Washington Post*, 2013). Snowden claimed that

> The NSA has built an infrastructure that allows it to intercept almost everything. With this capability, the vast majority of human communications are automatically ingested without targeting. If I wanted to see your emails or your wife's phone, all I have to do is use intercepts. I can get your emails, passwords, phone records, credit cards. I don't want to live in a society that does these sort of things . . . (*Guardian*, 2013b).

- On 18 September 2015, the United States Environmental Protection Agency (EPA) issued a 'Notice of Violation' of the Clean Air Act 1990 to various Volkswagen group companies, which alleged that certain Volkswagen and Audi 2.0 litre diesel cars included software that by-passed EPA emissions standards for nitrogen oxides (EPA, 2015). On 22 September, Volkswagen issued the following statement:

Photo © rvlsoft. Courtesy of Shutterstock

> Discrepancies relate to vehicles with Type EA 189 engines, involving some 11 million vehicles worldwide. A noticeable deviation between bench test results and actual road use was established solely for this type of engine (Volkswagen, 2015).

It would appear that seemingly large and respected companies have ethical issues to consider, and sometimes do not act in a correct manner. So how should a researcher in a business and management discipline approach a research topic to ensure that their research is undertaken in an ethically credible manner?

The research process

For a researcher, the recognition of ethical issues, and deciding what actions need to be taken, is a problematic area. On the one hand, there is the desire to complete the research project and provide timely findings using pertinent data, to the agreed timescales. On the other hand, there is the desire to behave ethically, which may impact on timescales due to the requirements of the ethical considerations the researcher is obliged to consider.

Researchers can find it problematic to resolve this predicament, unless steps are taken to consider the relevant ethical issues early on in the planning stage of the research, and should actively manage a considered response to ethical issues throughout the research process.

Most universities and professional bodies provide guidance on how to conduct ethical research. Table 12.1 gives a selection of sites that you may want to visit to help inform your understanding of ethics in the context of academic research.

TABLE 12.1 Selection of websites offering ethical guidance

Academy of Management Code of Ethics (2006)	http://aom.org/
American Psychological Association Ethical Principles of Psychologists and Code of Conduct (2010)	http://www.apa.org/
British Educational Research Association Ethical Guidelines for Educational Research (2011)	https://www.bera.ac.uk/
British Sociological Association Statement of Ethical Practice (2002)	http://www.britsoc.co.uk/
Economic and Social Research Council Framework for Research Ethics (ESRC) (2012)	http://www.esrc.ac.uk/
ISO 20252:2012 Market, opinion and social research – Vocabulary and service requirements (2012)	http://www.iso.org/
ISO 26362:2009 specifies the terms and definitions, as well as the service requirements, for organisations and professionals who own and/or use access panels for market, opinion and social research	http://www.iso.org/
Joint Information System Committee (JISC) Code of Practice for the Further and Higher Education Sectors on the Data Protection Act 1998 (2008)	http://www.jisc.ac.uk/
Market Research Society Code of Conduct (2014)	https://www.mrs.org.uk/
Research Councils UK (RCUK) Policy and Guidelines on Governance of Good Research Conduct (2015)	http://www.rcuk.ac.uk/
Social Policy Association Guidelines on Research Ethics (2009)	http://www.social-policy.org.uk/
Social Research Association Ethical Guidelines (2003)	http://the-sra.org.uk/

The British Psychological Society Code of Ethics and Conduct (2009)	http://www.bps.org.uk/
The Higher Education Academy – A Resource Guide in Exploring Ethics (2009)	https://www.heacademy.ac.uk/
Universities UK – The Concordat to Support Research Integrity (2012)	http://www.universitiesuk.ac.uk/

Research ethics overview

The UK Economic and Social Research Council (ESRC) states six key principles of ethical research that must be adhered to (ESRC, 2012: 2), and that the ethical issues must be addressed at the research proposal stage:

1. Research should be designed, reviewed and undertaken to ensure integrity, quality and transparency.
2. Research staff and participants must normally be informed fully about the purpose, methods and intended possible uses of the research, what their participation in the research entails and what risks, if any, are involved.
3. The confidentiality of information supplied by research participants and the anonymity of respondents must be respected.
4. Research participants must take part voluntarily, free from any coercion.
5. Harm to research participants and researchers must be avoided in all instances.
6. The independence of research must be clear, and any conflicts of interest or partiality must be explicit.

The six ESRC principles above are used by many UK universities and professional bodies as the starting point for the code of ethics to be adopted by researchers. The general principles here are that:

1. Risk should be minimised: the sort of risks to look for are what physical or psychological harm could be caused to the participants; how the research will affect their personal social standing, privacy, personal values and beliefs, their links to family and the wider community, and their position within work-related situations; as well as any adverse effects of revealing sensitive information relating to illegal, sexual or deviant behaviour. Risks cannot always be avoided, but it is important that the researcher is aware of the potential risks to the participants, and develops an appropriate strategy to quantify and minimise them, and to discuss them with the participants before obtaining consent to participate in the research.
2. Informed consent must be obtained: this means giving the potential participants full information concerning the research so that they can make a free and informed decision whether to participate in the research, or not.
   It may not always be practical to obtain informed consent if this would compromise the research findings (e.g. in the case of a mystery shopping exercise, or in psychological experiments). Care will also need to be taken when obtaining

consent from vulnerable potential participants (e.g. children, older persons or adults with learning difficulties). In such cases the researcher should refer to their research supervisor for guidance on the institutional ethics requirements.

3. Involvement is voluntary and free from coercion: this means that the researcher must inform the participant that they have the right to not to participate in the research, to not answer particular questions, and that they may withdraw during participation, or after having participated. There should be no coercion on potential participants to participate in the research.

4. Conflicts of interest must be made clear: the research should, wherever possible, be independent of outside bias, and any conflicts of interest should be made clear to potential participants prior to being involved in the research, and in presenting the findings.

The six key ESRC principles of research ethics are underpinned by the ideas of non-malfeasance and beneficence. Non-malfeasance is the principle of doing, or permitting, no official misconduct, and is the principle of doing no harm. Beneficence is the requirement to serve the interests and well-being of others, including respect for their rights, and is the principle of doing good.

However, as well as the ESRC requirements, a UK-based researcher must also be compliant with the requirements of the Data Protection Act (1998), which are that:

1. Personal data shall be processed fairly and lawfully.

2. Personal data shall be obtained only for one or more specified and lawful purposes, and shall not be further processed in any manner incompatible with that purpose or those purposes.

3. Personal data shall be adequate, relevant and not excessive in relation to the purpose or purposes for which they are processed.

4. Personal data shall be accurate and, where necessary, kept up to date.

5. Personal data processed for any purpose or purposes shall not be kept for longer than is necessary for that purpose or those purposes.

6. Personal data shall be processed in accordance with the rights of data subjects under this Act.

7. Appropriate technical and organisational measures shall be taken against unauthorised or unlawful processing of personal data and against accidental loss or destruction of, or damage to, personal data.

8. Personal data shall not be transferred to a country or territory outside the European Economic Area unless that country or territory ensures an adequate level of protection for the rights and freedoms of data subjects in relation to the processing of personal data.

The Data Protection Act (1998) therefore imposes a number of responsibilities on researchers who are collecting and processing personal data, including ensuring that the data is only used for the purpose for which it was collected, that only data relevant to the research should be collected, that personal data is accurate, is securely held, and is not kept for longer than is necessary.

Other legal requirements that may be relevant to UK researchers include the Computer Misuse Act (1990), the Equalities Act (2010), the Obscene Publications Act (1959), the Employment Rights Act (1996), the Human Tissue Act (2004) and the Human Rights Act (1998), along with relevant legislation on Disabilities, Health and Safety, Animal Rights and the Environmental Protection Act (1990).

Ethical case studies

Mini-case 12.1

Anti-Corruption Bureau

You are a dissertation supervisor with a Masters student based in a sub-Saharan African country who is a senior officer in the Anti-Corruption Bureau. One of the issues facing the Bureau is that it is believed that import duties are not being levied at the correct rate at customs posts, and that customs officials are accepting bribes from the lorry drivers, which reduces the money paid to the government. The customs officials are not paid a living wage, and quite often have two or three jobs just to buy the basics needed to support themselves and their families. The research was designed to investigate whether the corruption exists or not, and, if it does, to assess how much is being lost in revenue and how this can be stopped.

The initial proposal is to install a hidden CCTV camera and microphone in the customs posts. The senior officer has an official letter from the head of the Anti-Corruption Bureau agreeing to this approach.

Is this research ethical?

What if he interviewed the customs officers and asked them about any bribes they may have taken, or observed being taken by other officers, or given by lorry drivers?

© R. Gino Santa Maria. Courtesy of Shutterstock

Mini-case 12.2

Customer relationship management in banking

You are a dissertation supervisor with a part-time Masters student based in a UK clearing bank. The bank fully funds her studies, and gives her extra time off work to attend university lectures and prepare for assignments and examinations. One of the issues that the bank has is that it does not collect much data from high-value customers who have successfully taken out business loans. The aim of the research was to assess about how the loan process was aligned to the customer's needs, and what changes could be made to improve the relationship that the bank has with its business customers.

The initial proposal was for her to access the bank database and identify which high-value customers had taken out a business loan from the bank in the past 18 months, and to contact them to assess how the loan process had worked, how the customer thought the bank had understood their business needs, and how the customers viewed their relationship with the bank.

In conversation with the student it becomes apparent that she has not yet obtained formal agreement in writing from the bank to conduct the research.

What would you do?

What if she said she was going to conduct the research anyway, and did not need written approval from the bank as she works there, they fund her studies and know that she is undertaking research for her dissertation, and that the findings will be useful to the bank?

© Yuriy Vlasenko. Courtesy of Shutterstock

Mini-case 12.3

Multinational financial institution

You are a dissertation supervisor for a part-time Masters student based in a multinational financial institution. He obtained written permission from the relevant director at work for research into assessing the service quality at the bank by surveying customers and members of staff. The data was successfully collected from both the staff and the customers and the research was nearly completed when he offered a job by a competitor; he accepted the job and tendered his resignation ten days before the dissertation hand-in date.

His previous employer immediately wrote to the student and to his supervisor at the university, withdrawing the authority to conduct the research and publish its results, with immediate effect. The dissertation had not at that point in time been formally submitted.

Can he still submit?

What advice would you give him?

If the letter from the employer was sent after the student had submitted the dissertation, what would your response be?

Photo © Monkey Business Images. Courtesy of Shutterstock

Research ethics checklist

Having looked at the ethical guidelines and requirements of the Data Protection Act (1998), what questions do you need to ask about your research to help you to research in an ethical manner?

1. Are you looking to do 'good' (beneficence) and not do 'harm' (non-malfeasance)?
2. Have you agreed the roles of researchers and responsibilities for management and supervision?
3. Is your research design appropriate for the question(s) being asked and do you have a process to review and approve any changes to the agreed research design?
4. Have you conducted a risk assessment to determine:

    a. whether there are any ethical issues;
    b. the potential for risks to the organisation, the research, or the health, safety and well-being of researchers and research participants; and
    c. what legal requirements govern the research?

5. How will you obtain informed consent from all participants prior to collecting data?
6. How will participants be told that they do not have to answer particular questions and can leave the study at any time?
7. How will participants be able to withdraw their data in retrospect?
8. How will you ensure that the participants are not at risk of physical or psychological harm (greater than encountered in ordinary life)?
9. How will you ethically manage the collection of data from vulnerable potential participants (e.g. children, older persons or adults with learning difficulties)?
10. If you are using a covert or deceptive approach, have you explained why no other method is appropriate?
11. How will the participants be de-briefed?
12. How has your research undergone an ethics review, especially if it involves human participants, animals, human material or personal data?
13. Where have all conflicts of interest relating to your research been identified, declared and addressed?
14. How are you following best practice for the collection, storage, management and confidentiality of data?
15. How will research data be retained in a secure and accessible form and for the required duration?
16. Will your research and its findings be reported accurately, honestly and within a reasonable time frame?

Bibliography

BBC (2002). See http://news.bbc.co.uk/1/hi/business/2047122.stm. Saturday, 15 June 2002, 22:09 GMT 23:09 UK Andersen guilty in Enron case.
Collins (2015). *Collins English Dictionary*. Available at http://www.collinsdictionary.com/dictionary/english/ethics.
Daily Telegraph (2009). 'Gordon Brown calls for inquiry into MPs allowances', 23 March. Available at http://www.telegraph.co.uk/news/politics/5039535/Gordon-Brown-calls-for-inquiry-into-MPs-allowances.html.
EPA (United States Environmental Protection Agency) (2015). http://www2.epa.gov/vw.

ESRC (Economic and Social Research Council) (2012). *ESRC Framework for Research Ethics (FRE)* 2010, updated September 2012. Swindon: ESRC UK.

Forbes (2013). 'Enron Ethics and Today's Corporate Values' (Ken Silverstein), 14 May. Available at http://www.forbes.com/sites/kensilverstein/2013/05/14/enron-ethics-and-todays-corporate-values/.

Guardian, (*The*) (2013a). 'NSA Prism program taps in to user data of Apple, Google and others' (Edward Snowden), 6 June 2013.

Guardian, (*The*) (2013b). 'NSA files source: "If they want to get you, in time they will"' (Edward Snowden), 10 June 2013.

Miller, T., Birch, M. and Jessop, J. (2012). *Ethics in Qualitative Research*. London: Sage.

Oliver, P. (2010). *The Student's Guide to Research Ethics*. Milton Keynes: Open University Press.

Rennie, F. and Smyth, K. (2015). *How to Write a Research Dissertation: Essential Guidance in Getting Started for Undergraduates and Postgraduates*. London: ETips.

Time (2015). http://content.time.com/time/specials/packages/completelist/0,29569,190 3155,00.html.

UK Government (1998), Data Protection Act 1998, http://www.legislation.gov.uk/ukpga/1998/29/schedule/1.

Volkswagen (2015). Press release, 22 September. Available at http://www.volkswagenag.com/content/vwcorp/info_center/en/news/2015/09/Volkswagen_AG_has_issued_the_following_information.html.

Washington Post (*The*) (2013). 'NSA slides explain the PRISM data-collection program' (Edward Snowden), 6 June.

INDEX